Mara W. Cohen Ioannides
Jewish Reform Movement in the U.S.

Mara W. Cohen Ioannides

Jewish Reform Movement in the U.S.

The Evolution of the Non-Liturgical Parts of the
Central Conference of American Rabbis Haggadah

DE GRUYTER

ISBN 978-3-11-064557-6
e-ISBN (PDF) 978-3-11-052470-3
e-ISBN (EPUB) 978-3-11-052321-8

Library of Congress Cataloging-in-Publication Data
A CIP catalog record for this book has been applied for at the Library of Congress.

Bibliographic information published by the Deutsche Nationalbibliothek
The Deutsche Nationalbibliothek lists this publication in the Deutsche Nationalbibliografie; detailed bibliographic data are available on the Internet at http://dnb.dnb.de.

© 2019 Walter de Gruyter GmbH, Berlin/Boston
This volume is text- and page-identical with the hardback published in 2017.
Printing and binding: CPI books GmbH, Leck
♾ Printed on acid-free paper
Printed in Germany

www.degruyter.com

Contents

Acknowledgements —— VII

Introduction —— 1

Chapter 1: History of the Passover Holiday and the Passover Seder Service as Reflected in the Haggadah —— 3

Chapter 2: Development of the Non-Liturgical Portions of the Haggadah in the Context of the Evolution of Jewish Education —— 22

Chapter 3: Development of the German Reform Movement and its Liturgies —— 45

Chapter 4: Growth of the American Reform Movement and Its Liturgies Including the Non-Liturgical Elements in CCAR Haggadot – The Early Years —— 55

Chapter 5: Development of the American Reform Movement and Its Liturgies Including the Non-Liturgical Elements in CCAR Haggadot the Middle Years —— 78

Chapter 6: Evolution of the Reform Movement and Its Liturgies Including the Non-Liturgical Elements in CCAR Haggadot – The Modern Period —— 112

Chapter 7: The Reform Movement and the Non Liturgical Elements in the CCAR Haggadot in the New Millennium —— 140

Conclusion —— 161

Bibliography —— 168

Index of Names —— 199

Index of Subjects —— 202

Acknowledgements

A project of this size does not happen magically overnight. There are numerous people and organizations I must thank for their assistance.

My dissertation advisor, Prof. Dean Bell, encouraged me and believed in my work and for that I am eternally thankful. My readers, Dr. Peter Haas, Rabbi Peter Knobel, and Dr. Elliot Lefkowitz, were not only immensely helpful with their comments, but considerate and speedy. My brother, Dr. Stephen M. Cohen, was gracious enough to edit my dissertation. All the faculty I was lucky enough to study with at the Spertus Institute of Jewish Learning and Leadership and my Hebrew professor, Dr. Pauline Nugent, at Missouri State University, provided background for this work, as well.

The majority of my research was funded by the Marguerite R. Jacobs Fellowship at the Jacob Rader Marcus Center of the American Jewish Archives at the Cincinnati Campus of the Hebrew Union College-Jewish Institute of Religion. I thank the staff there for their assistance and the head archivist, Kevin Proffit, for his patience and continued aid. Missouri State University's Faculty Research Grant provided me with the ability to spend a summer working on my research. The Rodef Shalom Congregational Archives in Pittsburgh, Pennsylvania were generous as well with their time and materials. The list of people who consented to be interviewed for this work is long, but because they were giving of their time and expertise I must thank: Rabbi Herbert Bronstein, Rabbi Sue Levi Elwell, Rabbi Peter Knobel, Rabbi Richard Levy, Rabbi Hara Person, Alan Yoffie, and Rabbi Mary L. Zamore.

My colleagues at the Midwest Jewish Studies Association, Western Jewish Studies Association, Conference on College Composition and Communication, the Missouri Philological Association, and the Annual Klutznick-Harris Symposium were patient and helpful as I presented various parts of my research at numerous meetings. I appreciate their feedback and encouragement.

I cannot forget the people who supported me emotionally and financially through this process. My mother, Brenda Cohen, and cousins, Mark and Carol Entman, kindly offered some financial aid. My mother, brother, husband Robert Anderson and daughter Sasha Cohen Ioannides suffered through my struggles as I completed my course work. Thankfully both my husband and daughter are patient people who understood my distraction and didn't mind late dinners and my endless ramblings about American Reform Judaism.

As I turned this from a dissertation to a monograph, I must thank my editors. I must thank Robert Anderson Photography for the cover art.

All of these people made it possible for me to complete my part-time degree in less than a decade. Thank you.

Introduction

"The Haggadah is in many ways the most popular and beloved of Jewish books. Scholars have meditated on it, children delight in it...
[It is] a book for philosophers and for the folk."

Yosef Hayim Yerushalmi[1]

Passover is a special mystical celebration for Jews. Its purpose is to bind Jews to their history and their god by retelling the Exodus story. Because of its nature as a home-centric holiday resulting in each family creating their particular interpretation, the nostalgia for past family experience is also tied to this celebration. For many American Jews this is one of the few Jewish holidays they celebrate regularly, because of its emphasis on freedom and its home-centric nature. All American Jews have an immigrant past, whether it was 350 years ago or 20 years ago, that began with the desire for religious freedom. Thus, Passover has an even tighter grip on American Jewish sensibilities than perhaps for non-American Jews.

The Reform Movement in Germany was also based on the idea of religious freedom. The founders of this movement want the freedom to make Judaism accessible to a bi-cultural, rather than the mono-cultural, Jew. When Reform Judaism arrived in the United States and collided with the independent spirit of Americans, it found its home and thrived, ultimately becoming the largest Jewish Movement in the world. As a movement that works to address the changing needs of its constituency, its leaders have worked to create a vibrant appropriate liturgy that meets the changing needs of its followers. Numerous rabbis and scholars have argued that Reform theology is influenced by changes in American culture and this in turn "required...a new spiritual pedagogy."[2] Joseph Tabory, emeritus professor of Talmud at Bar-Ilan University, has argued that analyzing what is contained within a *Siddur* (prayerbook) will show the needs and desires of Jews over their entire history.[3] Since the Haggadah is a liturgy, the liturgy of the Seder, this book responds to Tabory's statement in context of the Seder.

---

1 Yosef HayimYerushalmi, *Haggadah and History: A Panorama in Facsimile of Five Centuries of the Printed Haggadah from the Collections of Harvard University and Jewish Theological Seminary of American* (Philadelphia: JPS of American, 1975), 13.
2 Herbert Bronstein, "Platforms and Prayer Books: From Exclusivity to Inclusivity in Reform Judaism," in *Platforms and Prayer Books: Theological and Liturgical Perspectives on Reform Judaism*, ed. Dana Evan Kaplan (Lanham, Maryland: Rowman & Littlefield, 2002), 26.
3 Joseph Tabory, "The Prayer Book (Siddur) As an Anthology of Judaism." *Prooftexts* 17 (1997): 115–132.

The Haggadah is a reflection of the Jewish community in that the liturgy developed over time in response to events that happened to Jews. As Haggadot became more accessible to people because of the creation of the printing press, the rate of change in the liturgy and appendices sped up. Considering the importance to American Jews of the Seder experience, there has been little research done on the development of modern Haggadot liturgy. Modern Haggadot contain not only the Seder, the liturgy for the Passover ceremony, but also instructional material to guide the leader and participants in appropriate observation. Even less research has been done on the non-liturgical parts of the Haggadah. The non-liturgical materials, introductory matter and appendices, tells just as much, if not more, about the needs of a particular generation of Jews. It is this material that this study focuses on.

Because the Central Conference of American Rabbis (CCAR) made a conscience effort to address the changing needs of its constituency, an examination of its seven Haggadot – especially the non-liturgical parts – should give insight into the forces internally and externally, that shaped the American Reform Seder experience. The five Reform Movement platforms, 1885, 1937, 1976, 1997, and 2000 are reflected in the editions of the Reform Haggadah: 1892, 1905 (1907/1908), 1923, 1974, 2002, 2012, and 2014. Sometimes the platforms led the way and sometimes the Haggadot seem to have impacted the Platforms. The changes in American Jewry—not only Reform Jewry but largely in this group—can be seen not just in the Passover liturgy and non-liturgical material, but in how this material is presented to the public. It is this presentation that will be examined here.

My hope is that through this examination, we can better understand the agents that influenced changes in Reform theology and practice and American Jews, which then were expressed in the instructional and educational parts of the CCAR Haggadot. This in turn should illustrate how flexible the Reform Movement is, how popular the Seder has become as it has been developed to address the needs of American Jews, and how American Jews have changed over time. Maybe then this will guide Jews and Jewish leaders on how to read the signs in the Jewish and gentile communities in order to predict or quickly respond to the shifts in American Reform Jewry's beliefs.

Chapter 1:
History of the Passover Holiday and the Passover Seder Service as Reflected in the Haggadah

[The Seder] "is the founding ceremony of the Jewish people."

Joseph Tabory[1]

The story of the Exodus of the ancient Hebrews from the oppression of the Egyptians is one that has resounded among Jews throughout their history. The tale of freedom and redemption as told in the Book of Exodus and the commandment to remember it was later transformed into the Passover ceremony called the Seder. The adaptation of this ceremony is very telling about changes in Jewish practice over time. By understanding how the Seder came to be as we celebrate Passover currently, we can better appreciate the non-liturgical material in the Haggadah and the reasons for it.

The idea of remembrance is central to the Seder. The rabbis asserted "that a Seder act is performed in memory of something as a means to reconnect with an unavailable object or experience."[2] In fact, the phrase "in remembrance of the (ZKR) Temple according to Hillel" is in the Mishnah to emphasize that this and what follows is what the rabbis have decided.[3] The Seder has worked as a tool to bind the Jewish people together and promote remembrance of the Exodus. Because it has been so effective at creating a continuous connection to the past, the ceremony has maintained its structure since at least 1038 C.E.

Biblical References to Passover

In its earliest form, the Passover ceremonies that later developed into the Seder, are described in the Torah in Exodus 12:1–20 where G-d commands Moses and Aaron to instruct the people on how to take a lamb and prepare it and the community for the feast:

---

[1] Joseph Tabory, *JPS Commentary on the Haggadah: Historical Introduction, Translation, and Commentary* (Philadelphia: JPS, 2008).
[2] Baruch M. Bokser, "Ritualizing the Seder." *Journal of the American Academy of Religion* 56, no. 3 (1988): 447.
[3] Ibid.

> 1 And HaShem spoke unto Moses and Aaron in the land of Egypt, saying:...
> 5 'Your lamb shall be without blemish, a male of the first year; ye shall take it from the sheep, or from the goats;
> 6 and ye shall keep it unto the fourteenth day of the same month; and the whole assembly of the congregation of Israel shall kill it at dusk.
> 7 And they shall take of the blood, and put it on the two side-posts and on the lintel, upon the houses wherein they shall eat it.
> 8 And they shall eat the flesh in that night, roast with fire, and unleavened bread; with bitter herbs they shall eat it.
> 9 Eat not of it raw, nor sodden at all with water, but roast with fire; its head with its legs and with the inwards thereof.
> 10 And ye shall let nothing of it remain until the morning; but that which remaineth of it until the morning ye shall burn with fire.
> 11 And thus shall ye eat it: with your loins girded, your shoes on your feet, and your staff in your hand; and ye shall eat it in haste–it is HaShem's passover....
> 15 Seven days shall ye eat unleavened bread; howbeit the first day ye shall put away leaven out of your houses; for whosoever eateth leavened bread from the first day until the seventh day, that soul shall be cut off from Israel.
> 16 And in the first day there shall be to you a holy convocation, and in the seventh day a holy convocation; no manner of work shall be done in them, save that which every man must eat, that only may be done by you....
> 18 In the first month, on the fourteenth day of the month at even, ye shall eat unleavened bread, until the one and twentieth day of the month at even.
> 19 Seven days shall there be no leaven found in your houses; for whosoever eateth that which is leavened, that soul shall be cut off from the congregation of Israel, whether he be a sojourner, or one that is born in the land.
> 20 Ye shall eat nothing leavened; in all your habitations shall ye eat unleavened bread."[4]

The stipulations made here of how to eat the sacrifice (roasted) and not to destroy the bones are polemics against the pagan sacrificial practices of the period. Because early Semites believed that the life force was in the blood, eating the raw meat and consuming the bones would be a way to ingest the life force of the sacrificial animal.[5]

It is interesting that in the Torah Jews are given the instructions for performing a ceremony. This is not true everywhere. For example Leviticus 9:8–14 tells about the sacrifice Aaron made, but does not go into great detail about it:

> 8 So Aaron drew near unto the altar, and slew the calf of the sin-offering, which was for himself.
> 9 And the sons of Aaron presented the blood unto him; and he dipped his finger in the

---

4 All translations, unless noted otherwise, are from the Jewish Virtual Library.
5 W. O. E. Oesterley and Theodore H. Robinson, *Hebrew Religion: Its Origin and Development* (New York: Macmillan, 1937), 131.

blood, and put it upon the horns of the altar, and poured out the blood at the base of the altar.
10 But the fat, and the kidneys, and the lobe of the liver of the sin-offering, he made smoke upon the altar; as HaShem commanded Moses.
11 And the flesh and the skin were burnt with fire without the camp.
12 And he slew the burnt-offering; and Aaron's sons delivered unto him the blood, and he dashed it against the altar round about.
13 And they delivered the burnt-offering unto him, piece by piece, and the head; and he made them smoke upon the altar.
14 And he washed the inwards and the legs, and made them smoke upon the burnt offering on the altar.

By including, in Exodus details as to the ceremony, there has developed a history of written detailed instruction on how to conduct a public rite. Since the public is to perform this, not a secret society like the Kohenim, the proscribed rite must be recorded in a place the public can easily obtain it and, since the Torah was to be publically read, this was the perfect place.

In Leviticus 23 the focus is also on the unleavened bread:

5 In the first month, on the fourteenth day of the month at dusk, is HaShem's passover.
6 And on the fifteenth day of the same month is the feast of unleavened bread unto HaShem; seven days ye shall eat unleavened bread.
7 In the first day ye shall have a holy convocation; ye shall do no manner of servile work.
8 And ye shall bring an offering made by fire unto HaShem seven days; in the seventh day is a holy convocation; ye shall do no manner of servile work.

In Numbers 9:1–14, these celebrations are commanded to continue as a way of remembering the Exodus. These celebrations were incumbent upon all Israelites.

2 'Let the children of Israel keep the passover in its appointed season.'...
4 And Moses spoke unto the children of Israel, that they should keep the passover.
5 And they kept the passover in the first month, on the fourteenth day of the month, at dusk, in the wilderness of Sinai; according to all that HaShem commanded Moses, so did the children of Israel....
10 'Speak unto the children of Israel, saying: If any man of you or of your generations shall be unclean by reason of a dead body, or be in a journey afar off, yet he shall keep the passover unto HaShem;
11 in the second month on the fourteenth day at dusk they shall keep it; they shall eat it with unleavened bread and bitter herbs;
12 they shall leave none of it unto the morning, nor break a bone thereof; according to all the statute of the passover they shall keep it.
13 But the man that is clean, and is not on a journey, and forbeareth to keep the passover, that soul shall be cut off from his people; because he brought not the offering of HaShem in its appointed season, that man shall bear his sin.
14 And if a stranger shall sojourn among you, and will keep the passover unto HaShem:

> according to the statute of the passover, and according to the ordinance thereof, so shall he do; ye shall have one statute, both for the stranger, and for him that is born in the land.'

Not until after the nomadic Hebrews had settled into Canaan and had become agriculturalists were the sheep sacrifice and the festival of matzah joined.[6] Before this time, more than likely these were, at first, festivals celebrating the newly born animals for pastoralists and first harvest for farmers.[7]

While there was no central temple at the time Leviticus was composed, by the time of the composition of Deuteronomy 12 there was a focus on a central cultic place:

> 5 But unto the place which HaShem your G-d shall choose out of all your tribes to put His name there, even unto His habitation shall ye seek, and thither thou shalt come;
> 6 and thither ye shall bring your burnt-offerings, and your sacrifices, and your tithes, and the offering of your hand, and your vows, and your freewill-offerings, and the firstlings of your herd and of your flock;
> 7 and there ye shall eat before HaShem your G-d, and ye shall rejoice in all that ye put your hand unto, ye and your households, wherein HaShem thy G-d hath blessed thee....
> 11 then it shall come to pass that the place which HaShem your G-d shall choose to cause His name to dwell there, thither shall ye bring all that I command you: your burnt-offerings, and your sacrifices, your tithes, and the offering of your hand, and all your choice vows which ye vow unto HaShem.

Thus, the push for a central cult had been established. The presumption in these two passages is that "the worshiper is free to return home to observe the Feast of Unleavened Bread."[8] This demanded a standardized ceremony surrounding the sacrifice.

Seder Beginnings in the Talmud

The Seder, as modern Jews understand it, was first outlined in the Talmud. There are sections in the Haggadah, like that about "the wandering Arameans," that

---

[6] Ze'eve Weisman, "Reflection of the Transition to Agriculture in Israelite Religion and Cult," in *Studies in Historical Geography and Biblical Historiography*, ed. Gershon Galil and Moshe Weinfeld (Boston: Brill, 2000), 252.
[7] Jacob Milgrom, comm., "The Second Passover," in *The JPS Torah Commentary: Numbers* (Philadelphia: JPS, 1990), 371.
[8] Ibid., 371.

date back to the latter half of the 3rd Century C.E.[9] Tractate Pesachim Chapter 10 focuses specifically on the structure of the Seder and why participants do what they do.

The Jews of the Talmudic period interpreted the destruction of the Temple as retribution by G-d against the sinful Jews. Thus, to rebuild the Temple required redemption of the Jews after a period of chastisement. Hence part of the purpose of the Talmud was to show the people how to behave in order to achieve redemption. Judaism had to be redesigned because no longer could sacrificial offerings be made because there was no longer a Temple. The proto-rabbis had to refashion the sacrificial part of the Pesach celebration. They had the opportunity to enforce what they believed: that the Temple cult was not the only way to reach G-d. They had to incorporate the sacrifice—the Temple cult practice—into the Passover celebration somehow. The rabbis "made the Seder independent of the sacrifice... [and] turn[ed] the celebration into a kinship gathering in the home instead of in the capital city."[10] They also decided to focus the message of the Seder on redemption, rather than on the sacrifice. Because of the milieu they existed in, the Greco-Roman style symposium, or meal and intellectual discussion, became the mode the proto-rabbi chose as the Seder. It makes sense. There is a way to incorporate symbolic food and the Biblical command to explain the story.

The drinking of wine, reclining requirement, eating of certain foods, and discussing of the meanings of the celebration parallels the Greek *symposium*. Scholars like David Arnow believe that "the Mishnah's interest in story telling reflects greater influence of the Greek symposium [which]...included dipped hors d'oeuvres eaten while reclining, praises to the gods, and stylized conversations."[11]

However, Baruch M. Bokser argues that the discussion recommended by the rabbis is not a symposium. He notes that "the editor of the Mishnah and his sources were aware of the similarities but strove to differentiate between the Jewish rite and other types of banquets so as to maintain the distinctive character of the Passover celebration."[12] One of his strongest arguments is that symposia were drinking orgies, while the religious nature of the Seder was maintained

---

9 Louis Finkelstein, "The Oldest Midrash: Pre-Rabbinic Ideals and Teachings in the Passover Haggadah." *The Harvard Theological Review* 31, no. 4 (1938): 293.
10 Bokser, "Ritualizing," 443.
11 David Arnow, "Passover for the Early Rabbis: Fixed and Free," in *My People's Passover Haggadah: Traditional Texts, Modern Commentaries*, vol. 1, ed. Lawrence A. Hoffman and David Arnow (Woodstock, Vermont: Jewish Lights Pub., 2008), 17.
12 Baruch M. Bokser, *The Origins of the Seder: The Passover Rite and Early Rabbinic Judaism* (New York: JTS 2002), 50.

through "the prescribed recitation of seven blessings" that ensured the divine nature of the ceremony was maintained.[13]

The description of the Seder in the Talmud, Pesachim 10, begins with a statement as to the basic requirement that each participant "shall have [no] less than four cups of wine." The Talmudists used the recitation of blessings as a "way to ensure that religious acts would involve an experience of the divine"[14] and, thus, help Jews as they struggled with the loss of the Temple and the sacrificial rites.

With the loss of the Temple, much of what the priests did had to be reassigned to the populace. The priestly purification acts became hand-washing before meals. There is much discussion in Pesachim 10 concerning hand-washing and when it should take place. The first hand washing represented the Temple practice of the priests washing their hands before the sacrifice. The rabbis felt this had to be maintained for the time when the Temple would be rebuilt and the practices were re-instituted. In addition, the rabbis equated the dining table to the altar in the Temple, making the act of eating equivalent to the sacrifice because the table is now the altar and the meal represents the sacrificial animal; thus the act of eating became the actual sacrifice. Therefore, washing one's hands re-enacted this important part of the sacrificial process.[15]

Pesaḥim 10 instructs Jews to break the *maṣah* and say *hamôṣî* (the blessing for bread) over part of it because the poor, who do not have a whole piece of bread over which to say *hamôṣî*, must be remembered. Some rabbis also suggested that the breaking of the *maṣah* is a reminder that Jews are not complete, that the Seder is not complete until it is finished. The *maṣah* is broken, but made whole by eating some at the beginning and some at the end,[16] just as Jews are not complete until they observed all the Commandants.

Pesaḥim 10 introduces the Four Questions. The Four Questions "reflect the rabbinic concern that parents teach their children what they know"[17] and are in-

---

[13] Ibid., 75.
[14] Baruch Bokser, *From Sacrifice to Symbol – and Beyond*. (Paper presented at the Solomon Goldman Lectures) ed. Byron L. Sherwin and Michael Carasik, vol. 5 (Chicago: Spertus College of Judaica Press, 1990), 74.
[15] Tabory, *JPS Commentary*, 22; David Arnow, "The World of Midrash," in *My People's Passover Haggadah: Traditional Texts, Modern Commentaries*, vol. 1, ed. Lawrence A. Hoffman and David Arnow (Woodstock, Vermont: Jewish Lights Pub., 2008), 119.
[16] Neil Gillman, "Theologically Speaking," in *My People's Passover Haggadah: Traditional Texts, Modern Commentaries*, vol. 1, ed. Lawrence A. Hoffman and David Arnow (Woodstock, Vermont: Jewish Lights Pub., 2008), 125.
[17] Bokser, *From Sacrifice*, 69.

cluded in response to the 4 times the Jews are told to tell the story to their children in Exodus 12:26–27, Exodus 13:8, Exodus 13:14, and in Deuteronomy 6:20–21. In this way, a father can guide the discussion if no discussion is forthcoming. Consider the beginning of this section, "the son should then inquire of his father (the reasons for the ceremony). If the son is mentally incapacitated to do this, the father is bound to instruct him as follows."[18]

The Gemara for this Mishnah goes into detail concerning how one can end the meal. What are the foods that constitute a dessert? One must be satiated by the meal, by the Torah, as is explained.

It was by the 2nd Century C.E. that *maṣah* was the last food eaten.[19] The implication of R. Joseph's statement in the Gemorah is that one should keep in his or her mouth the taste of the lamb or the *maṣah* as a reminder of the sacrifice. The importance here is that the sacrifice must be remembered. Some scholars speculate that the *maṣah* "may also represent a taste of *s'udat ha-tsadikim*, the feast that G-d prepares for the righteous in the world-to-come."[20] Thus, we want to keep that holy taste in our mouth and not subvert it by another. That, of course, would be disrespectful. This has been carried through to the modern Seder where the last item eaten just before the Grace after Meals is a piece of matzah.

Haggadah Additions in the Medieval Period

The Seder ceremony did not remain stagnate. As Jews spread across Europe and encountered persecution and acceptance, they added to the Festival of Freedom prayers, songs, and rites that spoke to them about their experiences.

The song *Dayēnû* was a very early medieval addition to the Haggadah. The first mention of this song is as an option to extending the list of the ten plagues in *Siddur Saadiah* in which is the oldest complete version of the Haggadah.[21] The

---

18 Lawerence Hoffman, "From Enslavement...," in *My People's Passover Haggadah: Traditional Texts, Modern Commentaries*, vol. 1, ed. Lawrence A. Hoffman and David Arnow (Woodstock, Vermont: Jewish Lights Pub., 2008).
19 Ibid., 201.
20 David Arnow, "Redemption: Blessing and Meal," in *My People's Passover Haggadah: Traditional Texts, Modern Commentaries*, vol. 2, ed. Lawrence A. Hoffman and David Arnow (Woodstock, Vermont: Jewish Lights Pub., 2008), 118.
21 Yosef Hayim Yerushalmi, *Haggadah and History: A Panorama in Facsimile of the Five Centuries of the Printed Haggadah from the Collections of the Harvard University and Jewish Theological Seminary of America* (Philadelphia: JPS, 1975), 13.

great Jewish philosopher and poet Saadiah explained this song as a contemporary addition to the Haggadah.[22]

While the rabbis identified the Seder with messianic redemption, it wasn't until the Early Middle Ages that mention of Elijah was added to the Seder. In fact both Elijah and "Pour out my wrath" appeared during the Crusades when the rise of anti-Semitism turned violent and Jews felt particularly persecuted. Opening the door for Elijah was also added at this period. The *kisel elîyahû* (chair for Elijah), while already present at a *běrît měîlah*, now arrived at the Seder as did the custom to open the door to invite the awaited herald of the messiah.

The dipping of the lettuce did not appear in the Haggadah until the 13th Century. The Jews felt so abandoned by the end of the Second Crusade in the 12th Century that they added to the end of the Seder: "Next year in Jerusalem." At this time, Haggadot became separate books; no longer were they included in prayerbooks as one of the liturgies.

The invention of the printing press by Gutenberg in 1445 had a huge impact on Jews and the Haggadah. The 1st printed Haggadah of which only pieces of the manuscript still exist was produced in 1480 by an unknown printer. This was only 5 years after the 1st Hebrew book was printed, pointing to the importance of the ceremony and the potential sales of the product.

Once the Haggadah was produced mechanically, the number of editions available to the public exploded. In the 16th Century there were 25 new editions of Haggadot; in the 17th Century 37, the 18th Century 234; the 19th Century 1269; and between 1960 and 1974 there were 1,100 new editions.[23] All of these were stand-alone manuscripts, not part of larger *sidûrîm* (prayerbooks). Since accessibility expanded with the reduction in price and the quantity of books available, not only were people able to acquire at least one Haggadah for their home, but rabbis were able to produce new versions with local traditions.

With the printing press came the popularity of illustrations. The first Passover illustrations in Haggadot can also be dated from around 1480. They are a pair of woodcuts showing Jews and a series of Passover themes: the smearing of blood on lintels, a Passover meal, the plague of darkness, and the slaying of the first born. They have been dated to the 1480s and are most likely Venetian in origin.[24] Woodcuts were included in most early printed Haggadot, but only 3 or 4 images in any one edition. However, Gershon Cohen's 1526 printing of the

---

22 Ibid., 67.
23 Ibid., 23–24.
24 Yerushalmi, *Haggadah and History*, 25–26.

Haggadah, commonly called the Prague Haggadah, includes 60 graphics by an unknown illustrator. The Prague Haggadah had a huge impact on those Haggadot that followed. The 1560 Mantua Haggadah (published in Mantua) copies the Prague Haggadah text exactly, and the idea that illustrations are integral to the Haggadah followed. The illustrations of this edition are copied in all 4 editions of the Venetian Haggadah (1599, 1601, 1603, and 1604). These illustrations were poorly redone for the 1662 Amsterdam Haggadah.

Translations of the Haggadah into the local language, so that those who were not fluent in Hebrew could follow, were significant in both Jewish and Christian circles and began within 2 centuries of the first printing. The 1st Latin version was produced for the Catholic Church, which emphasizes how interested the Church was in this ceremony and that while Passover is important, it is not sacred because non-Jews were translating and observing the festival. However, the first complete translation for a Jewish audience was the 1609 Venice Haggadah[25] that was translated into Judeo-Italian, Judeo-Spanish, and Judeo-German to meet the needs of the residents of the Venice Ghetto. The Judeo-Italian translation was prepared by the famous Rabbi Leone da Modena and the noted printer Daniel Zifroni.[26]

Haggadah in the Modern Period

The 1st English language Haggadah was published in 1770 by W. Gilbert of London. Alexander Alexander completed the translation himself after the success of his earlier prayer book. The complete title reads: *The* הגדה של פסח *Containing the Ceremonies and Prayers which are used and read By all Families, in all Houses of the Israelites, the Two first Nights of Passover.* The copyright date is given in the Hebrew: 5530.

In 1842, the West London synagogue of British Jews published the 1st Reform Haggadah in English. It is unclear if this publication was encouraged by a need to financially support the synagogue, thus a fundraising effort, or a desire to meet the needs of its constituency. However that it was published only a year after Leopold Stein's German Liberal Haggadah[27] suggests the latter over the for-

---

25 Ibid., 61.
26 Nanette Stahl, *The Venice Haggadah of 1609: A Treasure for the Ages* (Yale Univ. Library, 2008), accessed 29 March 2014, http://www.library.yale.edu/judaica/site/exhibits/venicehaggadah/VeniceHaggadah.html.
27 Joel Gereboff, "One Nation, with Liberty and Haggadahs for All," in *Key Texts in American Jewish Culture*, ed. Jack Kugelmass (New Brunswick: Rutgers Univ. Press, 2003), 277; Hara Person,

mer. This is more strongly supported by the 1897 *The Revised Hagada: Home Service for the First Two Nights of Passover* published in 1897 by Rev. A. A. Green of London. He is explicit that there "has long been a distinct want in the Ritual literature of English Jews" and offers not only an "entirely new" translation, but also "the critical notes and the explanations of the ceremonies [that] are intended to invest the whole of the function with a living interest for parents and children and [to] serve as a helpful guide."[28]

American Jews were not a unified group. America had required German, Russian, Lithuanian, and Sephardic Jews to pray together, so a new Judaism was created. They felt the need to make the Haggadah their own and altered it to fit their varied requirements. The 1st Haggadah published in the United States appeared in 1837 and states on its English title page that it is the "First American Edition." Published by S. H. Jackson, it has both Hebrew and English title pages noting that it is a: "Service for the two first nights of the Passover, in Hebrew and English: According to the Custom of the German & Spanish Jews." The service is presented in both English and Hebrew. Jackson gives credit to David Levi[29] who had translated a Haggadah and published it in London in 1794.

The Haggadah in America

Most Jews in America, during the first half of the 19th Century, used 1 of 3 Haggadot: Jackson's 1837 translation into the English as published by Solomon H. Jackson, Leopold Stein's German Liberal Haggadah published in 1841 in Bavaria, or Haim Liebman's 1878 (or later edition) Americanized Haggadah. An American version of Stein's Haggadah was produced that was particularly popular with the German Jewish community.[30] There were other Haggadot, of course. For example Rabbi David Einhorn, a leader in the American Reform Movement, published a Haggadah in 1856 in his prayer book *Olat Tamid* and titled it "Domestic Service on the Eve of Passover." Interestingly, it was entirely in German with only one

---

"CCAR Haggadot: A Feast of Haggadah Choices." *Reform Rabbis Speak* 21 February 2014, accessed 29 March 2014, http://ravblog.ccarnet.org/2014/02/ccar-haggadot-a-feast-of-haggadah-choices/.

28 A. A. Green, *The Revised Hagada: Home Service for the First Two Nights of Passover* (London: Greenberg & Co., 1897), 4.

29 S[olomon] H. Jackson, *Service for the two first nights of the Passover, in Hebrew and English: According to the Custom of the German & Spanish Jews*, trans. David Levi (New York: S.H. Jackson, 1837).

30 Ibid.

line of Hebrew and did not follow the traditional order of a Seder. It was popular enough that Einhorn worked with Bernard Felsenthal to translate the entire prayerbook into English. That the British Reform Haggadah did not gain popularity in the United States while the German ones did, underscore the German demographic of the American Jewish population. L. H. Frank published a Haggadah in the midst of the Civil War (1863) with the statement that "on this night it is customary to allow even the meanest Hebrew servant to sit at table during the ceremonial part: For as we were all equally alike in bondage, it is proper that we all return thanks to G-d for the redemption."[31]

Over time, the Seder in America took on a new meaning, that of family reunion, while the religious ceremony became relatively unimportant. In fact, the Seder is one of "the two most popular forms of personal American Jewish practice."[32] The mixture of the ancient story of freedom tied to the promise of religious tolerance to a community that was historically opened is understandably appealing.

Merchants great and small realized the potential of catering to Jewish women for Passover. They advertised everything from food to special table linens and even vacations where one could "celebrate the Passover festival amid delightful country surroundings by the sea, avoiding the usual annoyance of ritual household preparation."[33] Publishing a Haggadah for a food company gave their food products a place in the kosher kitchen. The kosher Jewish housewife would feel more comfortable believing a product was kosher, if that company offered a Haggadah.

In the 1930s, Maxwell House decided to combat the false notion that coffee was not kosher for Passover by offering free Haggadot with the purchase of their product. The 1st edition of the Maxwell House came out in 1912 and was a copy, with parts removed, of Dr. A. Th. Philips' *Seder Haggadah Shel Pesah* also printed in 1912. Maxwell House published over 50 million copies of its Haggadah between 1930 and 2008[34] with 1 million alone published in 2009.[35] This particular

---

31 הגדה של פסח *Passover Haggadah Service for the Two First Night of Passover with an English Translation*, 7th (Stereotype) Edition (New York: L.H. Frank, 1863): 71.
32 Lawrence Hoffman, "Peoplehood with Purpose: The American Seder and Changing Jewish Identity." In *My People's Passover Haggadah: Traditional Texts, Modern Commentaries*, vol. 1. Edited by Lawrence A. Hoffman and David Arnow (Woodstock, Vermont: Jewish Lights Pub., 2008), 47.
33 Jenna Weissman Joselit, "The Call of the Matzoh," in *The Wonders of America: Reinventing Jewish Culture, 1880–1950* (New York: Henry Holt and Co., 1994), 223.
34 Elie Rosenfeld, "Elie Rosenfeld- Maxwell House Haggadah." *Jinsider*, 13 November 20098, accessed 29 June 2010, http://www.youtube.com/watch?v=1_PL7PjL6NE.

Haggadah has become so popular that it was smuggled into Russia during the 1970s, used on *kibbutzim* in Israel, by the US military, and in 2010 it graced President Barak Obama's Seder. The State Bank of New York's reprint of the Haggadah published by Philip Cowen, translated by his wife Lillie, was perhaps the 1st to publish a Haggadah, and Streits' Matzoh and Chase & Sanborn Coffees had theirs by the 1950s. Various rabbis and religious groups saw the potential to promote their religious views and/or make a profit on this popular holiday. Along with Liebman's, Einhorn's, and Frank's Haggadot, the Diskin Orphan Home of Israel reprinted a series of early modern Haggadot as a fundraiser for the education of their wards.[36] The Central Conference of American Rabbis' (CCAR) הגדה של פסח: *A Passover Haggadah* edited by Herbert Bronstein has sold over a million copies.[37] These 2 texts, the CCAR and Maxwell House, are the ultimate examples of 2 different modern perspectives of Judaism.[38] The Maxwell House being the traditional presentation on which "Orthodox Rabbis and scholars...have worked so many hours"[39] and the Bronstein, the Reform. Bronstein considers his Haggadah "an attempt at *renovation ab origine:* a return to the creative beginning."[40]

Making the Seder American

American Jews, enamored by their adopted country, felt compelled to Americanize the Haggadah. The first such Americanization was the addition of both "America the Beautiful" and "The Star-Spangled Banner" to those songs one could select from to sing after the Seder. These were added by Isaac Moses in

---

35 Joan Alpert, "Maxwell House Hagaddah: Good to the Last Page." *Moment* March/April 2009, accessed 29 June 2010, http://www.momentmag.com/maxwell-house-hagaddah-good-to-the-last-page/.

36 *The Matteh Aharon Haggadah 1710* (New York: The Disken Orphan Home, 1982), "Acknowledgement," back cover.

37 *A Passover Haggadah Second Revised Edition Edited by Herbert Bronstein Illustrated by Leonard Baskin.* (CCAR Press, 2010), accessed 20 July 2010, http://ccarnet.org/ccar-press/all-books/passover-haggadah/.

38 Interestingly, Bronstein used the Maxwell House edition as a child (Herbert Brontstein, "Re: Ltr. To Mara W. Cohen Ioannides–CORRECTED VERSION 8/22 Bronstein," email to author, 24 August 2000.).

39 *Passover Haggadah*, DeLuxe Edition (n.p.: General Foods, 1988), 3.

40 Herbert Bronstein, הגדה של פסח: *A Passover Haggadah: A New Union Haggadah* (New York: Grossman Pub., 1974), 5.

his 1898 Haggadah.[41] The American Gospel song "Let My People Go" very much resonated with American Jews as it spoke of the Exodus story.

Singing struck a chord with American Jews. Eventually, they composed their own songs, similar to "Adir Hu." One of these songs is "The Four Sons" that is set to the tune of the American folk song "Clementine," written by Ben Aronin in 1948[42] and first published in 1954.[43] This song faithfully recounts the requirement in the Talmud that the Seder leader explain the Exodus story to four different sons (wise, wicked, disinterested, and simple).[44] This parody has become amazingly popular, so much so that other parodies have been composed. For example, Rabbi Dan Liben composed "There's no Seder like our Seder" (sung to "There's no business like show business") and "Elijah" (sung to "Maria" from *West Side Story*).[45] Some of these parodies have gone mainstream and are included in such Haggadot as Alan Yoffie's *Sharing the Journey: The Haggadah for the Contemporary Family*.[46] In 1988, CLAL (the National Jewish Center for Learning and Leadership) produced *Dayenu: A Special Contemporary Dayenu Created in Honor of the 40th Anniversary of the Birth of the State of Israel*. It was designed to "celebrate some of the small steps taken by our people towards the not yet complete redemption in our own day."[47]

American Jews were not the only ones to make Haggadot in their own image. Residents of *kibûṣîm* (Israeli secular communes), who had reimagined the model of the ideal Jew into a physically strong and anti-traditionalist, produced about 1500 Haggadot between 1930 and 1948. These were never produced for public consumption, as they were meant for use within the *kibûṣ*, but they did take into account the Holocaust and that the audience lived in a modern Israel.

---

41 I[saac] S. Moses, *Seder Hagadah: Domestic Service for the Eve of Passover*, 2nd ed. (Chicago: I.S. Moses, 1989).
42 *Funny Passover Songs*, n.d., accessed 5 April 2014, http://holidays.jua.com/passover-songs.shtml.
43 Hannah Bluver, "The Ballad of the Four Sons." *The Jewish Magazine* April 1998, accessed 5 April 1998, http://jewishmag.com.
44 Pesachim 10:4
45 *Funny*.
46 Alan S. Yoffie, *Sharing the Journey: The Haggadah for the Contemporary Family*, ill. Mark Podwal (New York: CCAR, 2012).
47 *Dayenu: A Special Contemporary Dayenu Created in Honor of the 40th Anniversary of the Birth of the State of Israel* (New York: CLAL, 1988).

Haggadot with Political and Social Agenda

Because of the Seder's focus on freedom and slavery, it became a forum for groups to forward their agenda about oppressed communities. The 1970s and 1980s saw a series of Haggadot produced to make the public aware of the oppression of Jews in the Soviet Union. For instance, Tamra L. Morris edited *Freedom Haggadah for Soviet Jewry* published by CLAL and The National Conference on Soviet Jewry[48] and Congregation Ohr Kodesh in Chevy Chase, Maryland produced *A Soviet Jewry Freedom Seder* in 1974.[49] In the 1970s, Aviva Cantor, Itzhak Epstein, and Jerry Krischen put together a Haggadah with socialist leanings,[50] not the 1st such one. Roberta Kalechofsky put together in 1985 *Haggadah for the Liberated Lamb* which is "both Haggadah and manifesto.... For vegetarians and for those whose knowledge of the suffering of animal life in this century divides them from a public which is not addressed itself to this problem."[51] The Religious Action Center of Reform Judaism put out a social-action Haggadah in 2004.[52]

A new century brought even newer concerns, such as, how to address the interfaith family. Alan Yoffie, and Cokie Roberts and Steven Roberts created Haggadot with this in mind. The Roberts' idea was that "our Haggadah is a practical guide for interfaith families, whether they're celebrating their very first Passover or starting a new tradition."[53] Yoffie is quite clear that since "85% of our HUC rabbis perform interfaith marriages" there is a need for Haggadot "to address that community at Passover.[54]

Nor could the feminist movement let this decisive moment in Jewish history and the Jewish year pass without commentary from them. Feminist Haggadot maintain the traditional Seder order, but focus on the women in the Exodus

---

48 Tamra L. Morris ed., *Freedom Haggadah for Soviet Jewry* (New York: CLAL and The National Conference on Soviet Jewry, 1987).
49 *A Soviet Jewry Freedom Seder* (Chevy Chase: Congregation Ohr Kodesh, 1974).
50 Aviva Cantor, "Jewish Women's Haggadah," in *Womanspirit Rising: A Feminist Reader in Religion*, ed. Carol P. Christ and Judith Plaskow (New York: Harper & Row, Pub., 1979). 185.
51 Roberta Kalechofsky, *Haggadah for the Liberated Lamb* (Marblehead: Micah, 1985), "Introduction."
52 Marcie Bellows, and Marla J. Feldman, *Pesach: a season for justice*. Religious Action Center of Reform Judaism (2004), accessed 21 April 2014, http://rac.org/_kd/Items/actions.cfm?action=Show&item_id=331&destination=ShowItem.
53 Cokie Roberts and Stephen V. Roberts, *Our Haggadah: Uniting Traditions for Interfaith Families* (New York: HarperCollins, 2011), book jacket.
54 Alan Yoffie, Interview by author, 24 January 2014.

story and women's issues.[55] Both E. M. Broner and Marcia Freedman wrote of their experiences celebrating in 1976 with the same feminist Haggadah, one in English in New York and one in Hebrew in Haifa.[56] Portions of the original photocopied Haggadah were published in *Ms.* in 1977.[57] Cantor also created a women's Haggadah that concentrated on "connecting links between Jewish women of the past and us here in the present."[58]

However, Cantor was "dissatisfied" with the experience of using her feminist Haggadah because it was a "take over of its single 'predecessors' [men's] account of the Exodus" while the Seder "marks a *specific*... liberation from a *specific* oppression" that does not necessarily include women, but should include women who were still oppressed at the time. Cantor felt that feminist Seders mitigated the joy in unity presented in the Haggadah.[59] She felt the exclusion of men in her Haggadah was divisive and so the Seder should be reconsidered altogether in a different form to address the issues women have.[60] In 1982, she composed *An Egalitarian Hagada* to address these issues.[61]

The feminist movement eventually affected American Haggadot. Editors and publishers of Haggadot, starting the in 1990s, began to introduce gender neutral language. By 2011, the most popular Haggadah in the United States—*The Maxwell House Haggadah*—had been reworked. Elie Rosenfeld, of Joseph Jacobs Advertising that represents Maxwell House, explained, "We wanted to make sure everyone who uses it feels comfortable with it....The fact of the matter is, G-d doesn't have a gender."[62]

The modern era brought with it additions to the text of the Seder as well. The Miriam's Cup was introduced to a Rosh Chodesh group in 1979[63] based on the midrash of Miriam's uncanny ability to locate water during the 40 years of crossing the desert after the Exodus from Egypt and the desire of feminists to create a hero of their own.[64] Shortly thereafter, the Miriam's Cup was added by feminists

---

55 E. M. Broner, *The Telling* (San Francisco: HarperSanFrancisco, 1993), 193–216.
56 Ibid.; Marcia Freedman, *Exile in the Promised Land* (Ithaca: Firebrand Press, 1990).
57 Broner, *The Telling*, 24.
58 Cantor, "Jewish Women's Haggadah," 187.
59 Ibid.
60 Ibid., 188.
61 Aviva Cantor, *An Egalitarian Hagada* (New York: Lillith Pub., 1982).
62 Sue Fishkoff, "New haggadot and a face lift for an old favorite." *Washington Jewish Week* 7 April 2011, 30.
63 Penina V. Adelman, "A Drink from Miriam's Cup: Invention of Tradition among Jewish Women." *Journal of Feminist Studies in Religion* 10, no. 2 (1994), 156.
64 Ibid., 157.

to the Haggadah.⁶⁵ In the spring 2000 issue of *Lillith* magazine, Rabbi Susan Schnur, a Reconstructionist rabbi and co-founder of *Lillith*, published a ceremony and blessing for the Miriam's cup to be included or inserted into any other Haggadah.⁶⁶

In the 1980s, some Jews added an orange to the Seder Plate because

> to celebrate being gay or lesbian as one of many great ways to be Jewish, and to mark the fruitfulness created in human society by the diversity of our sexualities. ... an orange because it suggests the fruitfulness for all Jews when lesbians and gay men are contributing and active members of Jewish life. "Be fruitful and multiply" is the Bible's first commandment, and we need to recognize the fruitfulness of gay and lesbian presence, and encourage that presence to multiply.⁶⁷

Each person takes a segment, says the blessing, and then spits out the seeds. This process "symbolize[s] our solidarity with Jewish lesbians and gay men, as well as others who are marginalized within the Jewish community" and by spitting out the seeds Jews would understand that "homophobia...poisons too many Jews."⁶⁸ Ruth Simkin's *Like An Orange on the Seder Plate: Our Lesbian Haggadah*⁶⁹ shows the placement of the orange on the front cover. It sits proudly in the center of the Seder Plate dominating the image.

In 2016 Le'Or Education Fund published the Cannabis Passover Seder Haggadah, which Le'Or saw as continuation of the 1960s Civil Rights Seders. Their goal was to "apply our story to the world today."⁷⁰ The lettuce leaf on the Seder Plate is replaced by a marijuana leaf or bud as a "symbol of freedom... to control one's own body."⁷¹ The 4 sons are replaced by activist children and the 10 plagues by 10 modern interpretations of personal liberty.⁷²

---

65 Ruth Gruber Freedman, *The Passover Seder* (New York: New American Library, 1983), 108–109.
66 Susan Schnur, "Miriam's Goblet (Kos Miriam)." *Lillith* (spring 2000).
67 Susannah Heschel, "Orange on the Seder Plate," in *The Woman's Passover Companion: Women's Reflections on the Festival of Freedom*, ed. Catherine Specter, Sharon Cohen Anisfeld, and Tara Mohr (Woodstock, Vermont: Jewish Lights, 2003), 211, accessed 11 April 2014, http://www.etzchaimflorida.org/wpress/wp-content/uploads/Orange-on-the-Seder-Plate.pdf.
68 Ibid.
69 Ruth Simkin, *Like An Orange on a Seder Plate: Our Lesbian Haggadah* (n.p.: Ruth Simkin, 1999).
70 Le'Or Education Fund, *Cannabis Passover Seder* (Portland, OR: Le'Or Education Fund, 2016), cover letter.
71 Ibid., 10.
72 Ibid., 17, 18.

All of these additions are clear reflections of current issues that Jews have been involved in. They follow in the traditions of addressing concerns Jews had in the Haggadah. Especially in America, where there is a freedom to publically address what people feel are wrongs and petition to correct them. These social and political agenda additions are included with some frequency.

It is extraordinarily rare for something to be removed from the traditional Haggadah. Certainly, no one would dare remove anything as found in the Talmud. However, one could possibly delete later, i.e., medieval, additions. Only one group would even consider taking such a radical path: Reform rabbis. In the 1st official Haggadah published by the CCAR, 3 traditional Medieval elements of the Haggadah were removed because of theological beliefs: the ceremony welcoming Elijah, the counting of the plagues, and the closing statement – "Next year in Jerusalem." The 1905 CCAR Haggadah did not include the welcoming of Elijah because:

> The attitude of mind of the modern man has completely changed....He can no longer regard rites and symbols with the awe that vested them with mystic meaning, or supernatural sanction. ...much of the old Pesach Haggadah is obsolete and tasteless. At times it is even objectionable to our sense of devotion.[73]

Since the theology of the Reform Movement was to examine religion scientifically and historically, the arrival of Elijah to the Seder was seen as superstitious nonsense. What these religious leaders wanted was a religious practice more structured and staid akin to their Protestant neighbors. The CCAR's Haggadah Committee's intent was to "fill a want that had long been felt" among American Reform Jews and to "restore the *Seder* evening to the distinguished place it once held."[74]

Additionally, the Reform Movement had shed the concept of a person as Messiah and adopted the concept of a messianic age. Thus the place of Elijah himself became problematic. Elijah's Cup was returned in the 1923 addition because:

> The Seder service was never purely devotional. Its intensely spiritual tone mingled with bursts of good humor, its serious observations on Jewish life and destiny with comments

---

[73] Central Conference of American Rabbis, *The Union Haggadah: Home Service for the Passover Eve* (Cleveland: CCAR, July 1905), 9.
[74] Joseph Krauskopf, "Appendix B: Message of Rabbi Jos. Krauskopf, President of Central Conference of American Rabbis, to its Sixteenth Annual Convention, Cleveland, Ohio, July 3, 1905." Cleveland, Ohio, 2–6 July 1905 Convention. *CCAR Yearbook*, vol. 15 (Cincinnati: Bloch, 1906): 198.

in a lighter vein, and its lofty poetry with playful ditties for the entertainment of the children.[75]

The Haggadah Committee of the CCAR was "guided by the desire of making the work...rich in those traditional elements that lend color to the service."[76] This shows the development of Reform Jewish philosophy, returning to Elijah place in the theology of the end of time and the desire to attract more traditional Jews to the Movement.

The recitation of the Ten Plagues was removed from *The Union Haggadah* because it was "unworthy of enlightened sensitivities."[77] One can presume that the Ten Plagues were considered another sign of superstition. However, Bronstein returned it to the Seder ceremony because it "is integral with the celebration of redemption." He wanted a "fusion" of deliverance and universal redemption that met the needs of an "enlightened" Jew.[78]

The 1905 CCAR Haggadah did not include this closing statement, "Next Year in Jerusalem," because the Reform Movement had shed Zionism as part of Judaism's outlook.[79] For American Reform Jews, America was the holy land. Here, they could be openly Jewish without fear of reprisal (for the most part) and participate in government and society. Jerusalem thus became a mythological place. While this was definitely the official Union of American Hebrew Congregations' (UAHC) stand, the reality was different. Reform Jews, both clergy and lay persons were becoming involved in the Zionist movement in the early part of the 20th Century.[80] "Next year in Jerusalem" was included in the 1974 Bronstein Haggadah[81] because there was a return, as stated in the 1976 Platform,[82] to Zionism as part of

---

[75] Central Conference of American Rabbis, *The Union Haggadah: Home Service for the Passover*, revised edition (n.p.: CCAR, 1923), vii–ix.
[76] Samuel S. Cohon, Samuel N. Deinard, Solomon B. Freehof, and Samuel Schwartz, Report of the Haggadah Committee, 38 Annual Convention, Washington, D.C., 13–17 April 1921. *CCAR Yearbook*, vol. 31. (Richmond, Virginia: Old Dominion Press, 1921), 38.
[77] CCAR, *The Union* (1905), 9.
[78] Bronstein, הגדה של פסח, 7.
[79] Henry Berkowitz, "Why I Am Not A Zionist," in *Reform Judaism: A Historical Perspective. Essays from the Yearbook of the Central Conference of American Rabbis*, ed. Joseph L. Blau (New York: KTAV Publishing House, 1973), 371–378.
[80] Yaakov Ariel, "Miss Daisy's Planet: The Strange World of Reform Judaism in the United States, 1870–1930," in *Platforms and Prayer Books: Theological and Liturgical Perspectives on Reform Judaism*, ed. Dana Evan Kaplan (New York: Rowman & Littlefield Pub., 2002): 54.
[81] Bronstein, הגדה של פסח.
[82] *Reform Judaism: A Centenary Perspective*, (CCAR, 1976), accessed 5 December 2010, http://ccarnet.org/rabbis-speak/platforms/reform-judaism-centenary-perspective/.

the Reform theology, clearly a response to the American Reform constituency's beliefs. Bronstein stated that he "wanted to communicate the meaning of various symbolic statements such as 'next year in Jerusalem,' which is a messianic statement rather than merely a suggestion that all Jews would like to spend the Passover in Jerusalem."[83]

Conclusion

Over more than 2,000 years, the celebration for Passover has evolved and with it a ceremony and a liturgy called the Haggadah has developed. As the ceremony was being created, the rabbis felt a need to explain in detail how to perform the rites. This liturgy has reflected the theological orientation of the people using it, changing to meet their needs with the additions of prayers and readings to help understand the world around them or the deletion of ceremonies that seemed unimportant. However, the basic liturgy has remained the same since Talmudic times.

---

83 Bronstein, "Re: Ltr."

Chapter 2:
Development of the Non-Liturgical Portions of the Haggadah in the Context of the Evolution of Jewish Education

> "To the task of training Jews in Jewish ways, of molding Jewish character in accordance with traditional standards, of building the Judaism of the future, may we, both as individuals and as an organization, sincerely and honestly dedicate ourselves today."
>
> S. H. Markowitz[1]

The celebration of Passover is not as simple as sitting down to a ceremonial meal and reciting the words in the Haggadah. The house needs to be purged of all leavened foods, eating and cooking utensils for non-Passover foods exchanged for kosher for Passover utensils, and kosher for Passover food. For those Jews who are ignorant of these things, the Passover practices seem almost foreign. However, despite the arduous preparations, the importance of celebrating Seder did not diminish over time among American Jews, as some Jewish leaders feared it would. Despite falling synagogue membership, observance of Passover went from around 30 percent in 1930[2] to over 80 percent 60 years later.[3] Part of this resurgence can be attributed to the post-Holocaust American renewal interest in Judaism and part of it can be seen as the abundance of Haggadot designed for any religious and political leaning a Jew could have.

Domestic Religion[4]

Preparation for Passover is complicated because of the complexity of what may and may not be eaten during the course of the 8-day holiday (as required by Orthodoxy) celebration, though the Reform Movement has moved to a day 7 cele-

---

[1] S. H. Markowitz, "The Educative Process in a Jewish Community." *The Jewish Teacher: A Quarterly Magazine for Jewish Religious School* 2, no. 2 (1934): 8.
[2] Michael A. Meyer, *A Response to Modernity: A History of the Reform Movement in Judaism* (New York: Oxford Univ. Press, 1988), 322–323.
[3] Sidney Goldstein, "Profile of American Jewry: Insights from the 1990 National Population Survey." *Jewish American Year Book* (1992), 172, accessed 5 June 2014, http://www.jewishdatabank.org/Studies/downloadFile.cfm?FileID=3004.
[4] This term was coined by participant of a study done by Barbara Meyerhoff. (Barbara Meyerhoff, *Number Our Days* (New York: E.P. Dutton, 1978).)

bration. This entire Passover preparation process historically was the purview of the woman of the house, and she taught it to her daughters through informal educational practices: by example. This has been viewed as a key way Judaism has survived – the generational passing of knowledge from one woman to her daughters. After all, the proper role of a Jewish woman was to maintain the home and teach the children Jewish customs. This was a highly respected role because of the amount of influence a woman would have on her children.

An Overview of Jewish Education before Public Education

Before the advent of free public education, it was the responsibility of parents to provide education for their children. The Torah states in Deuteronomy 11:19, Deuteronomy 4:9, and Deuteronomy 33:4 that it is a father's obligation to teach his sons Torah. However, daughters are not required to be taught Torah. We do know that both boys and girls were taken with their parents on pilgrimages to sanctuaries and the Temple (Deuteronomy 16:12, 18; 16:11; 31:12; 1 Samuel 1; Nehemiah 12:43; Jeremiah 9:19) and it is through this practice that both genders would have learned customs. During the Biblical Period, the education of children was left to the parents and there was a large variance in the type of education received by the children of the priests and the children of farmers.

The Talmud contains a number of statements that suggest girls were educated in Torah and secular subjects. Beruriah, wife of Rabbi Meir and daughter of the martyred Rabbi Haninah ben Teradyon, is presented as the sole female scholar in the Talmud. Some scholars see her as literary device created by the Talmudic rabbis as an example of a bad woman (Rashi comments that she was seduced and committed suicide), while others see her as an example of what women in Talmudic times achieved. The Talmud includes others, like Ima Shalom in *Shabbat* 116 and the daughter of Rabbi Hisda in *Hagigah* 5a. Because the Talmudic material, the only Jewish literature we have of the period, was written by men, it is probably skewed. Therefore, women have been ignored and we do not have a clear picture of what women's lives were really like.

In Medieval times, Ashkenazi families who were wealthy enough would hire a tutor for their sons. Girls might listen in on the lessons, either with or without the approval of their parents. If there were no sons, then a family might consider educating the daughters and hiring a tutor for them to learn Torah and Talmud.

The Sephardim believed in teaching their sons all the subjects their Muslim neighbors were taught so that they could compete for the same jobs, which under Muslim rule they could have. Thus, they studied astronomy, literature, and science. In the 12th Century, Joseph Ben Judah ibn Aqnin, a Spanish courtier, designed a curriculum of study for Jewish Spaniards to train their sons to be courtiers: reading and writing was to be done in Arabic; Torah, Mishnah, and Hebrew grammar were required subjects with Talmud added at the age of 15; poetry; philosophy, logic; mathematics; astronomy; music; mechanics; metaphysics; and medicine and natural sciences. Judah ibn Tibbon, in his will circa 1190, reminded his son to "examine the Hebrew books at every new moon, [and] the Arabic volumes once in two months."[5] Even in Muslim countries, where a strict separation of sexes existed, there are cases of girls being learned and teaching others, even men. While most Sephardic women were illiterate, they were still business-savvy. Some Jewish women were midwives to royalty and others practiced medicine under authorization of the king. Thus, there were different types of education; clearly some were apprenticed, like midwifery, and others more formal, like Talmudic study.

There were women leaders of the women in synagogues during the Middle Ages who were able to read and chant Hebrew and knew the prayers by heart. Rashi's daughters are some of the most famous Talmudically educated women. There were other daughters of rabbis who learned from their fathers. Common women also studied, as Eleazar ben Samuel of Mayence's (d. 1357) will attests to. He directs his children to live with other Jews "so that their sons and daughters may learn the ways of Judaism...they must not let the young of both sexes go without instruction in Torah."[6] There were even women who practiced medicine. Ashkenazic girls during the Middle Ages and early Modern Period were expected to be able to run a business, and so often had some education in business skills (basic mathematics, reading, and writing). During the Medieval Period, Jewish women in Christian lands were involved in business, which required some education. They were also involved through public religious life including educating other women. However, their education was limited. They did not learn, for example, science, advanced mathematics, law, or other matters that would provide them a way into the social sphere of men.

During the early Modern Period, literature in Yiddish began to take hold in Eastern Europe. Hebrew was reserved for prayer and international business and Yiddish for community communication. This was a language that women were taught to read and write because it was the language the Jewish community spoke. In early 16th Century Prague, Rebecca Tiktiner, a prominent scholar and preacher, taught women Talmud and ethics. In the late 16th Century, Jacob ben

---

[5] William Hallo, David Ruderman, and Michael Stanislawski, *Source Reader Heritage: Civilization and the Jew* (Westport: Praeger, 1984), 141.
[6] Ibid., 187.

Isaac Ashkenazi composed *Ze-enuah U-Re'enah* (*Come and See*) a work on the Torah that was intended for the use of both sexes as he explains in his front piece, but was used primarily by women as something to read on Shabbat. Hava Bacharach (c. 1585–1652), the daughter of Rabbi Isaac ben Simeon Katz and the granddaughter of Rabbi Judah Löwe, was revered throughout the Jewish world as a scholar. The Jewish community of Minsk was famous for educating its girls in Torah in the same way as the boys in the 16th Century.

Glückel of Hameln (1646–1724), a business woman now remembered for her singular diary, remarked that she and her sisters and brothers received both a religious and a secular education, and her stepsister spoke French and played the clavichord.[7] This is clearly the expectation of a liberal-thinking wealthy merchant-class family. Documents of the period show, at least in the elementary-school level, that girls and boys studied together. Calls began in the late 1700s for equal religious education for boys and girls. Rabbi Elijah Gaon instructed his wife on the education of their daughters, which was to include reading on the Sabbath.

However, 150 years later Mary Antin wrote in her memoir about her jealousy of the boys of the Pale of Settlement in the late 1800s who were privileged to attend school while she could not. "There was no free school for girls,"[8] she moaned, "for a girl it was enough it she could read her prayers in Hebrew, and follow the meaning by the Yiddish translation."[9] Instead, "a girl's real schoolroom was her mother's kitchen...and while her hands were busy, her mother instructed her in the laws regulating a pious Jewish household."[10] Esther Singer Kreitman, sister of Isaac Beshivas Singer, wrote in her autobiographical novel *Deborah* set in pre-World War I Poland, "it was an accepted view among pious Jews that there was only one achievement in a life a woman could hope for – the bringing of happiness into the home by ministering to her husband and bearing him children."[11] While there is a clear difference in social class between Glückel, who came from a wealthy and international family, and Antin and Kreitman, who came from poor and provincial families, that an entire community, Minsk, had Talmud lessons for girls, shows that expectations for girls' education fell over time, forcing them into the private world of home.

---

7 Glückel of Hameln, *The Memoirs of Glückel of Hameln*, trans. Marvin Lowenthal (New York: Schocken Books, 1977), 6, 11, 12.
8 Mary Antin, *The Promised Land* (Boston: Houghton Mifflin Co., 1912), 26.
9 Ibid., 34.
10 Ibid.
11 Esther Singer Kreitman, *Deborah*, trans. Maurice Carr (New York: St. Martin's Press, 1946), 6.

In the New World, the first Jewish school was opened in New York at Shearith Israel in 1731. The board demanded that their teacher be able to teach Hebrew, have the ability to translate from Hebrew to English, and be able to speak English. They were following the practice of the time that religious institutions were the place children went for education.

Both genders were included, which shows the importance of teaching Jewish theology and history to girls had gained a stronghold in the New World.

Public Education and Its Effect on Jewish Education

The Emancipation of Jewry in Europe came in the wake of the Enlightenment. The idea that secular education was for everyone brought with it an opportunity for poor boys and girls to become literate. Free public schools were opened in Italy before 1800. In Hungary, compulsory education was decreed in 1783 (though these schools were sponsored by religious groups and required to teach a certain list of secular subjects by the government). Government-funded schools were instituted in Hungary by 1884, by England in 1870, by Germany no later than 1872, by France in 1881, and after the Communist Revolution in Russia.

Just because these schools existed did not mean the Jewish population took full advantage of them. For example, poverty kept many children in France away from schools during the early 19th Century, although they had better attendance than their poor Gentile counterparts. Their parents either could not afford clothes and shoes and school supplies or needed the income their children could provide to subsist. Despite numerous attempts to organize after-school religious education, this did not take hold in France. Only in the 1930s among the newly arrived Eastern European Jewish immigrants to Paris did it succeed.

Free public education was problematic because of its Christian leanings and secular subject matter. Often religion, meaning Christian doctrine, was one of the required subjects. By the early 1800s, Hungarian Jewish leaders were concerned "about the dangerous decline of their [children's] Jewish knowledge and religious practice" even with private instruction and after-school programs.[12] Additionally, the girls who attended public schools while their brothers attended *cheder* and *yeshiva* developed a more enlightened view of the world and this

---

[12] Ruth Kestenberg-Gladstein, "The Jews Between Czechs and Germans in the Historic Lands, 1848–1918." In *The Jews of Czechoslovakia: Historical Studies and Surveys*, vol. 1 (Philadelphia: JPS of America, 1968), 369.

brought conflict into the home concerning what one should believe and how one should understand the world around them.

In 1850, the United States instituted a national public-education system. However, in New York there had been a Board of Regents and a state superintendent by 1800. The states of Pennsylvania, Ohio, and Massachusetts followed suit and set up these free public schools by 1837. The public-education laws mandated that every child attend school. In the United States, this resulted in a general increase in the literacy of Americans, both black and white. Students attending private Jewish schools were not affected. Jews were particularly committed to education and public education was, therefore, an enticement to them. Additionally, American Jews "believed in education as the precondition of status and prosperity."[13] However, because Jewish girls were now required to attend school, it did change their education patterns drastically.

As girls were spending less time with their mothers and grandmothers learning domestic religion because they were in school or doing their homework and their parents were less concerned with the traditions, they were absorbing less informal education. The result for girls was that when they were ready to marry, they were unable, and even unwilling, to run a household in the traditional Jewish way because they had not learned the customary homemaking skills.

There were effects on the boys as well. Their knowledge of Torah and Talmud fell as time was spent studying secular subjects instead. As various governments demanded that more secular subjects be taught, government funding for religious schools that did not comply was withdrawn. Thus, those Jewish schools that could remain open had to charge tuition and the poorer boys ended up going to the state schools rather than the Jewish private schools. Therefore, after-school programs were introduced to teach the boys the religious knowledge they had not learned in the public schools.

Israel Joseph Benjamin of Moldavia was a trader by profession and then decided to become a wanderer and preacher (*magîd*). In 1859, he arrived in the United States. In 1861, he returned to Europe and the following year he published his memoir about his travels: *Three Years in America*. His insights into American Jewish life are unusual and enlightening. He included a chapter, "About the Up Bringing of Jewish Women in America," in which he derides American Jewish parents for the lack of religious education for their daughters that has resulted in a group of young women who "are at present unable to undertake and fulfill wor-

---

[13] Stephen J. Whitfield, "American Jews: Their Story Continues," in *The American Jewish Experience*, ed. Jonathan D. Sarna (New York: Holmes & Meier, 1986), 286.

thily the place in life for which they are intended,"¹⁴ meaning being a Jewish homemaker and mother according to the traditional standards as he understood them. He explains the situation thusly: a girl stays at home with her mother until the age of 5,

> then the child, it is obvious, must be sent to a public school....the child begins the usual course of studies.... After school, she studies her lessons for the next day or, like all children, plays. Upon going to bed or arising in the morning, she may very likely recite for her mother some Hebrew or English prayers; but as for Judaism, the child experiences nothing and knows nothing....On her fifteenth birthday...the longed-for day arrives at last...she... shall leave school...What useful knowledge has she gained during this time? Extremely little in fact....She does not know how to sew, has no knowledge of household affairs, and still less of higher things.¹⁵

He was horrified that girls knew no Hebrew or Jewish practices. Benjamin blamed the parents who had no "true religious feeling"¹⁶ and even more the entire Jewish community.¹⁷ He had found the central problem for the continuation of Judaism in America: the combination of an interest in continuing Judaism, rather than devoting all energies to assimilation, and education to enforce the practice and understanding of Judaism. It should be pointed out that Benjamin did not give parents positive feedback concerning their sons' educations. He is appalled that boys were not given religious training unless they live in a large urban area.¹⁸

Development of Jewish Religious Education in the United States

Jewish educators realized they had to address this need for religious education by providing religious schools. Rebecca Gratz opened the first free Jewish Sunday School in Philadelphia in 1838 following the example set by the American Sunday School movement (a Christian movement) founded in 1791 also in Philadelphia. In 1871, Esther Levy published the *Jewish Cookery Book, on Principles of Economy, Adapted for Jewish Housekeepers*, for which she believed a need had

---

14 [Israel Joseph] Benjamin, *Three Years in America 1859–1862*, vol. 1, trans. Charles Reznikoff (Philadelphia: JPS of America, 1956), 86.
15 Ibid., 86–87.
16 Ibid., 87.
17 Ibid., 88.
18 Ibid., 88.

"been felt in our domestic circles" for some time. This work was her attempt to assist a new generation of Jewish uneducated homemakers.[19] The Reform Jews brought with them David Friedländer's concept of Jewish education as subordinate to secular subjects. They turned away from the traditional *cheder* and turned toward the Protestant idea of catechism.

The Union of American Hebrew Congregations (UAHC) realized the need for Jewish education and in 1886 supported the creation of the Hebrew Sabbath School Union (HSSU). In 1905, the UAHC's Department of Synagogue and School Extension (DSSE) replaced the HSSU. When Emanual Garoran, a graduate of the Teachers Institute of the Jewish Theological Seminary (JTS), was appointed director of the UAHC–DSSE, he developed an emphasis in the program on Jewish observance and Hebrew. It was so much better than other available curricula that the Conservative and Orthodox schools used it.

Alexander Dushkin, employed by the Department of Jewish Education in New York City, wrote in 1916 on the front page of the 1st edition of *The Jewish Teacher* a repetition of Benjamin's sentiment: "Education has probably never meant as much to the preservation of any group's life, as Jewish education means at this moment to the continued life of our people."[20] That year the Bureau of Jewish Education was founded in New York City. Duskin believed that education was important because he saw in the Jews of the turn of the 20th Century a lack of commitment "to the need for the Jewish literacy." Rather, they were interested in "belonging."[21] He estimated that in 1917, only 25 percent of the 400,000 Jewish adolescents in the United States participated in any Jewish institution.[22]

Harry Friedenwald, a Jewish philanthropist, wrote in the same edition of *The Jewish Teacher* that "the secular education of the child takes up almost all the time that child should devote to study" and that a new system for imparting Jewish literacy was desperately needed.[23] The following year, Dushkin estimated

---

19 Esther Levy, *Jewish Cookery Book, on Principles of Economy, Adapted for Jewish Housekeepers, with the addition of many useful medicinal recipes, and other valuable information, relative to housekeeping and domestic management* (Philadelphia: N.P., 1871 Reprint Cambridge, Connecticut: Applewood Books, 1988), 5.
20 Alexander M. Dushkin, "Editorial Statement." *The Jewish Teacher: A Quarterly Magazine for Jewish Religious School* 1, no. 1 (1916): 1.
21 Alexander M. Duskin, "Fifty Years of American Jewish Education – Retrospect and Prospects." *Jewish Education* 37, no. 1–2 (1967): 45.
22 Alexander M. Dushkin, Editorial Statement." *The Jewish Teacher: A Quarterly Magazine for Jewish Religious School* 1, no. 3 (1917): 133.
23 Harry Friedenwald, "The Problem of Jewish Education from the layman's point of view." *The Jewish Teacher: A Quarterly Magazine for Jewish Religious School* 1, no. 1 (1916): 13.

"that there are in this country over 400,000 Jewish adolescents between the ages of fourteen and twenty-one. Of these future members of the American Jewish community, probably less than one in twenty-five comes under the influence of any Jewish institution."[24]

Seventy years later, Walter Ackerman, professor at New York University, criticized the Jewish education system for the "distressing fact that few Jewish schools in this country have succeeded in imparting any real Jewish knowledge to their students, or in developing even the minimum of intellectual competence required of the literate Jew."[25] During the Interwar Period, Rabbi S. H. Markowitz of Fort Wayne, Indiana, told the Ohio-Michigan-Indiana Teachers Association that he was disappointed with his religious school. He understood that education is "the process of life adjustment" and the entire Jewish community must participate in the educational process.[26] However, because "Jews are today [in 1933] for the most part religiously barren, culturally ignorant, and socially insecure," they "are psychologically incapable of perpetuating Judaism in the lives of children."[27]

By 1949, the Reform Movement had renamed its curriculum committee the Education Department of the Union because its leaders realized they had to begin "paying special attention to the isolated Jews who, living in small communities, do not have the opportunity for pursuing courses of instruction in organized Jewish Centers."[28]

In 1950 Rabbi Gamoran, at this time Educational Director of the UAHC, praised American Jews for their support and participation in the American public school system, but also lamented the lack of Jewishly-trained leaders among Reform Jews.[29] In the 1960s, 90 percent of American Jewish children attended a re-

---

24 Dushkin, "Editorial Statement." *The Jewish Teacher*, no. 3: 133.
25 Walter I. Ackerman, *"Strangers to the Tradition: Idea and Constraint in American Jewish Education."Jewish Population Studies*, 77 (Jewish Education Worldwide: Cross-Cultural Perspectives) Avraham Harman Institute of Contemporary Jewry, 1989. Accessed 13 June 2014, http://www.bjpa.org/Publications/details.cfm?PublicationID=421.
26 Markowitz, "The Educative Process," 1–2.
27 Ibid., 3.
28 Emanuel Gamorn, "Progress and Prospects in Jewish Education" (presented at the American Association for Jewish Education and the National Council for Jewish Education, Atlantic City, New Jersey, June 1949); reprint *The Jewish Teacher: A Quarterly Magazine for Jewish Religious School* 18, no. 3 (1950): 3.
29 Emanuel Gamoran, "Liberal Judaism and the Day School" (presented at The Jewish Day School: A Symposium, Central Conference of American Rabbis, Cincinnati, June 1950); reprint *The Jewish Teacher: A Quarterly Magazine for Jewish Religious School* 2, no. 2 (1951): 1, 5.

ligious school associated with a synagogue once a week.³⁰ Ackerman attributed the rise in religious schools attached to synagogues to the growth of suburban synagogues and the desire of suburban Jews to identify with the American Jewish community. Because these religious schools were "attempting to persuade children to adopt a life style which their parents have rejected," the "school [was] regarded as a symbol of Jewishness," not a way of communicating how to be Jewish.³¹ Interestingly, the percentage of American Jewish children attending religious school dropped in the next decade. School-age children in the Reform Movement were receiving less education than their parents.³² Chaim I. Waxman, professor emeritus of Sociology and Jewish Studies at Rutgers University, discovered that pre-World War II Jewish Americans and Jewish American Baby-boomers, Americans born and raised between 1946 and 1964, had little supplementary (after-school program of) formal Jewish education.³³ These religious school programs did their best to incorporate Jewish traditions into the educational process; however, there is a difference between learning something and living it.

By understanding that there was ignorance on how to observe the holidays, Jewish religious leaders could then address the problem. There is much to be said for informal education in learn homemaking skills. What Benjamin, Dushkin, and Ackerman saw and, in their way, tried to combat was the combined factors of ignorance and contempt. Without observance, education has little meaning and only encouraged the lack of interest in observance.

The Development of Non-Liturgical Material in Haggadot

The lack of formal education combined with the lack of interest among many immigrant families for maintaining traditions encouraged ceremonial ignorance. Add to this the large number of Jewish immigrants who did not live in Jewish

---

30 Dushkin, "Fifty Years," 49.
31 Walter I. Ackerman, "Jewish Education–For What?" *Jewish American Year Book*, vol. 70 (1969), 5, accessed 13 August 2014, http://www.ajcarchives.org/AJC_DATA/Files/1969_3_Special Articles.pdf.
32 Fred Massarik, "Trends in U.S. Jewish Education: National Jewish Population Study Findings." *American Jewish Year Book*, vol. 77 (Philadelphia: JPS, 1977), 242, accessed 13 June 2014, http://www.bjpa.org/Publications/details.cfm?PublicationID=20843.
33 Chaim I. Waxman, *Jewish Education Does Matter* (Tel Aviv: Tel Aviv University, School of Education, 2003), 114–115, 117, accessed 13 June 2014, http://www.bjpa.org/Publications/details.cfm?PublicationID=3038.

communities or who lived in very small Jewish communities where practice was difficult to observe, and one can understand why 1st- generation Jews were Jewishly undereducated.

American rabbis, especially non-Orthodox rabbis, realized that if American Jews were going to observe the rituals, they were going to have to be instructed. Therefore, in 1967 the UAHC produced *Liberal Judaism at Home: The Practices of Modern Reform Judaism*. Rabbi Morrison David Bial "hope[d] that this presentation will have value to the Liberal Jew who is seeking a positive understanding of the rituals and practices of Liberal Judaism as he and his family observe them."[34]

Thus for the Seder information was needed to help guide the celebrant. Those Haggadot published before the creation of governmentally funded public education, like the Amsterdam Haggadah published in 1695, the Leipnik-Rosenthaliana Haggadah of 1738, and the Moshe Bamberger Haggadah of 1772, only have the 12th Century "קדש ורחץ" ("Blessing and Washing") as introductory material. Thus, it is really a part of the liturgy, rather than introductory material. Most interestingly, all these Haggadot include the "קדש ורחץ" in Hebrew and Yiddish. The Amsterdam and Leipnik-Rosenthaliana Haggadah include this in Judeo-Spanish also because the publishers wanted as broad an audience as possible for their publications and there were many Sephardim in Amsterdam at the time. The presumption was that preparing for the holiday was learned by girls as part of their domestic education.

However, with the advent of Emancipation and public education, we can see the inclusion of more informative materials develop. This is especially true in American Haggadot because American Jews were more readily accepted into American society and became secularized more quickly. For example, A. Th. Phillips' 1859 Haggadah includes not only an image of the search for leavening, where a father and son stand together – the father with a feather and prayer book and the son with a candle – and a page entitled "בדיקת חמץ" ("The search for leavening"), but also the prayers and instructions are provided to the reader. In fact, the reader is reminded "on the evening preceding the Fourteenth day of the month Nissan, it is requisite for the master of every family to search after leavened bread in every place where it is usually kept, gathering all the leaven lying in his way."[35] Philips then instructs the reader on how to set the table with a plate for "three cakes, (generally called *Mizvos* [sic])," a Seder Plate, a glass of

---

34 Morrison David Bial, *Liberal Judaism at Home: The Practices of Modern Reform Judaism* (New York: UAHC, 1971), v.

35 A. Th. Philips, פסח הוסדר של הגדה *Form of Service for the Two First Nights of the Feast of Passover with English Translation*, New Illustrated Edition (New York: Hebrew Publishing Co., 1859), 2–3.

wine for every person, and that "even the lowest Hebrew servant [is] to sit at table during the ceremonial part."[36]

In 1886, Rabbi H. M. Bien published *Easter Eve or The "New Hagodoh Shel Pesach." A Metrical Family-Fest Service*. The title is itself enlightening. Here Bien is attempting to equate Seder with Easter to make it more appealing to Americanized Jews of the period. His solution was to turn the Seder into a play, with characters explaining the ceremony and story and interspersing the Hebrew prayers with English readings. Bien is not the only Jew to call Passover Easter. In her memoir about Jewish communal colony in 1883 outside of Newport, Arkansas, Kate Herder describes the holiday as Easter.[37]

Sometimes the only non-liturgical material is a paragraph at the opening of the Haggadah that directs one how to set the table. For example, Isaac S. Moses included this as the only introduction in his 1898 Haggadah:

> In the center of the festive board will be placed the following articles: Matzoth, or the unleavened bread, covered with a white cloth; a piece of meat, roasted over the fire; bitter herbs and early spring garden fruit; a cup with salt-water; a boiled egg; and a little dish containing a mixture of apples, almonds, and nuts. In front of each participant will be placed a wine-glass. With bread and wine, the two most precious fruits of earth, and with the symbols of Israel's checkered career, shall we celebrate the return of this oldest and most significant Festival of Judaism, in happy family reunion.[38]

This Haggadah was a popular one, as by 1907 it was in its 5th revision. However, there were no more non-liturgical parts added.

The Central Conference of American Rabbis (CCAR) in their effort to create a uniform American Judaism "in the mode of public and private worship"[39] published a prayerbook in 1892 that included a Haggadah.[40] This too included a paragraph on instruction on how to set the table.[41] With this simple statement, we can see the beginning of the need for instruction, but both Moses and the

---

[36] Ibid., 4.
[37] Kate Herder, "Memories of Yesterday." *OzarksWatch: Documenting Jews of the Ozarks* 12, nos. 1 & 2 (1999): 61.
[38] I[saac] S. Moses, *Domestic Service for the Eve of Passover*, 2nd revised and enlarged ed. (Chicago: n.p., 1898), 1.
[39] Mannheimer, S. and I. Schwab."On Prayer-Book." (presented at the Convention of the Central Conference of American Rabbis, Cleveland, Ohio, 14 July 1891). *Year Book of the Central Conference of American Rabbis 1890 – 91* (Cincinnati: Bloch Pub., 1891); reprint *Central Conference of American Rabbis Year Book Volumes I, II, III 1890 – 1983* (New York: CCAR, n.d.), 26.
[40] Central Conference of American Rabbis, *Union Prayer Book* (Chicago: Bloch Pub., 1892).
[41] Ibid., 227.

CCAR did not believe that their audience needs much explanation on how to prepare for Passover.

Rabbi William Rosenau, president of the CCAR between 1915 and 1917, "believ[ed] that the demand for a new English version of the Hagadah as existed for some time" and, thus, published his in 1905[42] in competition with the CCAR edition. No longer is there a "בדיקת חמץ" section, rather it is titled: "The Search for Leaven" and includes just the blessings to say before, after, and in the morning as the leavening is burnt.[43] Then there is a 2 page list of how the Seder table is organized with explanations of what each of the Seder foods symbolize.[44] Rosenau's Haggadah is arranged with Hebrew on one page and the English translation on its facing page. The text is "fully traditional in the Hebrew text, but reflective of the ideology of classical Reform in the English version."[45]

Many more traditional American Haggadot had some kind of non-liturgical materials. The 1910 Behrman's Jewish Bookshop הגדה של פסח, also with Hebrew and English on facing pages, begins with the "בדיקת חמץ".[46] While Rosenau was a leader of the Reform community and he and the Movement were purposely reaching out to the undereducated, this Orthodox text also has a paragraph on how to set the table and arrange the Seder Plate. Interestingly, the paragraph appears in English on the Hebrew page and does not have the corresponding illustration, although there is an arrangement of the words in a circle representing the Seder Plate.[47] One could speculate that this author presumed that those who understood the Hebrew did not need instruction or such instruction in Hebrew would be far too advanced Hebrew for the reader. In either case, this points to those Jews who are secularly educated and Jewishly undereducated.

The 1929 "thoroughly revised" Haggadah published by the Star Hebrew Book Company begins with "דיני בדיקת חמץ" ("Test for Leavening") that presents the laws and blessings for the cleansing of the house.[48] Then there is a page of "The Preparation of the Table and the Four Cups" beginning with the admonition that "the table must be prepared during daylight, but the ceremony should

---

[42] William Rosenau, הגדה סדר *Home-Service for Passover Eve* (New York: Bloch Pub., 1905), "Preface."

[43] Ibid., 1–2.

[44] Ibid., 2–3.

[45] Joel Gereboff, "One Nation, with Liberty and Haggadahs for All," in *Key Texts in American Jewish Culture*, ed. Jack Kugelmass (New Brunswick: Rutgers Univ. Press, 2003), 280.

[46] הגדה של פסח (New York: Behrman's Book Shop, 1910); reprint as הגדה של פסח (New York: KTAV, 1951), ב–2.

[47] Ibid., א–3.

[48] הגדה של פסח סדר *Service for the First Two Night of Passover*, New Ed. (New York: Star Hebrew Book Co., 1929), 1–2.

not begin until after nightfall" and concluding with "women as well as children ought to take part in the ceremonial."[49] This passage contains much to consider. Firstly, is the idea that one must be done with the labor of preparation before the beginning of the festival. This implies that the first day of Passover is a holy day when work is forbidden. This is the hidden message to the constituency. Finally, the conclusion reminds the readers, or leaders, that women and children are expected to sit at the table and participate. This is not a man's ceremony, but a family ceremony.

American Jewry was not the only Jewish community in need of instruction. In 1897, the Reverend A. A. Green, minister of the Hampstead Synagogue, published, under the authorization of the Chief Rabbi of England: *The Revised Hagada: Home Service for the First Two Nights of Passover*. Green is clear that "the present edition of the Hagadah for Passover aims at supplying what has long been a distinct want in the Ritual literature of English Jews."[50] The manuscript is specifically "to invest the whole of the function with living interest for parents and children."[51]

Green's "Introduction" includes a history of Egypt and recounting of the Exodus story.[52] The Haggadah proper begins with "The Search for Leaven"[53] and is followed by detailed explanation of what is needed to perform the ceremony. Here, Green dispels the "popular error" that *charoset* (the mixture of nuts, dried fruit, and wine) is a symbol of the building materials of the slaves. Rather, he claims, "it is…a usual Oriental accompaniment of such dishes as bitter herbs and should be used in the Seder as a sauce into which to dip the horseradish."[54] There is a reminder to include "a spare cup of wine" for Elijah which "is a guest cup, set apart in readiness for any visitor who may enter the family circle in response to the invitation offered in the early portion of the Seder."[55] Like the Haggadot of the American Reform Movement, Green's Haggadah included no superstitions or folkways from the ceremony and so diminished the role of Elijah in the mythology of the coming of the Messiah. Finally, he mentions that one should not forget a pillow for the leader to lean upon because "this…is one of

---

49 Ibid., 4–5.
50 A. A. Green, *The Revised Hagada: Home Service for the First Two Nights of Passover* (London: Greenberg & Co., 1897), 4.
51 Ibid.
52 Ibid., 6–16.
53 Ibid., 17–18.
54 Ibid., 19.
55 Ibid., 20.

the many Orientalisms, pure and simple, the retention of which lends so much charm to the Seder."[56]

In 1917, a Haggadah in Arabic translation was published in Cairo entitled in Hebrew: הגדה של פסח כמנהג ק"ק ספרדי יצ"ו עם תרגום ערבי באותיות ערביות מאת דר' הלל פרחי. Dr. Hillel Farhi, a poet, translator, and physician, published it again in 1918 and 1922. In it are directions in Arabic for setting the table. There seem to have been customs and explanations for these customs in the 1922 edition. This was the first Egyptian Haggadah to use "high literary Arabic" unlike other Egyptian Haggadot that used a more common Arabic. It was also the first Arabic Haggadah to provide Seder instructions.[57] Haggadot in Arabic had become common beginning in the latter half of the 1800s because of the push for modernization in Egypt, which included the development of a public education system and the establishment of Arabic as the official language of the country. The number of public schools grew from 185 in 1863 to 4,685 in 1875, which included about 100,000 students.[58]

Egyptian Jewish children in the early 20th Century received minimal Hebrew instruction. Rather they studied in Arabic and learned French and English, so that this Haggadah with its explanations and instructions in Arabic was for the less Jewishly educated. In fact, the Arabic instructions are far more detailed than the Hebrew ones. For example, the Hebrew instruction for "Tikkun Erev Pesach" is simply: "If Erev Pesach falls on Wednesday, one takes aside two cooked portions of food and says this blessing." However, the Arabic explains what is "eruv tavshilim" and the customs concerning it.[59] Thus, Jews all over the world in the late 19th and early 20th Century were addressing similar problems that developed because of the reduction of Jewish education. Even such institutions as the Alliance Français Schools in Arab lands were teaching the standard curriculum of France, not a Jewish curriculum.

A revival of Judaism in India began when the remote Bene Israel, who had had no contact with other Jews for almost 1 thousand years, began moving to

---

56 Ibid., 21.
57 Nachum Ilan, "For Whom Was the 'Farhi haggada' Intended? On the image of Egyptian Jews during the First Half of the 20th Century." *Jewish Studies an Internet Journal* 4 (2005), accessed 20 June 2014, http://www.biu.ac.il/js/JSIJ/4-2005/Ilan.pdf.
58 Vladimir Borisovich Lutsky, "Chapter XII: Egyptian the Middle of the 19th Century (1841–76) Egypt After the Capitulation of 1840," in *Modern History of the Arab Countries*, trans. Lika Nasser (Moscow: Progress Publishers, for the USSR Academy of Sciences, Institute of the Peoples of Asia, 1969), "The Reforms of Said and Ismail," accessed 4 July 2014, https://www.marxists.org/subject/arab-world/lutsky/ch12.htm.
59 Ibid.

Mumbai in the first half of the 18th Century. In Mumbai there were British colonists, including British Jews and Jewish merchants from other countries, who taught the Bene Israel about Judaism. In the 1830s, Hebrew-Marathi dictionaries and grammars were published to help the Bene Israel learn Hebrew, as Judeo-Marathi had become their common language. In 1846, the first Haggadah printed in India was produced in Mumbai. It followed the opening of the first synagogue in 1796 and marked the reintroduction of Passover to the Jews of India. They had forgotten the ceremony of Seder and had turned the festival into one that centered on the cleansing of and the purging of leavening from the house. The result was "Anasi Dhakacha San," "The Covering of the Jar," which alluded to the process of taking all forbidden liquids and putting them into a pot and covering the pot until after the festival.[60]

This 1846 Haggadah then is a perfect example of the non-liturgical material that is necessary to teach the people how to recreate a ceremony that had been lost for generations. It follows the layout and uses the graphics of the Amsterdam Haggadah and presents the text in Hebrew and Marathi. "קדש ורחץ" is presented with Hebrew titles, Marathi explanations, and pictures.[61] Following this is a brief explanation of the "בדיקת חמץ" with blessings.[62] Then the directions for creating the Seder table are provided:

> Keep a plate in the middle with three small bowls in it. One of it should hold salt, other one should hold "date pudding" and the third one should hold "sour juice." On these three bowls keep three pieces of unleavened bread...One end of the plate should hold karpas and the other end maror. The other two sides of the plate should hold an egg on one side and bone on the other side.[63]

There is also a drawing of how the plate should look.[64] This Haggadah was so popular that it was reprinted in Poona in 1874 and again in Mumbai in 1935.[65]

---

60 Walter J. Fischel, "Introduction," in *"The Haggadah shel Pesach" in Marathi of the Bene-Israel* (New York: Orphan Hospital Ward of Israel, 1968).
61 הגדה של פסח (Bombay: n.p., 1846); reprint *"The Haggadah shel Pesach" in Marathi of the Bene-Israel* (New York: Orphan Hospital Ward of Israel, 1968). I am deeply indebted to Alka Amonker for her translation of the Marathi text.
62 Ibid., 4A.
63 Ibid., 4B.
64 Ibid., 4B.
65 Fishchel, "Introduction."

Modern Haggadot

Not all Haggadot include non-liturgical material. Dr. Marcus Lehmann's 1935 German *Hagadah Schel Pesach* begins with "דיניבדיקת חמץ" ("The Test for Leavening") and follows this with "ערו בסדר תבשילין" ("Foods not for Passover"). The material is produced in a double-column format of Hebrew and German,[66] but there is no material to explain about the Seder or Passover. Most American Haggadot, even if Orthodox like the Manischewitz *Passover Haggadah*, include the instructions on how to set the table.

However, not all American Haggadot have instructions. Z. Harry Gutstein's 1949 *Passover Hagadah* הגדה של פסח follows this example,[67] as does Rabbi Nathan Goldberg's *Passover Haggadah* הגדה של פסח, which originally came out in 1949 also.[68] The ShopRite הגדה של פסח *Passover Haggadah* has the facing Hebrew and English pages and two sentences: "The Seder Plate is placed on the table in front of the leader. A special Seder Plate or a regular large platter may be used. Illustrated above is a traditional assembly for the Seder Plate, which includes the following."[69] Philip Birnbaum does very much the same thing in both his 1953 and 1976 editions of the Haggadah. The first page includes the graphic of the Seder Plate and a list of the items.[70] Then his Haggadah moves directly into the "בדיקת חמץ."[71]

Rabbi Mordecai M. Kaplan, Rabbi Eugene Kohn, and Rabbi Ira Eisenstein, co-founders of the Reconstructionist Movement, worked together to produce *The New Haggadah for the Pesah Seder* in 1941,[72] the first liturgical work published by the Reconstructionist Movement.[73] They specifically wanted to support the claim that "the Pesah Haggadah has assumed once again a major role in the lives of Jews"[74] by adding "compelling content of present-day idealism and aspi-

---

[66] Marcus Lehmann, *Hagadah Schel Pesach* (Frankfurt am Main: J. Kauffmann Berlag, 1935), 7.
[67] Z. Harry Gutstein, *Passover Hagadah* הגדה של פסח (New York: KTAV Pub., 1949).
[68] Nathan Goldberg, *Passover Haggadah* הגדה של פסח, New Revised Ed. (New York: KTAV Pub., 1966).
[69] הגדה של פסח *Passover Haggadah* (Bloomfield Hills, MI: SKM Marketing., 2013), 3.
[70] הגדה של פסח *The Passover Haggadah*, ed. and trans. by Philip Birnbaum (USA: Hebrew Pub. Co., 1976), 1.
[71] Ibid., 2.
[72] Mordecai M. Kaplan, Eugene Kohn, and Ira Eisenstein, *The New Haggadah for the Pesah Seder* (New York: Behrman's Jewish Book House, 1941).
[73] *A Night of Questions – A Passover Haggadah*, ed. Joy D. Levitt and Michael J. Strassfeld (Elkins Park: Reconstructionist Press, 2000), 9.
[74] Ibid., vi.

ration" keeping "in mind the needs of the young American Jew."[75] Since Kaplan believed that the point of the Reconstructionist Movement is "to enable the Jewish people to function as a highly developed social organism,"[76] we can see how the Reconstructionist Movement would push to make Seder compelling. The authors include a chapter entitled "The Seder Table" that describes what each item on the Seder Plate is and the symbolic meaning of each.[77]

The Shulsinger Brothers Publishing Company addressed the Orthodox community in 1954 with their הגדה של פסח *The Haggadah of Passover*. There is a 5 line paragraph explaining what the word Haggadah means and then the blessings for the "Searching for Leavened Bread."[78] Since this Haggadah was produced for the supporters of the General Israel Orphans Home for Girls in Jerusalem,[79] one can presume the publishers believed their audience was more knowledgeable in the customs of and preparations for Seder.

In 1959, Rabbi Morris Silverman edited a Haggadah "for the family in the home, for the public Seder, for adult study groups, and for Passover institutes."[80] As promised in the Preface,[81] there are guidelines to follow starting with a page of "Preparation for Seder" that outlines how to clean the house and set the table, then tips and tricks to keep the Seder running smoothly.[82] For many families, the Seder had become a play or program, rather than an interactive family meal, and so these tips for a smooth Seder were clearly important. The same year, the internationally famous Soncino Press published *The Haggadah: A New Edition with English Translation* with an introduction by Cecil Roth.[83] The 17 page introduction provides not only a history of the Seder and the Haggadah, but also explains the purpose and custom of searching for the leavening, what is the *aphikoman*, and what the various items on the Seder Plate symbolize.

Rabbi Alfred J. Kolatch issued his Haggadah in 1967. In his "Preface," he admits to what was happening in the United States at the time:

---

75 Ibid., vii.
76 Mordecai M. Kaplan, "A Program for the Reconstruction of Judaism." *The Menorah Journal* 6 (1920): 181–193; reprint *The Jew in the Modern World: A Documentary History*, 3rd ed., ed. Paul Mendes-Flohr and Jehuda Reinharz (New York: Oxford Univ. Press, 2010), 559.
77 *A Night of Question*, ix–xv.
78 הגדה של פסח *The Haggadah of Passover* (New York: Shulsinger Brothers Pub., 1954).
79 Ibid., inside cover.
80 Morris Silverman, הגדה של פסח *Passover Haggadah with Explanatory Notes and Original Readings* (Hartford, Connecticut: Prayer Book Press, 1959), v.
81 Ibid.
82 Ibid., vi–x.
83 Cecil Roth, *The Haggadah: A New Edition with English Translation* (London: Soncino Press, 1959).

> The main motivation has been to make The Family Seder a meaningful and inspirational experience for the modern Jew. As such, even those whose knowledge of Hebrew is limited, and may prefer to skip many of the Hebrew sections, will find that the English portion stands as a complete entity.[84]

The chapter "The Seder Table and Its Symbols" includes not only the food required on the Seder Plate, but also the Biblical and Talmudic references with explanations so that the reader understands why these foods are important.[85]

Arthur M. Silver, rabbinic scholar, focused on the partially under-Jewishly educated audiences by creating a Haggadah in 1980 "for those who know how to conduct a Seder but would like to know more, the reasons for and the meaning behind every action, custom, and rite."[86] He understood the lack of education of American Jews and the desire of his generation to understand what they were doing. He included a 7 page chapter on setting the table that describes the differences between the Ashkenazi and Sephardic Seder Plates, what a *kittel* is, and the meaning of the symbolic foods.[87] Then he explained why one lights candles, what the order of "the Seder Program" is, and so forth. Interestingly, there are 101 pages of explanation before the Haggadah proper is introduced.

The exodus of Russian Jews beginning in the 1970s resulted in the publication of הגדה של פסח *Пасхальная Агада* in 1971 or 1972, printed in Israel.[88] Because of the anti-Jewish policies of the Soviet Union beginning in the 1920s, including the ban on teaching children Judaism and producing prayer books, the Soviet Jewish population was Jewishly uneducated. There were no rabbis because they could not be educated, which had further detrimental impact on the practices of the community.[89] Even in the 1960s, when synagogues were permitted, they were slandered by the Soviet authorities as places for drunks and criminals and those associating with them were arrested.[90]

The publishers were quite aware that the Russian Jews had little or no experience with any Jewish customs. They begin with an explanation of why Passover

---

84 Alfred J. Kolatch, *The Family Seder: A Traditional Passover Haggadah for the Modern Home* (New York: Jonathan David, Pub., 1967), "Preface."
85 Ibid., 1–5.
86 Arthur M. Silver, *Passover Haggadah: The Complete Seder* (New York: Menorah Publishing Co., 1980), v.
87 Ibid., 1–7.
88 הגדה של פסח *Пасхальная Агада* (Jerusalem: HotzotBkal, ©1971).
89 Leon Shapiro, "Soviet Jewry Since the Death of Stalin: A Twenty-five Year Perspective." *American Jewish Year Book*, vol. 79 (1979): 81–82, accessed 5 August 2014, http://ajcarchives.org/AJC_DATA/Files/1979_3_SpecialArticles.pdf.
90 Ibid., 82.

occurs during the month of Nissan.⁹¹ There is a short discussion of "הגדול שבת" ("the Great Sabbath"), the Sabbath before Passover that commemorates the Jewish slaves' purchases of lambs just before the exodus. Then there is an explanation of what *kameṣ* is and how one would clean the house to remove it.⁹² How one *qašēr* dishes for the festival is explained as is how to prepare *maṣâ*⁹³ in case one could not locate it in the local markets. Most interesting is the note that it is obligatory to eat *maṣâ* on the first two nights of Passover, but not after that.⁹⁴ There are also instructions concerning the Fast of the First Born.⁹⁵ Finally the setting of the table is explained. Apparently, in Russia the symbols are slightly different. The sacrificial lamb is represented by an undercooked piece of meat, the holiday sacrifice by a fried egg, and a potato or onion can stand in for the greens.⁹⁶

As Jewish education expanded during the 1980s, so did the appreciation for different Jewish traditions and a resurgence of Sephardic Jews reclaiming their heritage. In that vein, Rabbi Marc D. Angel produced הספרדים הגדה של פסח *A Sephardic PASSOVER HAGGADAH* in 1988.⁹⁷ Dedicated "to the continued vitality of the Sephardi tradition and all who experience it," the Haggadah includes the search for leavening with a detailed discussion of what is *kameṣ*, and a page on how to set the table. Then in each section there are explanations of the various Sephardic customs. For example, in some Sephardic circles at the end of the Seder the roasted egg is eaten by the firstborn child or head of the household. If there is no firstborn, some give it to an unmarried girl.

The 1970s and 1980s brought an explosion of feminist philosophies and independently-produced liturgies. The Wilshire Boulevard Temple in Los Angeles produced a Haggadah in the late 1980s. Rabbi Harvey J. Fields, the author, put in 2 pages at the beginning, "The Seder Table." These 2 pages introduce the food on the Seder Plate and the other items (e.g., candles, and Elijah's cup) that should be placed on the table. There are also hints on how to encourage guests to participate.⁹⁸ The *Tucson Jewish Feminist Haggadah*, published in the

---

91 הגדה של פסח *Пасхальная Агада*, 1. A special thanks to Dina Kravitz for her assistance with the translations.
92 Ibid., 1–5.
93 Ibid., 3.
94 Ibid., 4.
95 Ibid., 5.
96 Ibid., 6.
97 Marc D. Angel, הספרדים הגדה של פסח *A Sephardic PASSOVER HAGGADAH* (Hoboken, New Jersey: KTAV Pub., 1988).
98 Harvey J. Fields, *Festival of Freedom* הגדה של פסח (Los Angeles: Wilshire Boulevard Temple, 1988), ii–iii.

early 1990s and sponsored by a Hillel, has a "קדש ורחץ," but there are no instructional materials.[99] One could presume that since this manuscript is designed to be used by a specific group in a public setting, there is not the need to explain how to prepare as the community would be working together. The Workmen's Circle reissued their Haggadah in 1991. It was originally "prepared by a committee of Yiddish writers and teachers" and later revised by numerous directors of education.[100] The introductory material is a single page entitled "פסח" ("Passover") that includes historical commentary on the importance of the festival. For the Socialist Workmen's Circle, the festival is about freedom and justice.[101]

Roberta Kalochofsky, a Jewish feminist and animal rights activist, edited the 1985 *Haggadah for the Liberated Lamb*.[102] She believed her Haggadah to be "both Haggadah and manifesto"[103] in the same vein as Haggadot for Soviet Jewry and Jewish feminists. Thus, at the end of her 10 page "Introduction" that protests the treatment of animals in the modern world, she explains that "the seder setting for this Haggadah dispenses with the shankbone. Instead, we place olives, grapes, and grains of unfermented barley."[104] However, there is no instruction otherwise on how to prepare for the Seder.

Additionally, Shaare Rahamim, a Sephardic congregation in Brooklyn, New York, produced its Haggadah in 1999 "whose primary purpose is to put forth and clarify the Syrian-Aleppo *minhagim* and traditions."[105] This work has the most in-depth introduction of all the Haggadot presented here. Not only is there a detailed explanation of what in the house needs cleaning (from bookcases to garbage pails),[106] there are various methods explained on how to *kasher* utensils for Passover along with which method is to be used for what object (e.g., crystal versus the backyard grill).[107] Then the reader is given details as to how to search for the *kameṣ*.[108] Finally on page 22 of the Introduction, the reader finds instructions on "Seder Preparations" that guide the reader through specifics on what wine

---

[99] *Tucson Jewish Feminist Haggadah* (Tucson: Women's Division of the Jewish Federation of Southern Arizona and B'nai B'rith Hillel Foundation of the Univ. of Arizona, ©1994).
[100] א נייע הגדה של פסח (New York: Workmen's Circle, 1991).
[101] Ibid., 3.
[102] *Haggadah for the Liberated Lamb*, ed. Roberta Kalochofsky (Marblehead, Massachusetts: Micah Pub., 1985).
[103] Ibid., "Introduction."
[104] Ibid.
[105] *The Shaare Rahamin Haggadah* (Brooklyn: Congregation ShaareRahamim, 1999), 4,
[106] Ibid., 10.
[107] Ibid., 11–16.
[108] Ibid., 16–20.

may or may not be used,[109] and how to address the elderly "who cannot chew the matzah."[110] It is not until page 29 that we get the layout of the Seder Plate and the "קדש ורחץ."[111]

The new century began with a new Haggadah by the Reconstructionist Press. *A Night of Questions – A Passover Haggadah*, edited by Rabbi Joy D. Levitt and Michael J. Strassfeld, is "a Haggadah that is deeply rooted in the tradition of the Jewish people, responsive to those familiar with the tradition as well as to those whose connections to the tradition are just being made."[112] Clearly, the authors see Jews by Choice as an important component of their audience, as conversions to Judaism began to increase in the 1940s. They also see their work as an extension of the movement's 1941 edition and so work to once again "connect the generations and speak of the past to the future as though both were present."[113] The "Introduction" explains to the reader the importance of the festival.[114] Then "Planning Your Seder" helps the leader decide what parts of the Seder to include to make the experience meaningful. This section includes options of blessings from which to choose and how best to retell the story (the Haggadah includes numerous options including a play).[115] Then there is a page "Getting Ready for Pesaḥ" that explains the process of cleaning the house for *chametz*.[116] Finally, on page 19 we get to "Preparing the Seder Table." This includes the items on the Seder Plate and Miriam's and Elijah's Cups.[117] The editors promised that this would be a Haggadah for all 4 sons, Wise, Wicked, Simple, and Unknowing,[118] and in that vein is the section "Four Questions to Ask Before Starting the Seder" that addresses whether or not the story of the Exodus is true, what kind of god would permit slavery, and why celebrate Passover if the story is not true.[119]

---

[109] Ibid., 22–23.
[110] Ibid., 24.
[111] Ibid., 29.
[112] *A Night in Question*, 9.
[113] Ibid.
[114] Ibid., 11.
[115] Ibid., 12–14.
[116] Ibid., 16.
[117] Ibid., 19–20.
[118] Ibid., 9.
[119] Ibid., 21–22.

Conclusion

Jack Kugelmass, Sam Melton Professor and Director of the Center for Jewish Studies at the University of Florida, notes that "texts are resonant with the periods and issues in which they are produced."[120] Since the 1st Haggadah was published in the United States, over 300 editions of the text have been published and it is the most widely published book in the United States.[121] This text must resonate with the American Jewish population for it to be so popular. That there are numerous versions from the various movements, self-published, and those that address specific political issues (e.g., vegetarians, socialists, etc.), also speaks to its appeal. The Haggadah is not a book in the traditional way one thinks of a book. Rather, it is an interactive text. It has an audience not of readers, but of actors.[122] Clearly with over 300 versions in less than 200 years there have been many issues to address. In fact, Kugelmass sees the Haggadah is the ultimate text of the "indicator[s] of changing currents in Jewish life."[123]

---

[120] Jack Kugelmass, "Keys and Canons," in *Key Texts in American Jewish Culture*, ed. by Jack Kugelmass (New Brunswick: Rutgers Univ. Press, 2003), 11.
[121] Gereboff, "One Nation," 275.
[122] Marc Michael Epstein, "Illustrating History and Illuminating Identity in the Art of the Passover Haggadah," in *Judaism in Practice: From the Middle Ages through the Early Modern Period*, ed. Lawrence Fine (Princeton: Princeton Univ. Press, 2001), 298.
[123] Kugelmass, "Keys and Canons," 17.

Chapter 3:
Development of the German Reform Movement and its Liturgies

"No religious movement of this kind is isolated. It is the outcome of preceding causes."

David Philipson[1]

By understanding what social and intellectual developments affected the Reform Movement both in Europe and the United States, the evolution of the Movement can be better understood. By understanding the evolution of the Reform Movement, the changes in the Haggadot, specifically the non-liturgical parts, can be seen as a reflection of the needs of the community, rather than editors making changes because they are the editors putting their mark on their work. The impact of civil legal codes, immigration patterns, and international politics cannot be underestimated. These are what caused the acceptance of Jews in the larger society, although the acceptance was accompanied by tensions.

Reform in Europe

From the 16th to the end of the 18th Century in pre-Emancipation Europe, many Jews were forced into ghettos and, while they had more accesses to the ruling classes than the peasantry, and, thus, had some power, in society since some elite Jews were bankers, advisors, and physicians, they were not part of either the peasant or ruling classes. Because they were middlemen in the European society, working as tax collectors, pawnbrokers, and in petty trade, they were derided by the wealthy and poor. This reflected the Church's theological anti-Semitism and added to the tensions between the Jews and Christians. Jews were forbidden to study the majority language or secular subjects in Christian nations; and while education was not wide spread among Gentiles, education in secular subjects was even less widespread among Jews. Jacob Radar Marcus, former Professor of American Jewish History at Hebrew Union College (HUC), understood "the Jews lived a distinctive civil, religious, and social life of his own under the authority of rabbinic law. Jewry was a legal, national, and religious corpora-

---

[1] David Philipson, *The Reform Movement in Judaism* (London: MacMillan Co., 1907; Reprint Forgotten Books, 2012), 9.

tion within the state. It had little cultural contact with the world at large."[2] To join the outside world, a Jew had to shed Judaism and become Baptized in order to become a fully accepted member of Gentile society.

When in 1791, the National Assembly in France and in 1795 the Batavian Republic gave Jews full citizenship, "a complete revolution in Jewry resulted."[3] However, with the rights of citizenship, came the problem of assimilation that "is a threat to survival because it is an aspect of flight from prejudice, but by its very nature it also becomes a means of survival, as when it permits the individual to become so like his neighbor that he is no longer different."[4] Striking a balance of integration and assimilation became a concern for the Jews for the next 200 years.

Early Reformers

Moses Mendelssohn is often touted as the 1st modern reformer. Though he did not reform Judaism, he did alter how Jews perceived themselves and brought them closer to the world of the Enlightenment. He translated the Torah into German, a language already spoken by educated Jews. As Jews escaped their insular communities and the cause of Emancipation grew, German eventually displaced both Hebrew and Yiddish as the language of the German and other Central European Jewish communities. This then encouraged Jews to read other, non-Jewish texts in German and learn about the Gentile world. In 1786 David Freidländer, a disciple of Mendelssohn who fought assimilation but wanted a more enlightened Judaism, translated the traditional prayer book into German in hopes it would then be more accessible to Jews who knew German but not Hebrew. This was considered quite radical despite the fact he did not alter the service. These steps to bring Jewish materials to the Hebrew illiterate continue as the use of Hebrew fluctuates among Reform congregants and, especially American, Reform Jews question the need for Hebrew in their religious lives.

Those involved in the reforming of Judaism did not think of themselves outside the norm of traditional Jewish practice throughout Jewish history. They saw

---

[2] Jacob Rader Marcus, *Impacts of Contemporary Life upon Judaism* (paper presented at the Biennial, UAHC, Chicago, Illinois, 19 June 1933) (Cincinnati: American Jewish Archives, 1969), 3.
[3] David Philipson, "The Beginnings of the Reform Movement in Judaism." *The Jewish Quarterly Review* 15, no. 3 (1903): 477.
[4] Jacob Rader Marcus, *The Future of American Jewry* (Presented at Dropsie College for Hebrew and Cognate Learning, Philadelphia, Pennsylvania, 2 June 1955) (Cincinnati: American Jewish Archives, 1956), 2.

themselves as following what "the Bible indicates in many a passage the proneness of the Israelites to adopt the customs of the surrounding peoples and to understand their view-points of religion and life."[5] They wanted social equality, but not at the expense of assimilation.[6] They saw themselves as part of a great tradition of reform that included the 8th Century Karaites, who refused to follow rabbinic tradition, and Gaon Saadia ben Joseph of the 9th Century who incorporated philosophical thinking into his writings and translated the *Tanaḥ* into Arabic. Aaron Chorin, the 1st traditional rabbi to publically support reform both in action and writing, understood that "religion must be expressed in terms that appeal to the people and are consonant with the needs of life" and that we must "rescue our liturgical service from the ruin into which it has fallen."[7] For these men, Reform was the continued development of Judaism and they saw traditional Judaism as stagnate.

Not all Europeans were supportive of the Emancipation. Even after the passage of the French Declaration of the Rights of Man and the Citizen in 1789 that states "all men are born and remain, free and equal in rights...No person shall be molested for his opinions even such as are religious,"[8] there was debate in the French National Assembly concerning the rights that Jews should be afforded. While the Declaration of Rights legally gave them the rights of citizens, there were still those French citizens who considered the Jews to be foreigners. There was even fear that "a decree that would give the Jews the rights of citizenship could spark an enormous fire" because of the anti-Jewish feeling among the Catholic French.[9] Nevertheless, Jewish emancipation made headway.

The Jews of Prussia saw the March 11, 1812 edict of Frederick William III King of Prussia as a defining moment for change. By the edict, they were "considered

---

[5] David Philipson, "The Beginnings of the Reform Movement in Judaism." *The Jewish Quarterly Review* 15, no. 3 (1903): 476.

[6] W. Gunther Plaut, *The Rise of Reform Judaism: A Sourcebook of its European Origins* (New York: World Union for Progressive Judaism, 1963), 95.

[7] Aaron Chorin, "The Rational of Reform," July 1844; Reprint in *The Jew in the Modern World: A Documentary History*, 3rd ed., ed. Paul Mendes-Flohr and Jehuda Reinharz (New York: Oxford Univ. Press, 2010), 211.

[8] Declaration of the Rights of Man and of the Citizen. French National Assembly. Paris, France, 26 August 1789; Reprint in *The Jew in the Modern World: A Documentary History*, 3rd ed., ed. Paul Mendes-Flohr and Jehuda Reinharz, trans. Benjamin Flower (New York: Oxford Univ. Press, 2010), 123.

[9] Clermont Tonnerre, "Debate on the Eligibility of Jews for Citizenship," (paper presented at the French National Assembly, Paris, France, 23 December 1789); Reprint in *The Jew in the Modern World: A Documentary History*, 3rd ed., ed. Paul Mendes-Flohr and Jehuda Reinharz, trans. J. Rubin (New York: Oxford Univ. Press, 2010), 125.

natives [*Einländer*] and as *state citizens of Prussia*."¹⁰ With the confederation of the German states in 1815 came a serious question of what to do with the Jews. The Constitution of the German Confederation expected the Confederation to eventually grant "the enjoyment of civil rights [to the Jews] in the Confederated States in return for their assumption of all the obligations of citizens," although it accepted that at the signing of the Constitution "the rights of the adherents of this creed [Jews] already granted to them by the individual Confederated States."¹¹

German Enlightenment

The acceptance of Jews into German society was part of the German Enlightenment, which viewed all human beings as having natural rights and rejected what was considered superstition. The civil changes in the role of rabbis as demanded in the king's edict disqualified them from teaching because they weren't qualified according to the state.¹² Before Emancipation, rabbis were the legal authority in the *kehila* (community), but the changes in the civil law that moved many of the legal controls of the community to the civil courts and forbade them to teach non-religious subjects, narrowed the role that the rabbi played in the *kehila*'s government. Traditional rabbis also did not welcome the fact that laymen, albeit university educated laymen, were becoming religious leaders. In response, Friedländer wrote *On the Changes in the Service in the synagogues made necessary by the new Organization of the Jewish Schools in the Prussian State*.¹³ He explained that "the progress of the times, closer contacts, and the wisdom of the government aroused both spirit and love. The Jew, too, was aroused out of his slumber, and was no longer *regarded* as a stranger. He ceased *being* a stranger."¹⁴ This pamphlet and much of the new understanding of Judaism grew from *Glückseligkeit* – the idea that religion should bring happiness or contentment.

---

10 Frederick William III, "Edict Concerning the Civil Status of the Jews in the Prussian State," 11 March 1812, sect. 1, accessed 28 March 2014, http://germanhistorydocs.ghi-dc.org/sub_document_s.cfm?document_id=3650.
11 Article 16, Constitution of the German Confederation, Congress of Vienna, Vienna, 8 June 1815, reprint in *The Jew in the Modern World: A Documentary History*, 3rd ed., ed. Paul Mendes-Flohr and Jehuda Reinharz, trans. by Raphael Mahler (New York: Oxford Univ. Press, 2010), 165.
12 Frederick, sect. 8.
13 Philipson, *The Reform*, 32.
14 Jakob J. Petuchowski, *Prayerbook Reform in Europe: The Liturgy of European Liberal and Reform Judaism* (New York: World Union for Progressive Judaism, 1968), 132.

Until this time, Judaism "regarded observances [as] an end in itself," but now Jews were seeking spiritual fulfillment and not finding Jewish practice as an answer.[15]

In 1815, Israel Jacobson, who had initiated educational reforms among the Jews by creating a private intra-religious school, began religious reform. W. Gunther Plaut, a scholar of Jewish history, refers to him as "the father of Reform Judaism."[16] In his dedication address for the Seesen synagogue in 1810, Jacobson remarked that his concern was for religious education, custom, and worship without "any secret intention to undermine the pillars of your faith,"[17] meaning traditional Judaism. On the occasion of his son's confirmation, there were prayers in German, a choir, and an organ.[18] These reforms were followed by those of Jacob Herz Beer who invited Isaac Auerbach and Leopold Zunz, among others, to deliver sermons in German to his newly formed congregation.[19] While these reforms were not long-lasting in Berlin because of restrictive civil laws,[20] they continued in Southern Germany.[21] However, a number of Jews in northern Germany Jews sought religious reformation.

In 1818, the Hamburg Temple was founded by Eduard Kley, a follower of Jacob Herz Beer, and others. One of the goals of the leadership of this temple was a greater appeal to women and those who had not attended services for years.[22] It did just that and the leaders justified the use of German as a way to reach women who were Hebraically illiterate.[23] Hamburg Temple congregants had their own prayerbook, considered "the first comprehensive Reform liturgy." It included Hebrew, German, and some Ladino, which shows that the authors hoped to entice Sephardic Jews to their cause. This was how they addressed Friedländer's concerns that "the larger portion of our nation understands noth-

---

15 Meyer, *A Response*, 18.
16 Plaut, *The Rise*, 27.
17 Israel Jacobson, Dedication Address (presented at Temple of Jacob, Seesen, 17 July 1810), reprint in *The Rise of Reform Judaism: A Sourcebook of its European Origins*, ed. by W. Gunther Plaut (New York: World Union for Progressive Judaism, 1963), 29.
18 Philipson, *The Reform*, 33. Jewish confirmation had been adapted from the Christian confirmation and began as early as 1803 (Meyer, *A Response*, 39).
19 Philipson, *The Reform*, 33.
20 Ibid., 36.
21 Ibid., 42.
22 Constitution. New Israelitish Temple Association, Hamburg, 11 December 1817, reprint *The Rise of Reform Judaism: A Sourcebook of its European Origins*, ed. W. Gunther Plaut (New York: World Union for Progressive Judaism, 1963), 31–32.
23 Meyer, *A Response*, 55.

ing of those prayers."²⁴ Hungarian Rabbi Aaron Chorin was adamant that it was "obligatory to free the worship ritual from its adhesions, to hold the service in a language understandable to the worshiper, and to accompany it with organ and song."²⁵ What he felt dissuaded modern Jews from enjoying the prayers was that "they were generally written...at the time of the darkest persecutions. They bear the mark of the extreme suppression of the human spirit."²⁶

This establishment meeting of the Hamburg Temple created an outcry in the Hamburg Jewish establishment.²⁷ The founding rabbis attempted to enlist the assistance of the government to force the new synagogue to close, but that effort failed. The Hamburg Rabbinical Court even went so far as to make a declaration forbidding "pray[er] in any language other than the Holy Tongue" and invalidating any prayerbook that did so, banning "musical instrument[s] in the synagogue on the Sabbath and on the festivals," and barring any "change [to] the worship that is customary"²⁸ in an effort to end these reforms.

A synagogue following religious structure similar to the Hamburg synagogue was founded in Leipzig that was to have far reaching effects because Leipzig had an annual international fair. Thus, Jews from all over Europe could be exposed to Reform Judaism.

In 1822 Leopold Zunz, the founder of the *Wissenschaft des Judenthums* (Scientific Study of Judaism) movement, published the first issue of *Zeitschriftfür die Wissenschaft des Judenthums*, a short-lived publication that was very influential in expanding the *Wissenschaft des Judenthums*.²⁹ In 1835, Abraham Geiger, a German rabbi, started the magazine *Wissenschaftliche Zeitschrift für judische Theologie* (*Scientific Journal for Jewish Theology*) that became a major clearing house for Jewish reformers to express and exchange their views.³⁰ It was hailed "as the dawning of a new day."³¹ Geiger understood that there was "a battle in progress"

---

24 Abraham Geiger, "Israel's Native Energy," reprint in *The Rise of Reform Judaism: A Sourcebook of its European Origins*, ed. W. Gunther Plaut (New York: World Union for Progressive Judaism, 1963), 127.
25 Aaron Chorin, *A Word in its Time*, reprint in *The Rise of Reform Judaism: A Sourcebook of its European Origins*, ed. W. Gunther Plaut (New York: World Union for Progressive Judaism, 1963), 33.
26 Ibid.,153.
27 Philipson, *The Reform*, 42–43.
28 These are the Words of the Covenant. Hamburg Rabbinical Court, 1819, reprint in *The Jew in the Modern World: A Documentary History*, 3rd ed., ed. Paul Mendes-Flohr and Jehuda Reinharz, trans. S. Fischer and S. Weinstein (New York: Oxford Univ. Press, 2010), 187–189.
29 Ibid., 16.
30 Philipson, *The Reform*, 67, 157.
31 Ibid., 157.

concerning Judaism "between the elements of dissolution and destruction [traditional Judaism]...and the unifying, encompassing, and affirming action of reason [Reform Judaism]."[32] Through this magazine, he hoped that Judaism could be meaningful to Jews yet again.[33]

This movement, led by Jewish intellectuals, focused on a scholarly, objective approach to Judaism – a "positive historical" approach. The founders wanted a more historical understanding of the religion. Coupled with the 1823 Grand Duke Carl Friedrich of Saxe-Weimar's edict demanding Jewish services be in German, exclusive of the reading of the Torah and Haftorah,[34] a new more inclusive Judaism was being formed. This began what Plaut calls "a torrential stream which carved out the riverbed of modern Reform Judaism."[35]

In 1842, the Frankfurt Society of Friends of Reform was founded. This group of laymen, led by M. A. Stern, who was a friend of Geiger's, called on the rabbis to address the issues of the reformation of Judaism that they had already admitted should be resolved.[36] The purpose of this group was not to institute reforms, but to push the rabbis to do so.[37] They, like other reformers who were laymen, understood the importance of having the rabbis support the movement. Their major concern was that "thousands [of Jews] have renounced allegiance to Talmudic rabbinical Judaism and are connected outwardly with the Mosaic religious community only by habit or by the control of the state or by family ties," and that this was "destructive and immoral."[38]

The problem lay in the growing dissatisfaction among a certain circle of Jews who no longer found Judaism responsive to their needs[39] versus the traditionalists who refused to permit change. A new congregation in Berlin grew from Sigismund Stern's *Genossenschaft für Reform in Judenthum* (Association for the Reform of Judaism), which was the most radical of the reform groups and only later dissolved under pressure by the Nazis. The Proclamation of the Association notes that "we want Judaism...but we want to understand the Sacred Scriptures ac-

---

32 Abraham Geiger, "Jewish Movements Today." *Wissenschaftliche Zeitschrift für jüdische Theologie* 1 (1835), reprint in *The Rise of Reform Judaism: A Sourcebook of its European Origins*, ed. W. Gunther Plaut (New York: World Union for Progressive Judaism, 1963), 18–19.
33 Ibid.
34 Philipson, *The Reform*, 51.
35 Plaut, *The Rise*, 3.
36 Ibid., 171.
37 Ibid., 173.
38 Society of the Friends of Reform, Declaration of Principle, 1842, reprint in *The Rise of Reform Judaism: A Sourcebook of its European Origins*, ed. W. Gunther Plaut (New York: World Union for Progressive Judaism, 1963), 51.
39 Philipson, *The Reform*, 127.

cording to the divine spirit, not according to the letter."[40] They too published a prayerbook. Their goal was that "prayer should be like a clear, transparent mirror of the sea in which the sentiment of the worshiper can reflect itself."[41] In this vein, the Association removed more Hebrew from worship services than any Reform prayerbook of the period.

When Ludwig Philippson, rabbi and journalist, called for a rabbinic conference in 1844[42] the response was immediate and positive. This conference, held in Brunswick, and so dubbed the Brunswick Conference, resulted in the participants deciding to examine practical requirements to preserve Jewish life. Those in attendance were well aware of the problems Jewry was grappling with, namely internal dissention and external assimilation tendencies, and attended the meetings knowing it could harm their careers. In a direct challenge to traditional Jews, they affirmed that the "ordinary prayerbook, *Seder Tefillah*,...is no longer in a position to satisfy the religious needs of a progressively educated generation."[43] This first meeting came to no conclusions, but did set an agenda for future meetings.

The Frankfurt Conference took place the following year and addressed the specific questions of the use of Hebrew in the service, music, Sabbath, and the status of women. All of this part of the reformation of Judaism. This conference also addressed the question of recreating a new liturgy, or editing the existing ones, to reach the needs of the Jews of the period.[44] Rabbi Zacharias Frankel, a Hungarian rabbi, left after the 3rd day of the conference because he was disheartened by the lack of compromise among the others present. He wanted to keep Hebrew as the language of prayer though he felt German would be permissible at times. However, in Frankel's words, "the majority of the Rabbinical Conference decided that Hebrew prayer was only *advisable* and that it would be the task of the rabbis to eliminate it gradually altogether....In my opinion this is not

---

[40] Association for the Reform of Judaism, Proclamation of the Association, Berlin, 1844, reprint in *The Rise of Reform Judaism: A Sourcebook of its European Origins*, ed. W. Gunther Plaut (New York: World Union for Progressive Judaism, 1963), 57.

[41] Association for the Reform of Judaism, "Introduction," *Prayer Book* (Berlin: Association for the Reform of Judaism, 1848), reprint in *The Rise of Reform Judaism: A Sourcebook of its European Origins*, ed. W. Gunther Plaut (New York: World Union for Progressive Judaism, 1963), 59.

[42] Ludwig Philipson to the Directors of the Jewish Community in Brunswick, 26 March 1844, reprint in *The Rise of Reform Judaism: A Sourcebook of its European Origins*, ed. W. Gunther Plaut (New York: World Union for Progressive Judaism, 1963), 74–75.

[43] Joseph Maier, Statement for new prayer book, Brunswick Conference, June 1844, reprint in *The Rise of Reform Judaism: A Sourcebook of its European Origins*, ed. W. Gunther Plaut (New York: World Union for Progressive Judaism, 1963), 154.

[44] Philipson, *The Reform*, 272.

the spirit of preserving but of destroying positive historical Judaism."[45] The Conference was "astonished" by Frankel's decision, especially since the "the majority did not fail to recognize the high significance of the Hebrew language for the Israelites and the necessity of learning it in the schools; only it did not hold that it was unconditionally necessary for the worship service."[46] The majority felt that they were maintaining the spirit of positive historical Judaism by requiring the learning of Hebrew.

The 3rd Rabbinic conference in Breslau was a dare to those rabbis who refused to change. It focused on ways to mediate between the traditional regulations of Sabbath practice and the demands of the modern economy. As Philipson remarked, "the rabbinical conferences of 1844, 1845, and 1846 will remain for all time among the most remarkable gatherings in the history of Judaism. It was here that the great truth received public expression that Judaism contained in itself the power of adaptation."[47]

This community of German speaking Reform Jews forged "the dominant form of the faith in that part of the world," in the words of Jakob J. Petuchowski, professor of Jewish Theology at Hebrew Union College (HUC).[48] From this community came the founders of Reform Judaism in the United States. Rabbis like David Einhorn and Isaac Wise were part of the German reform movement that grew out of Enlightenment and Emancipation. They came to the New World with the expectation of creating a Judaism "which will be, the Judaism of your children and yet also that of our fathers," as Einhorn stated in his inaugural American sermon in 1855.[49] It was Einhorn who "was the father of American Reform, its theology and practice, its ideology and thrust."[50]

---

45 Zacharia Frankel, Letter to the Second Rabbinical Conference in Frankfort, 18 July 1845. Reprint W. Gunther Plaut. *The Rise of Reform Judaism: A Sourcebook of its European Origins*, ed. W. Gunther Plaut (New York: World Union for Progressive Judaism, 1963), 87–89.
46 Declaration of the Rabbinical Conference, Frankfort, July 1845, reprint in *The Rise of Reform Judaism: A Sourcebook of its European Origins*, ed. W. Gunther Plaut (New York: World Union for Progressive Judaism, 1963), 89–90.
47 Ibid., 315.
48 Petuchowski, *Prayerbook Reform*, 43.
49 Ibid., 96.
50 W. Gunther Plaut, "The Pittsburgh Platform in the Light of European Antecedents," in *The Changing World of Reform Judaism: The Pittsburgh Platform in Retrospect*, ed. Walter Jacob (Pittsburgh: Rodef Shalom Congregation, 1985), 18.

Conclusion

By understanding the conflicts among the Jewish communities in Europe, we can begin to conceptualize the impact this has on various liturgies. The question of the use of Hebrew versus Yiddish or German, for example, highlights these issues. The role of women in synagogue was not unimportant and would come into greater importance in the United States and ultimately change the liturgy. Perhaps most importantly, as these leaders argued how best to bring Judaism to the secularly educated Jew and make it meaningful affected more than the language used during religious services. It caused changes in the liturgies, including the Haggadah.

Chapter 4:
Growth of the American Reform Movement and Its Liturgies Including the Non-Liturgical Elements in CCAR Haggadot – The Early Years

"It was natural for reform Judaism, which found itself at variance with a number of passages in the Haggadah, to construct a ritual for Pesaḥ eve in keeping with its religious principles."

CCAR, Union Haggadah.[1]

The arrival of Reform Judaism in the New World had not only a profound effect on the Reform Movement and Judaism, but also on American Jewry. American Jews were involved in religious reform even before their European counterparts. With the addition of Reform rabbis and adherents, Reform in America expanded and developed. It grew into a powerful movement in the United States that demanded its own liturgy. The creation of the Central Conference of American Rabbis (CCAR) was a product of the *Wissenschaft des Judenthums* and first-generation American German Jews, but changed in accord with American Reform theology. They developed a Haggadah that they revised to meet the needs of their changing constituency.

Early American Jews

In the fall of 1654, the *St. Catrina* arrived in the port of New Amsterdam. The ship brought 23 Jews, fleeing the institution of the Inquisition, from Recife, Brazil to this fledgling city. For some years, Brazil had been a Dutch protectorate and recently had been recaptured by the Portuguese. Already in residence for only a few months in New Amsterdam were Jacob Barsimon and Solomon Pietersen, although there is some debate as to whether the 23 came 1st. After the *St. Catrina*, later in 1654 or maybe early 1655, another shipload of Jews arrived on the *Peereboom*, this time from Amsterdam; some of these Jews had significant ties to the Dutch West India Company. This influx of Jews into New Amsterdam would eventually change the laws of the city and, thus, help make religious diversity a foundation of the eventually to be created United States.

---

[1] Central Conference of American Rabbis, *The Union Haggadah: Home Service for the Passover* (n.p.: CCAR, 1923), 157.

Asser Levy and his colleagues wanted to be citizens, not tolerated outsiders. They conducted themselves as citizens, especially as Asser Levy and his contemporaries wanted more than toleration. They conceived of themselves as full-fledged citizens, especially because they had many more privileges in other parts of the Dutch empire. They were some of the earliest Jews who clothed themselves with the cloak of anticipated Emancipation. However, the Jews in New Amsterdam could not openly practice their religion, travel outside the city, or conduct business. Therefore, they petitioned numerous times for the various rights and freedoms they felt they deserved and that were accorded them in Holland and Dutch controlled Brazil. Once they had residency, the Jewish community decided to establish their presence in a more permanent manner. In July of 1655 the Jews requested permission to buy some land for a cemetery.[2] After receiving permission to travel and trade, the Jews wanted the right to defend themselves and the community in which they lived.

In the 1680s, a group of Jews left New Amsterdam to start a community in Newport, Rhode Island. It failed and it wasn't until the 1740s that New York Jews tried to establish this community again. The Jewish community spread to Philadelphia. Another group began a Jewish community in Savannah, Georgia, in the 1730s that didn't last. Charleston, South Carolina, gained a Jewish community in the 1740s that also failed, but was re-established a few decades later.

Jews were not treated the same in all the American Colonies, nor was the social acceptance of Jews a promise of political equality. For example, the Puritan communities were not welcoming to non-Puritans. In the English Colonies, Jews were taxed at the same rate as their British counterparts, and starting in 1740 Jewish colonists were eligible to apply for naturalization if they had been in the colonies for at least 7 years.[3] However, Jews, because of their exclusion from politics in Europe since the Middle Ages, did not seem as a group to aspire to be part of American politics until the Revolutionary War, when such men as Hayyim Solomon helped to fund the American government in that war effort. After this, American Jews participated in politics.[4]

---

[2] Samuel Oppenheim, *The Early History of the Jews in New York, 1654–1664: Some New Matter on the Subject* (New York: American Jewish Historical Society, 1909), 75.
[3] Eli Faber, *A Time for Planting: The First Migration 1654–1820*. The Jewish People in America (Baltimore: Johns Hopkins Univ. Press, 1992), 17.
[4] Jonathan D. Sarna, Marshal Sklare Memorial Lecture (paper presented at the annual meeting of the Association for Jewish Studies, 2002). Transcript.

Ezra Stiles, president of Yale University in 1762, "declared that Jews would never become citizens of America."[5] However, the Constitution's Article VI stipulates that the government may not require adherence to any particular religion as a stipulation to take office and President George Washington's letter to the Hebrew Congregation in Newport, Rhode Island where he refers to "all classes of Citizens [sic]"[6] ensured that Stiles' belief would not come to pass. Perhaps the most powerful weight supporting Jews as full citizens of the United States was President Washington's response to the letter by Levi Sheftal, president of the Hebrew Congregation of Savannah, congratulating Washington on his election. Washington understood that Jews were one of a number of religious minorities. He also knew that this was a wealthy community that had supported him, the Revolution, and the development of the new country's economy. In addition, Washington was also a product of the Enlightenment that religious tolerance was an important principle. Washington said to the congregation: "I rejoice that a spirit of liberality and philanthropy is much more prevalent than it formerly was among the enlightened nations of the earth; and that your brethren will benefit thereby in proportion as it shall become still more extensive."[7] The response to Moses Sexias and the Hebrew Congregation in Newport, Rhode Island was even more strongly worded. Not only did Washington call them citizens, but hoped they will continue to "enjoy the good will of the other inhabitants" of the United States.[8] Finally, in his letter to the congregations in Philadelphia, New York, Charleston, and Richmond, Washington calls the Jews "fellow citizens."[9]

These first citizens practiced their Judaism the way their families had for generations, but "American Jewry remained outside the cultural establish-

---

[5] Jacob Radar Marcus, *Impacts of Contemporary Life upon Judaism* (paper presented at the Biennial Union of American Hebrew Congregations, Chicago, Illinois, 19 June 1933)(Cincinnati: American Jewish Archives, 1969), 9.
[6] George Washington to the Hebrew Congregation in New Port, Rhode Island, 17 August 1790; reprint "Correspondence Between the Jews and Washington," in *A Documentary History of the Jews in the United States 1654–1875*, 3rd ed., ed. Morris U. Schappes (New York: Schocken Books, 1971), 80.
[7] George Washington to the Hebrew Congregation of the City of Savanah, 1789; reprint "Correspondence Between the Jews and Washington," in *A Documentary History of the Jews in the United States 1654–1875*, 3rd ed., ed. Morris U. Schappes (New York: Schocken Books, 1971), 78.
[8] George Washington to the Hebrew Congregation in Newport, Rhode Island, 1790; reprint "Correspondence Between the Jews and Washington," in *A Documentary History of the Jews in the United States 1654–1875*, 3rd ed., ed. Morris U. Schappes (New York: Schocken Books, 1971), 80.
[9] George Washington to the Hebrew Congregations in the Cities of Philadelphia, New York, Charleston and Richmond, 1790, reprint "Correspondence Between the Jews and Washington," in *A Documentary History of the Jews in the United States 1654–1875*, 3rd ed., ed. Morris U. Schappes (New York: Schocken Books, 1971), 83.

ment,"[10] which was Christian, in many ways. Despite their citizenship, they were denied, for example, the right to hold an office in many cities because they would not be sworn in on New Testament and many clubs would not accept non-Christians. Additionally, Christianity was taught in the public schools. Definitely far more integrated into the life of the country than most of their European counterparts, they still struggled with their bi-culturalism and often ended up disassociating from Judaism in order to gain full rights. During the 1700s in the United States, the Jewish community was small, barely making it to 0.1 percent of the American population.[11] Thus, as a tiny minority community, they were ignored because they were seen as numerically unimportant. Reform began early in American Judaism. As Jacob Rader Marcus, former professor of Jewish History at HUC, states: "America signified the ultimate frontier of Jewish life. Religious controls were inevitably relaxed here. There was much less concern about observance and ritual. The individual was far freer to do as he pleased."[12] Rabbi Richard Levy, past CCAR president, supports Marcus' view: "In this new environment, Jews could define their Judaism rather than be defined or limited by it."[13]

Shortly after the American Revolution, where people in the New World declared their independence from the way the Old World operated, American Jews began shaking off the traditions of the Old World. By the 1790s, there must have been calls for the use of English in the service because Shearith Israel in Philadelphia had to stipulate in its regulations that only Hebrew was acceptable to use in worship services.[14] This was not the only congregation to introduce polemical regulations against the incursion of Gentile ways. Other congregations had regulations against the eating of non-kosher foods and the breaking of Sabbath and holiday laws, as well as the promise to revoke synagogue privileges for those who intermarried.[15] In 1825, Congregation Shearith Israel had to stipulate that one could not be called for an *aliâ* (the honor of blessing the Torah) if he

---

10 Michael A. Meyer, "German-Jewish Identity in Nineteenth-Century America," in *The American Jewish Experience*, ed. Jonathan D. Sarna (New York: Holmes & Meier, 1986), 49.
11 Ira Sheskin and Arnold Dashefsky, *Jewish Population in the United States, 2010*, ed. Arnold Dashefsky, Sergio DellaPergola, and Ira Sheskin (Storrs, Connecticut: North American Jewish Databank, 2011), 3.
12 Marcus, "The American Colonial Jew," 13.
13 Richard N. Levy, *A Vision of Holiness: The Future of Reform Judaism* (New York: URJ Press, 2005), 182.
14 Eli Farber, *A Time for Planting: The First Migration 1654–1820*. The Jewish People in America (Baltimore: Johns Hopkins Univ. Press, 1992), 114.
15 Ibid., 121.

was not wearing a *talêt* (prayer shawl).[16] In Savanah, Georgia in 1820 an organ was used at a synagogue dedication. The established Sephardim in the 1700s had communal Seders at their synagogues to reinforce the sense of Jewish community. Intermarriage in the early 1800s was a serious problem: 1 in 3 Jews married Christians.[17]

In 1818 the American Jewish population was estimated to be 3,000, mostly Sephardim with a few Germans.[18] Only 12 years later the Jewish population had doubled, and by 1848, 30 years later, there were an estimated 50,000 Jews in the United States,[19] making Jews between 0.03 and 0.1 percent of the population in the first half of the 19th Century until the beginning of the wide scale German immigration.[20]

Charleston, South Carolina had the largest Jewish population in the United States in the early 1800s. Most of these Jews were affluent and interacted with the Gentile population both socially and economically. In 1750, Beth Elohim, a Sephardic congregation was founded. Nearly 75 years later, a large portion of its members petitioned for reforms:

> With regard to such parts of the service as it is desired should undergo this change, memorialists would strenuously recommend that the most solemn portions be retained, and everything superfluous excluded; and that the principal parts, and if possible all that is read in *Hebrew*, should also be read in *English*...so as to enable every member of the congregation fully to understand each part of the service.[21]

The Beth Elohim congregation saw reform as "indispensable to the preservation of our faith."[22] They had been following the calls for reformation in the German

---

[16] Malcom H. Stern, "The 1820s: American Jewry Comes of Age," in *The American Jewish Experience*, ed. Jonathan D. Sarna (New York: Homes & Meier Pub., 1986), 35.
[17] Arthur Hertzberg, *The Jews in America: Four Centuries of an Uneasy Encounter: A History* (New York: Simon and Schuster, 1989), 91.
[18] Joseph Jacobs, "Statistics of Jews: Jewish Population of the United States Memoir of the Bureau of Jewish Statistics of the American Jewish Committee." *American Jewish Yearbook*, vol. 16 (1914–1915), 339, accessed 11 June 2007, http://ajcarchive.org/AJC_DATA/FILES/1914_1915_7_Statistics.pdf.
[19] "Jewish Statistics." *American Jewish* Yearbook, vol. 1 (1899–1900), 283–285, accessed 4 November 2013, http://www.jewishdatabank.org/Studies/downloadFile.cfm?FileID=3024.
[20] Sheskin and Dashefsky, *Jewish Population in the United States, 2010*, 3.
[21] Israelites of the City of Charleston, Memorial to the President and Members of the Adjunta of Kaal Kadosh Beth Elohim of Charleston, South Carolina, 23 December 1824, reprint in *A Documentary History of the Jews in the United States 1654–1875*, 3rd ed., ed. Morris U. Schappes (New York: Schocken Books, 1971), 173.
[22] Ibid.

Jewish community and, as they acculturated, wanted to prove their Americanism by using English.

Because their demands were rejected, a dozen men left the congregation and formed the Reformed Society of Israelites in 1825.[23] This prayerbook was a hand-copied manuscript that combined communally agreed-upon prayers and personal additions. [24]

In 1830, Abraham Moïse, a leader of this congregation, published a volume of the group's prayer book, dubbed "American Jewry's first Reform prayer book and probably, the first prayer book to institute radical liturgical reform in modern Jewish history."[25] While the congregation ceased to exist by 1833, it had addressed some issues their European counterparts had yet to consider, such as Jewish prejudices against Gentiles. Eventually, the group's members returned to Beth Elohim. In 1841, Rabbi Gustav Poznanski, a Polish-born German-trained rabbi, was hired by Beth Elohim and he instituted such reforms as one-day observances of the high holidays. At this time, the Jewish population of Charleston rivaled even New York City, making it the largest collection of Jews in one city anywhere in the United States.[26] There were only 20 synagogues in the country at this time[27] and only about 15,000 Jews in the country.[28]

A group of Jews in Baltimore, Maryland, adopted the Hamburg prayerbook in 1842. Har Sinai Verein's use of the first published Reform prayer book shows the growth of liberal Judaism in the United States. Additionally, Leo Merzbacher, rabbi at Temple Emanu-El in New York City, produced a prayerbook for his congregation in 1854, publishing it in 1856.[29] The redesigns of prayerbooks shows the dissatisfaction American Jews had with the traditional liturgy and

---

23 Michael A. Meyer, *A Response to Modernity: A History of the Reform Movement in Judaism* (New York: Oxford Univ. Press, 1988), 227–229.
24 Ibid., 231.
25 Gary Phillip Zola, "The First Reform Prayer Book in America: The Liturgy of the Reformed Society of Israelites," in *Platforms and Prayer Books: Theological and Liturgical Perspectives on Reform Judaism*, ed. Dana Evan Kaplan (Lanham, Maryland: Rowman & Littlefield, 2002), 104.
26 Gemma Romain, "The Jews of Nineteenth Century Charleston: Ethnicity in a Port City" (paper presented at Seascapes, Littoral Cultures, and Trans–Oceanaic Exchanges, Library of Congress, Washington, D.C., 12–15 February 2003). Transcript, accessed 4 March 2008, http://www.historycooperative.org/proceedings/seascapes/romain.html.
27 "History." United Hebrew Congregation, 2012, accessed 24 March 2015, http://www.unitedhebrew.org/AboutUs/History.aspx.
28 "Jewish Statistics." *The American Jewish Yearbook*, vol. 1 (Philadelphia: Jewish Publication Society, 1899–1900), 283. Accessed 18 February 2015, http://wwww.ajcarchives.org/AJC_DATA/Files/1899_1900_7_Statistics.pdf.
29 Sefton D. Temkin, *Creating American Reform Judaism: The Life and Times of Isaac Mayer Wise* (Portland: Littman Library of Jewish Civilization, 1998), 149.

their desire to affect some reform. However, Reform growth was slow, as only 4 percent of the American congregations had introduced reforms by 1860.[30]

All of this shows that despite the desire to maintain Judaism, there has always been a push for reform of Jewish practice to permit bi-cultural American Jews. Because American Jews were always equal, or technically equal, citizens with their Christian counterparts, they desired to appear similar and this was part of the moment for such reforms as the use of English in services.

German Reform Arrives

The Second Wave of Jewish Immigration (1840–1880) brought a new kind of Jew to the New World; the early immigrants were anxious for Emancipation and the later ones were Emancipated. While the Jews in the United States were constitutionally guaranteed religious freedoms, the Jews in Europe had to fight for the privilege to practice their religion. In doing so, they had re-conceptualized Judaism.

At the beginning of the 1800s, Rabbi Max Lilienthal, a German-born proponent of reforms in Jewish education, instituted the ceremony of confirmation in the three synagogues that constituted the United Hebrew Congregations in New York City. He believed that "religion can not adhere autocratically to medieval tenets, when the whole tendency of our modern age is pointing to new developments. Religion, too, has to adapt itself to modern changes and modern ideas."[31]

Rabbi Isaac Mayer Wise arrived in the United States from Hungary in 1846 and was elected rabbi of Beth El in Albany, New York. He almost immediately dispensed with gender segregated seating and instituted confirmation and family pews. He felt that confirmation was a way to integrate Jewish girls into the synagogue and "extend its [the synagogue's] benevolent influence over the daughters of Israel as well as the sons,"[32] in addition by having families sit to-

---

30 Eli Farber, "Preservation to innovation: Judaism in America, 1654–1880." In *The Cambridge Companion to American Judaism*. Ed. Dana Evan Kaplan (New York: Cambridge Univ. Press, 2005), 35.
31 Max Lilienthal, "Modern Judaism" (paper presented at Indianapolis, Indiana, Thanksgiving 1865), reprint in *Max Lilienthal: American Rabbi: Life and Writings*, ed. David Philipson (New York: Bloch Pub., 1915), 452.
32 Isaac Mayer Wise, "The Confirmation and the Bar Mitzvah," *Asmonean* 1854, reprint in *The Jew in the Modern World: A Documentary History*, 3rd ed., ed. Paul Mendes-Flohr and Jehuda Reinharz (New York: Oxford Univ. Press, 2010), 518–519.

gether "decorum and devotion would be gained."³³ The co-educational confirmation was not accepted without much protest. In 1855, Einhorn was hired by Baltimore's Har Sinai Verein.

These 3 men laid the foundation for Reform Judaism in the United States. What these 3 rabbis instituted in the United States is part of what makes American Reform Judaism different than German. The divide in Charleston and the adoption of Reform liturgy in Baltimore, even the hiring of these rabbis, shows the push towards a new Judaism. Until this point, most congregations had no rabbis. They were led by ḥazānîm (cantors) or lay leaders. These leaders were not necessarily well versed in Jewish law and practice or Hebrew. However, the need of American congregations to hire German Reform rabbis as the catalyst required to create change is most telling of the need for a Jewish hierarchy in the United States.

In 1840, the estimate was that there were 15,000 Jews in the United States,³⁴ or just 0.09 percent of the American population.³⁵ The 1840's witnessed a large increase in the wave of German Jewish immigration and so was dubbed the Second Great Wave of Jewish immigration. Marcus called the period from 1841–1920 "The Age of the Rise and Dominance of the German Jew and the Challenge to His Leadership."³⁶ This was a particularly apt description. By 1877 there were an estimated 230,000 Jews,³⁷ about 0.5 percent of the American population,³⁸ and by 1888, 400,000,³⁹ between 0.6 and 0.75 percent of the American population.⁴⁰ Of these, nearly 2/3rds were from southern and western Germany and Prussia.⁴¹

Germans fled their homeland because of economic hardships and political turmoil. The added burden of being legally barred from various occupations

---

33 Ibid.
34 Joseph Jacobs, "Statistics of Jews: Jewish Population of the United States Memoir of the Bureau of Jewish Statistics of the American Jewish Committee." *American Jewish Yearbook*, vol. 16 (1914–1915), 339, accessed 11 June 2007, http://ajcarchive.org/AJC_DATA/FILES/1914_1915_7_Statistics.pdf.
35 Sheskin and Dashefsky, *Jewish Population in the United States, 2010*, 3.
36 Jacob Rader Marcus, *The Periodization of American Jewish History* (presented at the Fifty-Sixth Annual Meeting, American Jewish Historical Society, Coolidge Auditorium, Library of Congress, Washington, D.C., 15 February 1958) (Cincinnati: American Jewish Archives, 1958), 9.
37 Jacobs, "Statistics," 339.
38 Sheskin and Dashefsky, *Jewish Population in the United States, 2010*, 3.
39 Jacobs, "Statistics," 339.
40 Sheskin and Dashefsky, *Jewish Population in the United States, 2010*, 3.
41 Corinne Azen Krause, "The Historical Setting of the Pittsburgh Platform," in *The Changing World of Reform Judaism: The Pittsburgh Platform in Retrospect*, ed. Walter Jacob (Pittsburgh: Rodef Shalom Congregation, 1985), 10.

due to anti-Semitic discrimination also curtailed their economic success. In addition, there were legal barriers to marriage that forced the younger sons to seek employment outside their original residence. While there was an influx of Christian Germans and Irish during the 1840's as well, the German Jews had three major advantages: 1. They were literate, which made learning to read English easier; 2. They were peddlers who became merchants, not farmers seeking land they often could not afford or could not afford to get to; and 3. They came with some money with which to begin life in the new country. Peddling was an integral part of the European Jewish experience from medieval through modern times. Thus, Jewish peddling in America was a natural occupation:

> the less developed a region, the poorer the internal transportation networks, the fewer settled merchants present, the further the distance from one settlement to another, and the more agrarian the region, the more attractive immigrant Jewish peddlers found it. Certainly the southern region of the United States fits all of these criteria. The least urbanized part of the United States for the longest time, the most agrarian, and the one with the least articulated system of roads and railroads, it attracted Jewish immigrant peddlers well into the early twentieth century. In the absence of focused case studies of Jewish peddling, let alone comparative ones, one can at least begin with the hunch that the South's persistent agrarianism, its fairly small commercial class, and its lag in industrial and urban development as compared to other American regions, made it a particularly attractive magnet for young Jews looking to gain a foothold in American commerce.[42]

The first German Jews to arrive joined the Sephardic synagogues because those were established and the immigrants saw this as a way to Americanize. However, as the number of German Jews grew, those who came later had been exposed to more modern views. They founded German synagogues. In 1850 there were 37 Jewish congregations in the United States.[43]

The peddlers took advantage of American Western Expansion, which was halted temporarily by the Civil War (1861–1865) and the post-Civil War Reconstruction (1865–1877). They peddled across the Midwest and South and eventually settled down. They also became owners of factories, mostly of textile factories. While by 1877, California, Illinois, Maryland, New York, Ohio, and Pennsylvania all had over 10,000 Jews for a total of 154,785 Jews, the remaining

---

[42] Hasia Diner, "Entering the Mainstream of Modern Jewish History: Peddlers and the American Jewish South." *Southern Jewish History* 8 (2005), 12–13.

[43] Jim Schwartz, Jeffrey Scheckner, and Laurence Kotler-Berkowitz, "Census of US Synagogues, 2001." *American Jewish Yearbook* (2002), 112, 117, accessed 31 January 2014, http://www.jewishdatabank.org/Studies/downloadFile.cfm?FileID=3022.

74,302 (nearly 1/3rd of the United States' Jewish population) Jews resided in the 42 other states.[44]

More American Jews in 1877 lived in small communities than large urban Jewish communities. Part of the reason was that the German Jews had good relationships with the German Christians because those German Christians "who took the initiative to leave Germany were less likely to have been under the influence of anti-Jewish prejudices than those who remained, and once they arrived most of them readily accepted the American value of social equality."[45] German Jews tended to congregate where German Christians were to share in German cultural experiences. The relationships between the Christian Germans and the Jewish Germans were cordial because they shared a common heritage and celebrated this heritage together. Thus, German Jews scattered across the Midwest and South and integrated into American society, without abandoning their Judaism, often becoming the first Jews in a community. In fact, German Jewish merchants opened a store in just about every town from the Alleghenies westward.

These German Jews had adopted the Reform ideology that emphasized, among other religious practices, Protestant customs of decorum and brought them to America. They were not outwardly religiously different than their neighbors as their Jewish domestic observances became minimal and they focused their religious practices in the synagogue. For the Jewish homesteaders "holidays gave punctuation, order, and symmetry to life which was otherwise an endless ribbon of monotony…[and] it was incumbent on every Jewish father to see to it that his children grew up to perpetuate this heritage and tradition."[46]

About 73 percent of southern Jewish communities were historically aligned with the Reform movement and that "in many small-town Jewish histories the story of local Jewish life is inexorably intertwined with that of the local Reform temple."[47] Because of their choices to seek economic prosperity in growing towns with no Jews, Jewish "isolation is a prominent fact of [Southern and Midwestern] Jewish life; there are no strong connections with major Jewish communities."[48]

---

44 Jacobs, "Statistics," 352.
45 Meyer, "German-Jewish Identity," 48.
46 Jenna Weissman Joselit, "The Call of the Matzoh," in *The Wonders of America: Reinventing Jewish Culture, 1880–1950* (New York: Henry Holt and Co., 1994), 91.
47 Lee Shai Weissbach, "East European Immigrants and the Image of Jews in the Small-Town South." *American Jewish History* 85, no. 3 (1997): 250.
48 Amy Hill Shevitz, "Constructing Community, Constructing Section: Regional Culture and Jewish Community Across the United States" (paper presented at the 2006 Biennial Scholars'

This Jewish isolation, of course, influenced how Jews worshipped and thought about themselves. Jewish isolation led to intermarriage which was a great impetus towards assimilation. However, Wise discovered many of "these German Jewish immigrants,...have not lost their love for Judaism under the influence of their new political and social conditions. Hence their desire for organization."⁴⁹ Additionally, all the leaders of the early Reform Movement realized that there had to be some delineation between themselves and the Gentiles, whom in many respects they sought to emulate; otherwise Jews would disappear. Being Jewish became a private matter, rather than a public, or communal one. Some Jewish leaders argued that the longer Jews were in contact with Americans the more they lost touch with Judaism.

No matter how far flung Jews in the New World were, no matter how dire their circumstances the desire to maintain some semblance of Jewish practices persisted. Isaac J. Levy wrote home from Adams Run, South Carolina, where he and his brother Ezekiel made a Seder in the Confederate army camp in 1864.⁵⁰ Joseph A. Joel's letter about celebrating a Seder with fellow Jews as part of the Union Army in Fayette, West Virginia in 1862 was published in an edition of the 1866 *The Jewish Messenger.* In it he described his joy in not only receiving matzah with "two Hagodahs [sic]", but that he and his fellow Jews foraging for food that resulted in a local weed for the maror and cider for the wine.⁵¹ As far removed from other Jews as the *Am Olam* commune outside of Newport, Arkansas was, residents celebrated Passover with matzah and coffee, because they had no money to purchase wine, which they couldn't get in the area anyway.⁵² In the late 1800s, when kosher wine was extraordinarily difficult to obtain in various parts of the United States and on the frontier, Jews resorted to the making and consuming of raisin wine. This was an Old World custom that was rabbinically sanctioned when kosher wine was not available. On the Dakota Plains, Jews ordered their Passover food months in advance and drove miles in their wagons to collect their crates from the train station. Homesteader Gittel Turnoy

---

Conference on American Jewish History, Charleston, South Carolina, 5–7 June 2006), 8, accessed 11 October 2007, http://www.cofc.edu/~jwst/pages/Shevitz,%20Amy%20-%20constructing%20section%20+.pdf.
49 Isaac Mayer Wise, *Reminiscences*, trans. David Philipson (Cincinnati: Leo Wise and Co., 1901), 36–37.
50 Isaac J. Levy to Leonara and Ezekial Levy, 24 April 1864, reprint "Confederate Passover," accessed 7 February 2013, http://www.jewish-history.com/civilwar/seder.html.
51 Joseph A. Joel, "Passover in Camp: A Reminiscence of the Warm," in *An Anthology of Western Reserve Literature*, ed. David R. Anderson and Gladys Haddad (Kent: Kent State Univ. Press, 1992), 41–43.
52 Herder, "Memories of Yesterday;" 63.

would *kasher* her utensils and dishes for Passover, because she owned but one set.[53] Rachel Calof had special Passover dishes, at least by the time she sold the homestead.[54]

German Jews also understood that Americanization would ease their entry into American society, just as Emancipation and Germanization eased their way into German society. Entrée was facilitated by the fact that German culture came to be held in high regard by a number of Americans, especially in the latter decades of the 19th Century. Such esteem of German culture was true in the Jewish community as well. Subjects in Jewish religious schools were taught in German or had German language instruction, sermons were delivered in German and minutes for Jewish communal groups began to be taken in German. Non-German American Jews felt the need to follow suit with their fellow Americans and emulate German society. Thus, the newly arrived German Jewish immigrants could become integrated into American society, once they learned English, for the culture to emulate was the German one.

As Jonathan D. Sarna, Chief Historian of the National Museum of American Jewish History, explained, "It was during this period [the Second Great Wave] that Judaism underwent the radical transformation that reshaped it into the American Judaism that we have come to know."[55] The addition of German Reform beliefs to the free-thinking post-American Emancipation thinking permitted the evolution of Reform Judaism into something that perhaps could not have been considered before. Before 1850 the only German-educated rabbis in the United States were Isaac Leeser, Isaac Meyer Wise, Max Lilienthal, James Gutheim, Abraham Rice, and Leo Merzbacher. By 1880, there were 16 more German university-trained rabbis.[56] Wise described a rabbi in America as "an unknown quantity, and to the Bible-loving Americans he was an interesting personality."[57] In just 30 years, the number of university, secularly, educated rabbis almost tri-

---

53 Sophie Trupin, *Dakota Diaspora: Memoirs of a Jewish Homesteader* (Lincoln: Univ. of Nebraska Press, 1984), 89–90.
54 Kristene Peleg, "Prairie Harvests and Sukkoth: A comparison of Jewish holiday observances in three frontier memories" (paper presented at the 36thAnnual Conference of the Association for Jewish Studies, Chicago, Illinois, 20 December 2004). Transcript.
55 Jonathan D. Sarna, "American Jewish History." *Modern Judaism* 10, no. 3 (1990), 348.
56 Alan Silverstein, *Alternatives to Assimilation: The Response of Reform Judaism to American Culture, 1840–1930* (Hanover: Brandeis Univ. Press, 1994), 115.
57 Isaac Mayer Wise. *The World of My Books*, trans. Albert H. Friedlander (Cincinnati: American Jewish Archives, June 1954), 11.

pled[58] illustrating the need in the United States for Reform rabbis. Since American Jews, for the most part, were assimilated, they found this appealing.

Wise arrived with the intent of being a rabbi teacher, though not necessarily a congregational leader. However, he discovered "the Portuguese ritual just as antiquated and tedious as the German and the Polish, although more decorous, dignified, and classical."[59] He realized that the "reforming spirit" was part of his nature and felt he needed to fix American Judaism.[60] Established Jewish leaders like Leeser were not friendly to the reformers and viewed them and their practices as destructive.[61] Wise, however, believed that reform "convey[s] the idea of putting [Judaism] into a new and improved form and condition."[62]

Early Organizations

Lilienthal urged the creation of a *bêt hadîn* in New York in 1846, the year Wise arrived. A *bêt hadîn*, a rabbinic court, would have put the power of control of religious law in the hands of the rabbis, thus recreating the power the rabbis had in Europe.[63] Considering the fact that these rabbis were hired because of their Reform theologies and the lack of cohesiveness in American Judaism, one can understand Lilienthal's desire to create unity and hierarchy. However, the *bet din* collapsed before it had begun because it didn't include rabbis from around the United States, only the New York metropolitan region, and American Judaism had already developed without a rabbinic hierarchy. At least one member of the *bet din* moved west and could no longer attend meetings. American Judaism had so far existed with the rabbinic hierarchy that existed in Europe and could because the American concept of social equality and individualism.

Lilienthal assigned Wise the task of creating a *Minhag America* and gave him a year to do so.[64] The idea of a *Custom of America* prayerbook was that this was a way to unite American Jews. After all, Jews in Europe had prayerbooks published in their regions that included prayers specific to that area. Wise realized that "re-

---

58 William B. Hackenburg, et al. *Statistics of the Jews of the United States* (Philadelphia: UAHC, 1880), 57.
59 Wise, *Reminiscences*, 21.
60 Ibid., 49.
61 Ibid., 57.
62 Issac Mayer Wise, "Reformed Judaism." In *Selected Writings of Isaac M. Wise: With a Biography*. Ed. David Philipson and Louis Grossman (Cincinnati: Robert Clarke Co., 1900), 261.
63 Wise, *Reminiscences*, 50.
64 Wise, *Reminiscences*, 50.

form could be accomplished only by introducing reforms; that is, that the act must accompany the spoken word."[65] Wise had the *minhag* complete, but the *bet din* had disbanded. "It never occurred to [him] to prepare a prayer-book for [his] own congregation, because [he] considered such an autocratic proceeding wrong...[He] did not wish to sever the bond of synagogal unity" and so he kept the manuscript in his briefcase.[66]

The *bêt hadîn* concept was instead shifted into a conference concept. American rabbis had been organizing into regional conferences since 1848. The first such gathering was a failure, despite Isaac Leeser's of Philadelphia and Isaac M. Wise's, then of Albany, New York best efforts.[67] These conferences were mostly groups from a single urban area established as a Jewish legal authority. Wise and 8 other rabbis attempted to organize a synod, the United Jewish Congregations of America in 1855. Reform and Orthodox leaders were present.[68] Among the items on the agenda, they proposed "the articles of union for the American Israel in theory and practice" and the creation of a *Minhag America*.[69] Wise was pleased and "imagined that the battle had been fought and won... The position of Judaism was adjusted to the laws of the land."[70] However, dissent within the Reform camp began almost immediately between those who were more liberal and those who were less willing to abandon tradition – the latter would eventually create Conservative Judaism. Lilienthal was not as disillusioned as Wise by this dissension. He was convinced that "Reform, nowadays, has gained so much ground that it can not be haughtily overlooked nor indignantly disregarded."[71]

However, at the 1855 Conference of Rabbis, the *Minhag America* was back on the list of items to address.[72] When it was finally published in 1857, Wise was disappointed to find "it was attacked with all the weapons possible...and yet it is now used in at least one-third of all American Jewish congregations...and

---

65 Wise, *Reminiscences*, 50.
66 Ibid., 55.
67 Michael A. Meyer, "Thank You, Moritz Loth: A 125-Year UAHC Retrospective." *Reform Judaism* (fall 1998), 31.
68 Wise, *Reminiscences*, 312.
69 "American Conference." *Year Book of The Central Conference of American Rabbis 1890–91* (Cincinnati: Bloch, 1891), reprint *Central Conference of American Rabbis Year Book Volumes I, II, III 1890–1983* (New York: CCAR, n.d.), 123.
70 Wise, *Reminiscences*, 316.
71 Max Lilienthal to Isaac Leeser, 24 November 1856, reprint "Letters and Addresses. Letters on Reform Addressed to the Rev. I. Leeser," in *Max Lilienthal: American Rabbi: Life and Writings*, ed. David Philipson (New York: Bloch Pub., 1915), 367.
72 Ibid., 347.

made the use of the old ritual an impossibility in America."⁷³ The *Minhag* had 2 parts: 1 in Hebrew and 1 in English, plus a companion edition in German could be purchased.⁷⁴ This showed that the overwhelming number of German Jewish immigrants were a powerful force in American Judaism. Perhaps the most radical change to the prayerbook was the statement at the beginning declaring women could be counted in a *minyan*.⁷⁵

This failed attempt at a permanent national organization did spawn an 1869 conference, a series of meetings in 1870, and a conference in 1871 of Reform rabbis. Wise was not the only rabbi to desire uniformity. Leeser successfully created the Board of Jewish Ministers of Philadelphia in 1861. It merged, in 1885, with the Jewish Minister's Association. Jewish clergy in New York formed the Jewish Ministers' Association in 1884 that included rabbis from other major cities in the Northeast. The group decided to rename itself the Jewish Ministers' Association of America.⁷⁶ The point was to reinterpret the Reform Judaism brought to America by German Jews into something appealing to the fractured American Jewish community. Members of the Jewish Minister's Association envisioned themselves as a national group, but that never came to fruition because they could not gain members outside their metropolitan area.⁷⁷ It could also be that the desire for uniformity among the clergy was not important to the American Jewish who desired to be an individual in the American sense.

In 1880 Lilienthal created the Rabbinical Literary Association of America.⁷⁸ The Union of American Hebrew Congregations (UAHC) was organized in 1873 by the layman Moritz Loth who was president of Wise's temple. Loth noted it was created "to safe guard against the so-called [radical] reform, which if not checked, may become disastrous to our cause."⁷⁹ There were 34 founding Reform congregations; by 1875 there were 72 member congregations;⁸⁰ by 1879 118 member synagogues;⁸¹ and by 1905 144.⁸² Reform Judaism had taken a firm hold on

---

73 Ibid., 346.
74 Temkin, *Creating*, 150.
75 Levy, *A Vision*, 196.
76 Gary Phillip Zola, "Southern Rabbis and the Rounding of the First National Association of Rabbis." *American Jewish History* 85, no. 4 (1997): 355.
77 Ibid., 353–354.
78 Sidney L. Regner, "The History of the Conference Part I: 1889–1964," in *Tanu Rabbanan: Our Rabbis Taught: Essays on the Occasion of the Centennial of the Central Conference of American Rabbis*, ed. Joseph B. Glaser (New York: CCAR, 1990), 3.
79 Meyer, "Thank You," 31.
80 Ibid.
81 Hackenburg, et al. *Statistics*, 57.
82 Meyer, "Thank You," 31.

American soil. The Eastern Conference, founded in 1885, included two rabbinic powerhouses of the Reform Movement: Kaufman Kohler and David Philipson.[83] At the same time, The Conference of Rabbis of Southern Congregations was created.[84] It is clear that each of the 2 groups followed what the other was doing; it may have been that they hoped to work together. It should be noted, however, that some Jews in America became more and more dissatisfied with synagogue worship and founded social groups, like B'nai B'rith, that functioned as "secular synagogues."[85]

The opening of the American West and post-Civil War Reconstruction resulted in the disintegration of European Jewish tradition in the United States. With the intermingling of Jews from all over the Europe who had differing traditions, and the vast distances between small communities in the newly acquired territories, new traditions developed out of necessity and opportunity. Nor were there enough rabbis for these dispersed communities, and so those with little Jewish education became lay leaders of Jewish communities. In addition, once the local Christians realized that Jews were "just like" them, and the Jews established themselves firmly in the middle class, Jews became acceptable mates for the local Christian men and women. Thus intermarriage became common and resulted in many Jews leaving Judaism or permitting their children to be raised as Christians.

First American Reform Conference

In 1885, Rabbi Kaufman Kohler, a son-in-law of David Einhorn, convened the Pittsburgh Conference to bring together American rabbis who advocated for reform. Nineteen rabbis attended the conference, most of whom were Midwestern.[86] Kohler was also very concerned about the religious decline among Reform Jews and hoped that by creating some basic tenets for the movement this decline could be reversed.[87] The focus of the Pittsburgh Conference was to create an ideological platform.[88] It was based on the format and ideals of the Brunswick,

---

83 Zola, "Southern Rabbis," 355–356.
84 Ibid., 358.
85 Hackenburg, et al. *Statistics*, 349.
86 Meyer, *A Response*, 265, 268.
87 Dana Evan Kaplan, "Reform Jewish Theology and the Sociology of Liberal Religion in America: The Platforms as Response to the Perception of Socioreligious Crisis." *Modern Judaism* 20 (2000): 65–66.
88 Silverstein, *Alternatives*, 118.

Frankfurt, and Breslau Conferences of 1844–1846 in Germany. There was also concern that the traditional "chaotic" services where Jews did "what we would call *private* prayer in a *public* setting" were not appropriate in the Protestant America where there was more predictability and decorum in the Protestant service.[89]

No congregation ever formally adopted the Pittsburgh Platform, as it was dubbed, but it did illustrate differing views among Jewish American movements. The tenor of the Platform can be seen in the Sixth Resolution of the Pittsburgh Platform that states: "We recognize in Judaism a progressive religion, ever striving to be in the postulates of reason."[90] The Platform also rejected those Mosaic laws that "fail to impress the modern Jew with a spirit of priestly holiness," "recognize[d] ...the Bible [as] the record of the consecration of the Jewish people," and accepted the idea of a soul.[91] Kohler never thought of the Platform as a creed.[92] For him, it really was "more a temporary stand than a permanent document."[93]

Shortly after the Pittsburgh Conference, the Conference of Southern Rabbis met and presented principles that followed the spirit of the Pittsburgh Platform.[94] The philosophy of the Pittsburgh Platform was particularly pleasing to the Southern constituency because they were grappling with preserving Jewish life on a non-Jewish society, especially for their congregants who lived mostly in isolation.[95] However, the Pittsburgh Platform was an intellectual statement that laypeople really did not understand. The lay Jew was less concerned with theology and more with practice and the Pittsburgh Platform discussed many points that seemed irrelevant to the American Jew of the period.

The Platform caused dissention between the liberal and conservative members of the Eastern Conference of Rabbis.[96] It reflected the reformers' rejection of

---

89 Daniel Freelander, "Birth of a Synagogue Movement." *Reform Judaism* (summer 2011): 58.
90 Declaration of Principles, Pittsburgh Conference, Pittsburgh, Pennsylvania, 16–18 November 1885, reprint *Year Book of The Central Conference of American Rabbis1890–91* (Cincinnati: Bloch, 1891); reprint *Central Conference of American Rabbis Year Book Volumes I, II, III 1890–1983* (New York: CCAR, n.d.), 121.
91 Ibid.
92 Bernard Bamberger, "Introduction," in *Reform Judaism: Essays by Hebrew Union College Alumni*, ed. Abraham J. Feldman, et al. (Cincinnati: HUC, 1949), 16.
93 Walter Jacob, "The Influence of the Pittsburgh Platform on Reform Halakhah and Biblical Study," in *The Changing Face of Jewish and Christian Worship in North America*, ed. Paul F. Bradshaw and Laurence A. Hoffman (Notre Dame: Univ. of Notre Dame Press, 1991), 26.
94 Ibid., 25.
95 Zola, "Southern Rabbis," 371.
96 Ibid., 365.

Hebrew and traditional Jewish practice.[97] More conservative members did not approve. They did not believe Judaism to be an evolving religion in the radical ways the more liberal contingent wished. Some of these conservative members founded the Jewish Theological Seminary in 1886[98] in an effort to "create a Westernized, English-speaking Orthodox rabbinate to serve congregations in America."[99] On the other hand, some liberal intellectual reformers started the Ethical Culture movement, founded by a Reform rabbinical student. The Platform was completed partially as a response to this movement away from Reform Judaism.

Wise didn't entirely like the statements in the Platform, but understood "that the American Jewish community needed organizational structure more than anything else."[100] Thus, the Central Conference of American Rabbis (CCAR) was organized in 1889. This was now possible because Wise had a core group of Hebrew Union College (founded 1875) graduates as members.[101] The name "Central" was used because Wise did not wish to compete with the other regional groups. It grew from 30 to 90 members in one year.[102] In 1893, it could be considered a national organization, because all the members of the Southern Conference were members of the CCAR.[103]

The CCAR resolved at the first Annual Convention in 1891:

> to work out a uniform system for the practice of Judaism in the family, the school and the synagogue. In conformity with this declaration, which meets with our hearty approval, we deem it of the utmost importance that we devise means for establishing a uniformity in the mode of public and private worship of those congregations and individuals adhering to the reform principles of Judaism.[104]

---

[97] Herbert Bronstein, "Platforms and Prayer Books: From Exclusivity to Inclusivity in Reform Judaism," in *Platforms and Prayer Books: Theological and Liturgical Perspectives on Reform Judaism*, ed. Dana Evan Kaplan (Lanham, Maryland: Rowman& Littlefield, 2002), 29–30.

[98] H. Pereira Mendes, "The Beginnings of the [Jewish Theological] Seminary," in *The Jewish Theological Seminary of American*, Semi-Centennial volume, ed. Cyrus Adler (New York: JTS of America, 1939), 36; reprint *The Jew in the Modern World: A Documentary History*, 3rd ed., ed. Paul Mendes-Flohr and Jehuda Reinharz (New York: Oxford Univ. Press, 2010), 522.

[99] Hertzberg, *The Jews*, 277.

[100] Ibid., 27.

[101] Regner, "The History," 4.

[102] Meyer, *A Response to Modernity*, 276.

[103] Zola, "Southern Rabbis," 368.

[104] S. Mannheimer and I. Schwab, "On Prayer-Book" (presented at the Convention of the Central Conference of American Rabbis. Cleveland, Ohio, 14 July 1891) *Year Book of the Central Conference of American Rabbis 1890–91* (Cincinnati: Bloch Pub., 1891), 26; reprint *Central Conference of American Rabbis Year Book Volumes I, II, III 1890–1983*. New York: CCAR, n.d.

Those present also felt that "a Standard Union Prayer-book ...that such a uniformity in our ritual would serve as a powerful magnet to draw together the varying and disperate religious views and sentiments of American Reform Judaism."[105] The 1891 Conference was given an outline of a prayer book that did not include a Haggadah.[106]

Early American Reform Liturgy

At the 1st Annual Convention of the CCAR on the 3rd day, Dr. Aaron Hahn, a Cleveland rabbi, requested "that a committee be appointed to compile a new prayer-book, to be used on all occasions in the synagogue and the home."[107] The following resolution was then passed: "We deem it of the utmost importance that we devise means for establishing a uniformity in the mode of public and private worship of those congregations and individuals adhering to the reform principles of Judaism."[108]

This was a direct outgrowth of Wise's desire for a *Minhag America* (a set American Jewish practice) that he had completed in 1847 and had finally been published in 1857. His text was not well received by the American Jewish public, much to Wise's disappointment, but this did not deter him from believing it to be important to American Jewish unity. The call at the first CCAR pleased him enormously.[109] The constituency of the Reform Movement at this time was almost exclusively German and immigrant. This shaped the Movement profoundly. The 1857 *Minhag America* had a German edition, the same as the English one, but printed separately. Additionally, the immigrant status ensured an adherence to

---

[105] S[olomon] Sonneschein, Aaron Hahn, Low Schwab, Leo Mannheimer, and E. N. Calish, "Report by the Committee on Ritual," Convention of the Central Conference of American Rabbis, Cleveland, Ohio, 15 July 1891. *Year Book of the Central Conference of American Rabbis 1890–91* (Cincinnati: Bloch Pub., 1891), 29; reprint *Central Conference of American Rabbis Year Book Volumes I, II, III 1890–1983* (New York: CCAR, n.d.).
[106] "Plan of the Prayer Book." *Year Book of the Central Conference of the American Rabbis 1891–92* (Cincinnati: Bloch Pub., 1892), 15–16; reprint *Central Conference of American Rabbis Year Book Volumes I, II, III 1890–1983* (New York: CCAR, n.d.).
[107] Aaron Hahn, Motion, Convention of the Central Conference of American Rabbis, Cleveland, Ohio, 14 July1891. *Year Book of the Central Conference of American Rabbis 1890–91* (Cincinnati, Ohio: Bloch Pub., 1891), 26; reprint *Central Conference of American Rabbis Year Book Volumes I, II, III 1890–1983* (New York: CCAR, n.d.).
[108] Mannheimer and Schwab, "On Prayer-Book."
[109] Wise, *Reminiscences*, 316.

the Old World traditions, in this case early Reform Judaism, rather than instituting changes as had the established communities in the New and Old World.

Dr. Solomon H. Sonneschein moved that a committee of 5 be created to arrange such a manuscript and "that the Prayer-book thus contemplated will have to evince not only a thorough sympathy with the ideal of a Religion of Humanity, but must in its main features...adhere to the sacred language and living historic mission of Israel."[110] Sonneschein, Hahn, Dr. Isaac Schwab, Rev. S. Mannheimer, and Rabbi E. N. Calish were appointed to the committee.[111] These gentlemen returned the next day with a report that included a resolution that the prayerbook will be traditional in worship and include 3 or 4 alternate services for each holiday that the vernacular be offered with the Hebrew prayers, and "that an appendix be attached, containing rituals for...the Seder."[112] This motion was adopted and a committee of Sonneschein, Dr. Sale, Dr. Philipson, Adolph Moses, Dr. [Rudolph] Grossman, Dr. Machol, Dr. Landsberg, Dr. Berkowitz, Dr. Mayer, and Rabbi Charles Levi were appointed to make this happen.[113]

The following year Sonneschein, as chairman of the Ritual Committee, submitted a "Plan of Prayer Book" that did not include a Haggadah.[114] The committee was disbanded and a new one of Rev. M. Mielziner, Dr. Sale, Dr. Leucht, Dr. Max Heller, and Mannheimer was appointed with a reminder to consider both Isaac S. Moses' recent work and others by prominent European and American rabbis,[115] which they did.[116] In 1892 the Ritual Committee submitted a "printed pamphlet...[with] hope that the rituals as arranged in this pamphlet will meet

---

[110] S[olomon] H. Sonneschein, Motion, Convention of the Central Conference of American Rabbis, Cleveland, Ohio, 14 July 1891. *Year Book of the Central Conference of American Rabbis 1890–91* (Cincinnati: Bloc Pub., 1891), 27; reprint *Central Conference of American Rabbis Year Book Volumes I, II, III 1890–1983* (New York: CCAR, n.d.).
[111] Ibid.
[112] Sonneschein, Hahn, Schwab, Mannheimer, and Calish, "Report by the Committee on Ritual," 29–30.
[113] Ibid.
[114] "Plan of the Prayer Book."
[115] Resolution. *Year Book of the Central Conference of the American Rabbis 1891–92*, 18 (Cincinnati: Bloch Pub., 1892); reprint *Central Conference of American Rabbis Year Book Volumes I, II, III 1890–1983* (New York: CCAR, n.d.).
[116] [William] Rosenau, response to I[saac] S. Moses' response to Henry Berkowitz, J. Stolz, and H. G. Enelow, "Report of the Committee on Haggadah." *Year Book of the Central Conference of American Rabbis*, vol. 14, 18 (Cincinnati: Bloch Pub., 1904).

with…[the] approval" of the Conference.[117] They encouraged the use of Wise's *Minhag America* as the Union prayerbook.[118]

Wise's dream of a *Minhag America* slowly came to fruition when in 1892 the *Union Prayer Book* was published under the auspices of the CCAR[119] even though it relied more heavily on the more radical *'Olat Tamid* by Einhorn, than the traditional *Minhag America* by Wise.[120] Einhorn purposely discarded the traditional service structure and the Hebrew, instead inserting prayers in German, while Wise maintained the traditional structure, though shortened, and translated the text into both English and German.[121] It included a Haggadah,[122] which Rabbi Mielziner later agreed was "a mistake,"[123] because the Haggadah should be a separate book as it was used during a meal and was commonly published as a separate book. However, the inclusion of the Haggadah is significant because it shows the desire of the CCAR to create a standardized form of worship for all ceremonies.

The Ritual Committee sent out a letter to all member congregations in 1892 encouraging the purchase of this prayer book that "is intended to remove the prevailing diversity of rituals, and to give in their stead *one* book that will, it is hoped, satisfy the wants of progressive Jewish congregations of America."[124] Here the differing philosophies within the Reform Movement are expressed. The CCAR was composed mostly of American trained rabbis, at this point, who apparently believed in a more radical reform than their founder Wise.

Within a year of its publication, the *Union Prayer-Book* was used by 55 congregations[125] and it quickly "became the accepted ritual of the Reform movement

---

117 M. Mielziner, S. Mannheimer, S. Hecht, H[enry] Berkowitz, and Isaac S. Moses, "Report of the Ritual Committee," *Year Book of the Central Conference of the American Rabbis 1892–93*, 97 (Cincinnati: Bloch Pub., 1893); reprint *Central Conference of American Rabbis Year Book Volumes I, II, III 1890–1983* (New York: CCAR, n.d.)
118 Ibid., 100.
119 Central Conference of American Rabbis, *Union Prayer Book* (Chicago: Bloch Pub., 1892).
120 Temkin, "A Century," 47.
121 Ibid., 14–15.
122 Central Conference of American Rabbis, "Domestic service for the Eve of Passover," *Union Prayer Book* (Chicago: Bloch Pub., 1892), 227–257.
123 M. Mielziner to Central Conference of American Rabbis, 2 December 1892, reprint *Year Book of the Central Conference of American Rabbis*, vol. 4 (Cincinnati: Bloch Pub., 1894), 8.
124 M. Mielziner, Henry Berkowitz, et al., to P.P. ©1892. Jacob Rader Marcus Center of the American Jewish Archives, Cincinnati Campus, Hebrew Union College – Jewish Institute of Religion, MS coll. L. Mielziner, nearprint.
125 Zola, "Southern Rabbis," 386.

as a whole."[126] In fact, by 1900 125 congregations used this prayerbook.[127] By 1903, over 300 congregations, not all aligned with the Reform Movement, used the prayerbook and over 100,000 copies had been sold.[128] The large number of sales shows not only that there was a desire for a new American Reform liturgy, but the CCAR had met in some way the needs of their constituency. The CCAR was quite pleased with "the solidarity already secured in American Israel through the creation of the Union Prayer Book."[129] This publication reflected the image a number of American Jews had of themselves. As A. Stanley Dreyfus, former chair of the CCAR Liturgy Committee, notes, "they undertook to assimilate the style of Jewish worship to the pattern of the dominant culture. They appropriated much in the 1895 prayer book from Protestant churches."[130] The end result was a more universalist liturgy than any before it.[131]

However, the Haggadah in the *Union Prayer-Book* "had not been submitted to the Ritual Committee."[132] This 1892 "Domestic service for the Eve of Passover," as the Haggadah in the *Union Prayer* book was titled, had a note that it was "adapted from the German of the late Dr. Leopold Stein" published in 1841 in Bavaria,[133] a particular favorite of American Jews.[134] Moses "recast" Stein's Haggadah "as well as [he] could, Americanizing it."[135] There was a paragraph at the

---

[126] Sidney L. Regner, "History of the Conference Part I: 1889–1964," in *Tanu Rabbanan: Our Rabbis Taught: Essays on the Occasion of the Centennial of the Central Conference of American Rabbis*, ed. Joseph B. Glaser (New York: CCAR, 1990), 6.
[127] Zola, "Southern Rabbis,"386.
[128] Meyer, *A Response*, 279.
[129] Henry Berkowitz, J. Stolz, and H.G. Enelow, "Report of the Committee on Haggadah," Convention of the Central Conference of American Rabbis, 1903. *Year Book of the Central Conference of American Rabbis*, vol.14 (Cincinnati: Bloch Pub.,1904), 83.
[130] A. Stanley Dreyfus, "The *Gates* Liturgies: Reform Judaism Reforms Its Worship," in *The Changing Face of Jewish and Christian Worship in North America*, ed. Paul F. Bradshow and Lawrence A. Hoffman (Notre Dame: Univ. of Notre Dame Press, 1991), 144.
[131] Elliot L. Stevens, "The Prayer Books, They Are A' Changin'." *Reform Judaism* (summer 2006), accessed 17 November 2008, http://urj.org/Articles.
[132] Mielziner, to Central Conference of American Rabbis.
[133] Hara Person, "CCAR Haggadot: A Feast of Haggadah Choices." *Reform Rabbis Speak* 21 February 2014, accessed 29 March 2014, http://ravblog.ccarnet.org/2014/02/ccar-haggadot-a-feast-of-haggadah-choices/.
[134] Joel Gereboff, "One Nation, with Liberty and Haggadahs for All," in *Key Texts in American Jewish Culture*, ed. Jack Kugelmass (New Brunswick: Rutgers Univ. Press, 2003), 277.
[135] I[saac] S. Moses, response to Henry Berkowitz, J. Stolz, and H. G. Enelow, "Report of the Committee on Haggadah." *Year Book of the Central Conference of American Rabbis*, vol. 14 (Cincinnati: Bloch Pub., 1904), 87.

beginning explaining how to set the Seder table[136] and this was the only non-liturgical material in the Haggadah. At this point, American Jewish leaders were not concerned that the customs were disappearing; rather they were working on making them relevant to the populace as set out in the Pittsburgh Platform of 1885 that there is a "necessity of preserving the historical identity with our great past."[137] The Conference then approved the now separately printed Haggadah and sent it to a special committee for further review.[138] As Rabbi Walter Jacob, president of the Abraham Geiger College in Berlin/Potsdam, explained, "the movement felt it should present a version which would appeal to its new American constituency. English was widely used so that the text would be readily understandable."[139]

Conclusion

The Reform Movement in America grew very much as did its German counterpart – as a response to the needs of American Jews. Thus too the liturgies were designed with the needs of the congregants in mind. Additionally, the 1st Haggadot produced by the CCAR were in response to the needs of their immigrant and first generation constituents who were deeply ingrained with the German Reform Science of Judaism and the desire to Americanize by discarding the trappings of the Old World. Their needs to understand the why of Passover and the way to observe were minimal. However, that there was a need for a Haggadah that met the needs of the Reform Jewish community in the United States is clear.

---

136 CCAR, "Domestic service for the Eve of Passover," 227.
137 Declaration of Principles, Pittsburgh Conference, Pittsburgh, Pennsylvania, 16–18 November 1885. Reprint *Year Book of the Central Conference of the American Rabbis 1890–91* (Cincinnati: Bloch Pub., 1891), 121. Reprint *Central Conference of American Rabbis Year Book Volumes I, II, III 1890–1983* (New York: CCAR, n.d.).
138 Motion on the Letter to Central Conference of American Rabbis, 2 December 1892. *Year Book of the Central Conference of American Rabbis*, vol. 4 (Cincinnati: Bloch Pub., 1894), 9.
139 Walter Jacob, "70. Reform *Haggadah*," in *Questions and Reform Jewish Answers: New American Reform Responsa* (New York: CCAR, 1992), 110.

Chapter 5:
Development of the American Reform Movement and Its Liturgies Including the Non-Liturgical Elements in CCAR Haggadot the Middle Years

> "The Liturgy Committee of the Central Conference of American Rabbis hoped to prepare a Haggadah that would have the power to summon up for our time the Seder's potency of joy and meaning."
>
> Herbert Bronstein[1]

When Rabbi Isaac Mayer Wise died in 1897, the American Jewish community was in the midst of another great change. The Third Great Wave of Jewish Immigration was just beginning. Eastern European Jews were fleeing rising violent anti-Semitism in Russia. The Central Conference of American Rabbis (CCAR) realized this and the president, Joseph Silverman, asked for revisions of "several important publications" including the Haggadah because he feared that American Jews had "almost abandoned [the] Seder service."[2]

The Americanization of the Eastern European Jewish immigrants of this period and the assimilation of the German Jews created a fear among rabbis that Jewish practice was being abandoned. The division between the immigrant Jews and the established Jewish community created concern that American Jewish unity would never happen, but with the slow acceptance of 1st generation Eastern European Jews into the Reform Movement, their desires for tradition became a powerful motivator for change in the Movement. It is this that drove the need for more non-liturgical material in the Haggadah in the 1st half of the 20th Century.

---

[1] Herbert Bronstein, הגדה של פסח: *A Passover Haggadah*: *A New Union Haggadah* (New York: Grossman Pub., 1974), 5.

[2] Joseph Silverman, "Message of President Joseph Silverman" (presented at the Central Conference of American Rabbis Annual Convention, New Orleans, Louisiana, 5–10 May 1902) *Year Book of the Central Conference of American Rabbis*, vol. 12 (Cincinnati: Bloch Pub., 1902), 34–35.

The Influx of the Eastern European Jew

The Third Great Wave of Jewish immigration, from 1881 to 1910, brought in around 1,700,000 Jews, of whom nearly 70 percent were defined as Russians.[3] Most of these Eastern European Jews had not yet been exposed to the bi-cultural world of emancipated German Jews. They adhered to the tenets of traditional Judaism. This new population of American Jews who only achieved emancipation upon reaching American shores would have a large influence on American Jewish population. The huge number of provincial Russian and Austrio-Hungarian Jewish immigrants concerned the cosmopolitan German-American Jews. In one year, from 1899 to 1900, 60,764 Jews arrived in the United States.[4] In New York alone, 22,045 Jews arrived.[5] Between 1899 and 1907, 829,244 Jews entered the United States.[6] The existing largely German Jewish population was secularly educated, mostly middle-class by the 2nd generation, and thoroughly Americanized. At the door to the New World, The Statue of Liberty called these immigrants "the wretched refuse" in a poem written by a Sephardic American Jewess, part of an even older upper class Americanized Jewish community. These immigrants were perceived as a mix of Russian-educated socialists and ghetto-raised secularly uneducated Orthodox. In the New World, they tended to congregate, socially and religiously, with others from their home communities.

Celebrating Passover at the turn of the 20th Century

Community sponsored Seders began at the turn of the 20th Century to provide a Seder experience for those who were unable to cover the cost themselves, like these poverty-stricken Eastern European immigrants. Rabbis derided both the idea of taking a vacation during Passover and communal Seders sponsored by

---

[3] Joseph Jacobs, "Jewish Population of the United States Memoir of the Bureau of Jewish Statistics of the American Jewish Committee." *Jewish American Yearbook*, vol. 16 (1914–1915), 341, 346, accessed 31 January 2014, http://www.ajcarchives.org/main.php?GroupingId=10047.

[4] Mark Wischnitzer, "Jewish Immigration into the United States: 1881–1948," in *To Dwell in Safety: The Story of Jewish Migration Since 1800* (Philadelphia: JPS, 1948), 289, reprint in *The Jew in the Modern World: A Documentary History*, 3rd ed., ed. Paul Mendes-Flohr and Jehuda Reinharz (New York: Oxford Univ. Press, 2010), 532.

[5] "Jewish Statistics." *Jewish American Yearbook*, vol. 24 (1900–1901), 623, accessed 2 June 2014, http://www.jewishdatabank.org/Studies/downloadFile.cfm?FileID=3024.

[6] H. S. Linfield, "Statistics of Jews." *Jewish American Year Book* (1927–1928), 251, accessed 3 June 2014, http://www.jewishdatabank.org/studies/downloadFile.cfm?FileID=3025.

hotels because they felt that these chipped away at the family structure.[7] The CCAR Haggadah addressed this concern by providing information on how to prepare a Seder for those who were unsure.

In 1902, CCAR President Joseph Silverman called for a review of the Haggadah because it should "contain a clear exposition of the story of the Passover, and, at the same time, be sufficiently modern in tone to arouse interest in the almost abandoned Seder service."[8] Additionally, there was concern that "the strong traditional emphasis on Zion and Israel was" presenting a misinterpretation of Reform Judaism and so "more stress was placed on America."[9] However, because the Reform Movement had taken the stand that "Judaism [is] a progressive religion, ever striving to be in accord with the postulates of reason"[10] the motivation that the Seder needed to meet these modern needs was clear. There were other influences on this call as well. The Jewish population in the United States was exploding with the influx of the huge numbers of Eastern European Jews. The CCAR saw this as an opportunity to expand their dream of a *Minhag America*. At this point, Eastern European Jews were not part of the Reform Movement, but their arrival spurred the desire for a standardized ritual. The rabbis wanted to make Reform Judaism the Judaism of the New World and the new arrivals threatened this unity. The only way the Reform rabbis felt they could develop unity was by encouraging the use of the Reform prayer book. By 1903 over 300 congregations, some not aligned with the Reform Movement, used the prayerbook that included the Haggadah and over 100,000 copies of this book had been sold.[11]

Rabbis Joseph Krauskopf and Henry Berkowitz, of the 1903 Committee on Haggadah, "recommend[ed] that the work to be issued shall embody the quaint charm and traditional sentiment of the original Haggadah, as far as this is consonant with the spirit of the time. It furthermore recommends that the work shall offer as an appendix, historical material and additional literature of an interest-

---

[7] Jenna Weissman Joselit, "The Call of the Matzoh," in *The Wonders of America: Reinventing Jewish Culture*, 1880–1950 (New York: Henry Holt and Co., 1994), 224.
[8] Silverman, "Message of President Joseph Silverman," 35.
[9] Walter Jacob, "70. Reform Haggadah." Questions and Reform Jewish Answers: New American Reform Responsa (New York: CCAR, 1992), 111.
[10] Declaration of Principles. Pittsburgh Conference, Pittsburgh, Pennsylvania, 16–18 November 1885. Reprint *Year Book of The Central Conference of American Rabbis* 1890–91 (Cincinnati: Bloch, 1891); reprint *Central Conference of American Rabbis Year Book Volumes I, II, III 1890–1983* (New York: CCAR, n.d.), 121.
[11] Michael A. Meyer, *A Response to Modernity: A History of the Reform Movement in Judaism* (New York: Oxford Univ. Press, 1988), 279.

ing, instructive and inspiring nature."[12] The Haggadah was removed from the *Union Prayer Book* because the Conference considered the Haggadah "a book by itself."[13] After all, the 1904 Committee, which went through numerous changes in membership,[14] reasoned that "the attitude of mind of the modern man has completely changed...he can no longer regard ceremonials with the awe that vested them with mystic sanction or as supernatural ordinances."[15] What the Committee understood was that they had to reach out to the now 2nd-generation German Jews who were becoming assimilated and were inculcated with the Reform ideal that religious education is most important. However, they did believe in "the solidarity already secured in American Israel through the creation of the Union Prayer Book and Union Hymnal may be further strengthened by the production...of the Pesach Haggadah."[16]

They solicited completed Haggadah manuscripts from Isaac Moses[17] and William Rosenau.[18] Moses complied, but Rosenau, believing his text would only be used for translation purposes, refused.[19] Originally, Moses felt it would be inappropriate to publish his Haggadah version, after the CCAR had adopted their own.[20] Despite the Conference's discussion of buying the rights to Moses'

---

12 Joseph Krauskopf and Henry Berkowitz, "Report of the Committee on a Pesach Haggadah." *Year Book of the Central Conference of American Rabbis*, vol. 13 (Cincinnati: Bloch Pub., 1903), 64.
13 I[saac] S. Moses, Response to Henry Berkowitz, J. Stolz, and H. G. Enelow. "Report of the Committee on Haggadah." *Year Book of the Central Conference of American Rabbis*, vol. 14 (Cincinnati: Bloch Pub., 1904), 88.
14 William Rosenau, to Joseph Krauskopf, 4 September 1903. Jacob Rader Marcus Center of the American Jewish Archives, Cincinnati Campus, Hebrew Union College – Jewish Institute of Religion, MS coll. 34, 1/17; William Rosenau, to Henry Berkowitz, 24 October 1904. Jacob Rader Marcus Center of the American Jewish Archives, Cincinnati Campus, Hebrew Union College – Jewish Institute of Religion, MS coll. 34, 2/2; Henry Berkowitz, to William Rosenau, 8 December 1904, Jacob Rader Marcus Center of the American Jewish Archives, Cincinnati Campus, Hebrew Union College – Jewish Institute of Religion, MS coll. 34, 2/2.
15 Henry Berkowitz, J. Stolz, and H. G. Enelow, "Report of the Committee on Haggadah." *Year Book of the Central Conference of American Rabbis*, vol. 14 (Cincinnati: Bloch Pub., 1904), 84.
16 Ibid., 83.
17 Rudolph Grossman, to I[saac] S. Moses, 29 March 1903. Jacob Rader Marcus Center of the American Jewish Archives, Cincinnati Campus, Hebrew Union College – Jewish Institute of Religion. MS coll. 34, 1/17.
18 Rudolph Grossman, to William Rosenau, 30 March 1903. Jacob Rader Marcus Center of the American Jewish Archives, Cincinnati Campus, Hebrew Union College – Jewish Institute of Religion, MS coll.34, 1/17.
19 William Rosenau, to Henry Berkowitz, 24 December 1904. Jacob Rader Marcus Center of the American Jewish Archives, Cincinnati Campus, Hebrew Union College – Jewish Institute of Religion, MS coll. 34, 2/2.
20 Moses, response to Berkowitz, Stolz, and Enelow, 88.

text,[21] they apparently did not. Moses was upset that he did not receive recognition for his work[22] and so published it in 1898.[23] Rosenau composed his Haggadah after years of urging by his wife because of their dissatisfaction with the "then existing English versions" available.[24] He subsequently published his manuscript with Bloch Publishing.[25] He claimed it was not as competition with "the authorized text of the Conference."[26]

In 1905 a Haggadah draft[27] was distributed to the Conference[28] for which Krauskopf, now president of the CCAR, had high hopes. He believed it to be a "scholarly contribution by the Conference to the Liturgy of Israel, and will fill a want that has long been felt."[29] It included at the beginning a "Forward" and "The Seder Table."

The "Forward" explains the reasoning behind the CCAR's revision of the Haggadah: "In the course of the ages the ancient Haggadah came to be embellished with such accretions as reflect the ideas and tastes of different times and various conditions of life."[30] Thus, it "has become imperative, because the old work is so entirely out of accord with the feelings of many sincere Jews who are eager to preserve the old observance in a consistent and effective way."[31] The Conference went so far as to state: "much of the old Pesach Haggadah is ob-

---

[21] Joseph Krauskopf, response to Henry Berkowitz, J. Stolz, and H. G. Enelow, "Report of the Committee on Haggadah." *Year Book of the Central Conference of American Rabbis*, vol. 14 (Cincinnati: Bloch Pub., 1904), 86.

[22] Moses, response to Berkowitz, Stolz, and Enelow, 88.

[23] I[saac] S. Moses, *Seder Hagadah: Domestic Service for the Eve of Passover*, 2nd ed. (Chicago: I.S. Moses, 1898).

[24] William Rosenau, to Max Heller, 6 April 1905, 1. Jacob Rader Marcus Center of the American Jewish Archives, Cincinnati Campus, Hebrew Union College – Jewish Institute of Religion, MS coll. 33, 4/26.

[25] William Rosenau, סדר הגדה *Home-Service for Passover Eve* (New York: Bloch Pub., 1905).

[26] Rosenau, to Heller, 1.

[27] Central Conference of American Rabbis, *The Union Haggadah: Home Service for the Passover Eve* (New York: CCAR, July 1905). Manuscript.

[28] There were some problems with this distribution as some members of the Conference did not receive copies because there weren't enough. (T. Schanfarber, to M. J. Gries, 19 October 1905. Jacob Rader Marcus Center of the American Jewish Archives, Cincinnati Campus, Hebrew Union College – Jewish Institute of Religion, MS coll. 34, 3/4).

[29] Joseph Krasukopf, "Appendix B: Message of Rabbi Jos. Krauskopf, President of Central Conference of American Rabbis, to its Sixteenth Annual Convention, Cleveland, Ohio, July 3, 1905" (presented at the CCAR Conference, Cleveland, Ohio, 2–6 July 1905) *Year Book of the Central Conference of American Rabbis*, vol. 15 (Cincinnati: Bloch Pub., 1905), 198.

[30] CCAR, *Union* (1905), 7–8.

[31] Ibid., 8–9.

solete and tasteless. At times it is even objectionable to our sense of devotion."[32] Conference members found the expunged material to be childish and superstitious, and desired to "save the Seder."[33] This "Forward" is significant because it provides to the reader the authors' reasoning for the work's production and it is the first such "Forward." There is something curious about the need of an organization to justify their publication; however, considering the changes in the American Jewish demography from a largely emancipated bi-cultural middle-class Jewry to a mostly traditional mono-cultural lower class Jewry, one can see why the CCAR felt the need to provide validity for their work. While they were yet to reach out to and accept the new arrivals, they felt the need to polemicize against the influx of more traditional Judaism.

There is still presumption, however, that the community knows how to create the Seder, as "The Seder Table" is a single page and simple list of items and instructions, such as "adorn the table with the best of the family plate."[34] The Appendix contains "Passover in History and Tradition," "The Passover in Literature," and "The Child and the Seder." "Passover in History and Tradition" is a 9-page chapter that illuminates the difference between history and tradition. For example, the Committee makes it quite clear that there is "monumental evidence and traditions seem to justify the opinion that Abraham, and later, Jacob and his sons, went down to Egypt,"[35] while "popular legend" declares Elijah to be the Messiah.[36] This section explains that while Passover is "fundamentally a feast of historical memories," it is also closely tied with the agricultural lives the ancient Israelites lived.[37] In "The Child and the Seder" there is a full explanation of what the symbolic foods represent.[38]

In 1906, after reviewing the comments of the Conference from the previous years and numerous Haggadot, the Committee on Seder Haggadah resubmitted a manuscript after considering revisions suggested by members after the 1905 convention. Berkowitz was in charge of reworking the manuscript to "embody the agreements of the Committee on the conflicting opinions received."[39] This was

---

32 Ibid., 9.
33 Ibid.
34 Ibid., 11.
35 Ibid., 58.
36 Ibid., 59.
37 Ibid., 65.
38 Ibid., 72–76.
39 Henry Berkowitz, to Tobia Schnfarber, 23 March 1906. Jacob Rader Marcus Center of the American Jewish Archives, Cincinnati Campus, Hebrew Union College – Jewish Institute of Religion, MS coll. 34, 3/8.

a task he found both "tedious and difficult." Some members felt that the text did not "conform throughout with the principles, spirit and methods of the Union Prayer Book, which embodies the general standpoint of the Conference" and, so the Committee worked to make sure it did.[40] There were questions about the quality of the English, which was "carefully corrected," and the translations were made to follow the pattern in the *Union Prayer Book* to be "a liberal rather than a literal rendition."[41] This manuscript was produced in 1907[42] and with only 3 weeks of advertising[43] in Jewish papers[44] sold 2,738 copies.[45] This was a clear sign, as the Committee on Publication stated, that it has "supplied a long-felt want."[46] Berkowitz, chairman of the Committee on "The Union Seder Haggadah," was satisfied that the liturgy was "providing for the needs of the present day Jewish family...enabling it to observe this happy festival in the home in an edifying manner."[47] Unfortunately, this first edition has been overlooked by historians who list the first publication of the Haggadah in 1908.[48]

In this 1907 edition, while much of the progressive religious sentiment remained the same, the language had been softened. For example, there was no mention of "tasteless traditions"[49] as they were described in the 1905 edition, rather "the old work is so largely out of accord with the feelings of many sincere Jews" that "the effort has been made to embody the quaint form and the tradi-

---

40 Henry Berkowitz, K[aufmann] Kohler, et al., "Report of the Committee on Seder Haggadah," CCAR Conference, Indianapolis, Indiana, 3 July 1906. *Year Book of the Central Conference of American Rabbis*, vol. 16 (Cincinnati: Bloch Pub., 1906), 83.
41 Ibid., 84.
42 Central Conference of American Rabbis, *The Union Haggadah* (New York: Bloch Publishing, 1907).
43 Joseph Silverman, Isaac S. Moses, and Solomon Foster, "Report of the Committee on Publication," 26 June 1907, Central Conference of American Rabbis Annual Convention, Frankfort, Michigan, 2–8 July 1907. *Year Book of the Central Conference of American Rabbis*, vol. 15 (Cincinnati: Bloch Pub., 1905), 54.
44 Charles S. Bloch, to J. Morgenstern, 31 July 1907, Jacob Rader Marcus Center of the American Jewish Archives, Cincinnati Campus, Hebrew Union College – Jewish Institute of Religion, MS coll. 34, 3/18.
45 Silverman, Moses, and Foster, "Report of the Committee on Publication," 54.
46 Ibid.
47 Henry Berkowitz, "Report of the Committee on 'The Union Seder Haggada," Central Conference of American Rabbis Annual Convention, Frankfort, Michigan, 2–8 July 1907. *Year Book of the Central Conference of American Rabbis*, vol. 15 (Cincinnati: Bloch Pub., 1905), 95.
48 Regner, "History of the Conference," 6; for more see Mara W. Cohen Ioannides, "A Lost Liturgy," *CCAR Journal* (spring 1999): 79–83.
49 CCAR, *Union* (1905), 9.

tional sentiment of the Haggadah, as far as this is consonant with the spirit of the present time."[50] The single page "The Seder Table" had been retained.[51]

The appendix begins with the same material as the sample manuscript, though this historical section is now divided into explanatory sections that are easier for the reader to use:

- "The Passover in Egypt," which is a passage providing history of the Biblical period related to the Exodus story copied from C. J. Ball's 1899 *Light from the East*.[52]
- "Moses," which is 2 paragraphs about the man and how this story "never ceased to bring courage and to kindle faith in a guiding Providence."[53]
- "Elijah the Hero of the Passover," which provides background to the role this prophet had in Jewish history and theology.[54]
- "The Cup of Elijah," which elucidates the purpose of this "extra cup of wine upon the table."[55]
- "The Passover in the Middle Ages," which presents the importance of the understanding of redemption to Jews of the Middle Ages.[56]
- "The Blood Accusation," which is a section from Anatole Leroy-Beaulieu's "Israel among the Nations" that explains various episodes of blood libels in Europe.[57]
- "The Time of the Festival," which explains the time of the festival according to the Jewish calendar and how old the festival is.[58]
- "The Paschal Lamb," which provides the Biblical passages focusing on the lamb and the act of passing over Egyptian houses.[59]
- "The Unleavened Bread," which explains the Biblical passage Exodus 12:15–19 where the festival of unleavened bread is mentioned.[60]
- "Passover—The Spring Festival," which focuses on how this festival responds to spring.[61]

---

50 CCAR, *Union* (1907), vi.
51 Ibid., 10.
52 Ibid., 80–81.
53 Ibid., 82.
54 Ibid., 82–83.
55 Ibid., 83.
56 Ibid., 84.
57 Ibid., 84–85.
58 Ibid., 86.
59 Ibid., 87–88.
60 Ibid., 88.
61 Ibid., 80–89.

The sections allow easy access to the information in a way that is most likely of interest to the reader. They answer basic historic and theological questions.

Berkowitz was careful to keep "Rabbinical references" to a minimum because they "are barren of present day significance."[62] Since to him and the Reform Movement, Elijah is "purely legendary,"[63] the section "Elijah the Hero of the Passover" points out that "later tradition wove a garland of legends around his [Elijah's] image."[64] This was, of course, the philosophy of Reform Judaism. Reform Judaism has turned toward historical religion, meaning only that which is verifiable is included in the practice. The superstitious concepts, like the legends surrounding Elijah, were discarded.

The next part of the appendix, "Passover in Literature,"[65] is a series of passages quoted from various historians on such topics as "Freedom" with a passage by Wise[66] and "Israel's Journey" by Rabbi David Einhorn.[67] The final part of the appendix is "Rites and Symbols of the Passover." Here each symbolic food is explained. Perhaps most telling is the section on "The Four Cups" where it is explained that "this custom is supposed to be based upon Exodus VI-6 where there are four words expressing deliverance."[68] However, much more discussion is devoted to "the most interesting interpretation of the Four Cups is that they are four toasts:" one for Abraham, one for Moses, one for "the martyred people" of Israel, and the fourth for the future.[69] This is a clear expression of the rationalistic historical turn that Reform Judaism had taken.

This 2nd edition of the Haggadah was printed just in time for Passover of 1907. Five thousand copies were printed and almost 3,000 were sold. Berkowitz, chair of the committee of "The Union Seder Haggadah," requested "that a second edition of 5,000 copies be issued in ample time for next Passover."[70] He reminded the 1907 Conference that both the numbers of sales and the "reports received by your Committee from many of those who have made use of the Book" proves the Haggadah is a "practical success."[71] The Committee on President's Message com-

---

[62] Henry Berkowitz, to Committee of the Central Conference of American Rabbis on Revision of the *Union Haggadah*, ©1922, p. 2. Jacob Rader Marcus Center of the American Jewish Archives, Cincinnati Campus, Hebrew Union College – Jewish Institute of Religion, MS coll. 276, 3/7.
[63] Ibid., 3.
[64] CCAR, *Union* (1907), 82–83.
[65] Ibid., 92–100.
[66] Ibid., 94–95.
[67] Ibid., 93.
[68] Ibid., 104.
[69] Ibid.
[70] Berkowitz, "Report of the Committee on 'The Union Seder Haggadah," 95.
[71] Ibid.

mended the Haggadah as an example of a "helpful publication" that encourages "traditional observances of Jewish home life."[72] During the 2nd year, over 800 copies were sold.[73]

A new edition of *The Union Haggadah* was published in 1908.[74] The Committee on Union Haggadah changed the Hebrew font "in order to make the same [service] serviceable for instruction in the schools" and incorporated "suggestions, emendations and corrections received" by members of the Conference. Two thousand five hundred copies were ordered for sale.[75] The changes were minimal. Bloch Publishers sent out an advertisement explaining:

> It contains the quaint form and traditional sentiment of the ancient Seder Service, in a *modern* [emphasis theirs] setting.
>
> It aims to supply the demand of those to whom the old form of the Haggadah no longer appeals.
>
> The *symbols* [emphasis theirs] of the Passover are beautifully explained....
> Following the devotional part of the Seder is a *"Miscellany"* [emphasis theirs] of interesting and instructive selections concerning the *Passover* in *History, Tradition,* and *Literature*.[76]

This is an obvious appeal to the Reform Jews of the period who were looking for something modern, but were beginning to need explanations concerning the importance of the festival. By this time, the German Jewish community was 1st- or 2nd-generation Americans with many scattered in small communities around the country. Their religious education was minimal. In fact, Jewish children in these scattered communities often got their religious education from *The Sabbath Visitor*, which appeared in the latter part of the 19th Century. It was a publication specifically for children that provided Jewish lessons and activities.[77]

---

[72] "Report of Committee on President's Message," Central Conference of American Rabbis Annual Convention, Frankfort, Michigan, 2–8 July 1907. *Year Book of the Central Conference of American Rabbis*, vol. 15 (Cincinnati: Bloch Pub., 1908), 118.

[73] Joseph Stolz, et al., "Report of Publication Committee," 2 July 1908, Proceedings of the Central Conference of American Rabbis, Frankfort, Michigan, 1–8 July 1908, *Central Conference of American Rabbis Yearbook*, vol. 18 (Cincinnati: S. Rosenthal & Co., 1909), 39.

[74] Central Conference of American Rabbis, *The Union Haggadah* (New York: Bloch Publishing, 1908).

[75] Henry Berkowitz, "Report of the Committee on Union Haggadah." *Year Book of the Central Conference of American Rabbis*, vol. 18 (Cincinnati: Bloch Pub., 1908), 132.

[76] *The Union Haggadah* (New York: Bloch Publishing Co., 1908). Advertisement. Jacob Rader Marcus Center of the American Jewish Archives, Cincinnati Campus, Hebrew Union College – Jewish Institute of Religion, MS coll. 34, 4/8.

[77] Jacob Rader Marcus, *United States Jewry 1776–1985*, vol. 3 (Detroit: Wayne State Univ. Press,) 584.

By 1910, only 685 copies were left for sale.[78] Bloch Publishers sent out a letter to CCAR member rabbis encouraging them to urge their congregants to purchase the *Union Haggadah*.[79] The Conference leaders were correct that there was a need in the United States for a beneficial Reform Haggadah. The 1914–1915 sales report shows that nearly 1,000 Haggadot were sold[80] and so the Publications Committee requested more copies of the *Union Haggadah* be printed.[81] They were given permission to reprint 3,000 copies.[82] In fact, during the 9 years that it had been in print, 11,997 copies were sold.[83] The Publications Committee emphasized to the Conference that the Reform Movement was growing in "importance" because of the number of prayerbook and Haggadah sales and that 1915–1916 proved to be "the greatest [in terms of sales] in the history of the conference."[84] Even the rising of the price of the Haggadah "from 25¢ to 40¢" did not diminish sales, rather they increased.[85] The *Union Haggadah* met a need for its constituency that the public felt was very important. By 1915, The Publications Committee was recommending new editions of both the *Union Prayer Book* and *The Union Haggadah* because there were not enough copies in stock for projected sales,[86] a resounding vote of support for Wise's dream of a *Minhag America*.

---

[78] A. Guttmacher, et al., "Report of the Publication Committee," 5 June 1910, Central Conference of American Rabbis Annual Convention, Charlevoix, Michigan, 28 June–4 July 1910. *Year Book of the Central Conference of American Rabbis*, vol. 20 (n.p.: n.p., 1911), 41.

[79] Sales Agents for the Conference, Bloch Publishing Co., to Sir, 21 March 1910. Jacob Rader Marcus Center of the American Jewish Archives, Cincinnati Campus, Hebrew Union College – Jewish Institute of Religion, MS coll. 34, 5/12.

[80] Julian Morgenstern, Ephraim Frisch, Isaac Landman, and Isaac E. Marcuson, "Report of the Publications Committee," Central Conference of American Rabbis Annual Convention, Charlevoix, Michigan, 29 June–6 July 1915. *Year Book of the Central Conference of American Rabbis*, vol. 25 (New York: Bloch Pub., 1915), 50.

[81] Ibid., 52.

[82] Leo M. Franklin, Ephraim Frisch, I. E. Marcuson, et al., "Report of the Publications Committee," Central Conference of American Rabbis Annual Convention, Wildwood, New Jersey, 13 June–7 July 1916. *Year Book of the Central Conference of American Rabbis*, vol. 26 (New York: Bloch Pub., 1916), 51.

[83] Ibid., 55.

[84] Ibid., 50.

[85] Ibid., 52.

[86] Morgenstern, Frisch, Landman, and Marcuson, "Report of the Publications Committee," 52.

Post World War I American Jewry

The estimated American Jewish population just before the turn of the 20th century was 937,800.[87] Just before the First World War, there were over 2 million,[88] making Jews between 1.6 and 2.2 percent of the American population.[89] By 1920, there were over 3,600,000 Jews.[90] Between 1908 and 1926, 1,029,145 Jews arrived.[91] In New York City, which was home to over half the Jews in the United States, there were only 5 Reform synagogues. In fact, nationally, only 10 percent of American Jewish houses of worship belonged to the Union of American Hebrew Congregations.[92] However, 73 percent of congregations in small-towns in the south did align with the Reform Movement.[93]

The 2nd generation of Eastern European Jews did not stay in the enclaves of 1st settlement. They moved to better neighborhoods and worked towards assimilation.[94] For example, New York City's Jewish population on the Lower East Side dropped from 353,000 in 1916 to 121,000 in 1930 and the "ghetto" in Chicago lost half its population between 1914 and 1920.[95] These new immigrants did not like Reform Judaism because it rejected too much tradition. It was also German Jewish in origin and membership. They also viewed it as a religion of the upper-middle and upper class Jews. Instead, they turned towards the newly created Conservative Movement.

By the 1920s, a number of German based Reform synagogues were having problems maintaining membership. Their communities had low birth-rates and high defection-rates due to assimilation and intermarriage. In small Jewish communities, the influx of Eastern European immigrants expanded the population of the Jewish community, causing them to be reclassified as mid-sized Jewish com-

---

[87] "Jewish Statistics." *American Jewish Yearbook*, vol. 1 (1899–1900), 283–285, accessed 4 November 2013, http://www.jewishdatabank.org/Studies/downloadFile.cfm?FileID=3024.
[88] Joseph Jacobs, "Statistics of Jews: Jewish Population of the United States Memoir of the Bureau of Jewish Statistics of the American Jewish Committee." *Jewish American Yearbook*, vol. 16 (1914–1915), 339, accessed 31 January 2014, http://ajcarchive.org/AJC_DATA/FILES/1914_1915_7_Statistics.pdf.
[89] Sheskin and Dashefsky, *Jewish Population in the United States*, 2010, 3.
[90] Linfield, "Statistics of Jews," 241.
[91] Ibid., 251.
[92] Meyer, *A Response*, 292.
[93] Lee Shai Weissbach, "East European Immigrants and the Image of Jews in the Small-Town South." *American Jewish History* 85, no. 3 (1997): 233.
[94] Lloyd P. Gartner, "American Judaism, 1880–1945,"in *The Cambridge Companion to American Judaism*, ed. Dana Evan Kaplan (New York: Cambridge Univ. Press, 2005), 50.
[95] Nathan Glazer, *American Judaism* (Chicago: Univ. of Chicago Press, 1957), 81.

munities.[96] The Eastern European Jews kept to themselves, creating their own synagogues and social clubs. This segregation in Jewish communities did not last more than 2 generations. With the difficulties in maintaining *kashrut* in the hinterlands and the emigration of children, most small Jewish communities could not support 2 synagogues. The Orthodox congregations folded into the Reform ones. However, even when congregations merged, the rise in membership was short lived. The children of the Orthodox were just as eager to leave the small towns as their Reform counterparts.

Eventually, the German Reform synagogues in larger communities were forced to welcome the children of East European immigrants, as well as, did Hebrew Union College (HUC), because at least 80 percent of American Jews were East European.[97] This resulted in a rise of Reform Jews who yearned for the inclusion of more traditions. In Rosenau's presidential address to the 27th Annual Convention of the CCAR in 1916, he attested to the fact that "Reform, in its present aspect, makes itself felt among the Jewries on the other side of the Atlantic" and "Reform sounds a compelling message."[98] However, in the United States, the CCAR responded to this quite early by revising *The Union Haggadah* starting in 1916. The hope was to "get out an Haggadah that would be acceptable to all—orthodox as well as reform"[99] in keeping with the idea of a *Minhag America*. This did not work at least not for this iteration of the CCAR Haggadah. The Orthodox and Reform expectations of a Haggadah and Seder are different. At this point, the Reform Movement was discarding what they viewed as superstitious rituals and the Orthodox did not see such rituals as inviting Elijah into the house as superstitious. With the growth of Eastern European Jewry in the United States, the Reform rabbinate was afraid they would lose any unity in American Judaism they had achieved. If they could alter their Haggadah to reach the more traditional Eastern European Jews, then the Reform Movement would grow and the Reform Rabbinate could solidify their role in the unification of American

---

96 Weissbach, "East European Immigrants," 234.
97 Glazer, *American Judaism*, 83.
98 William Rosenau, "A Message of the President to the Twenty-Seventh Annual Convention of the Central Conference of American Rabbis" (presented at the Central Conference of American Rabbis Annual Convention. Wildwood, New Jersey, 1 July 1916) *Year Book of the Central Conference of American Rabbis*, vol. 26 (New York: Bloch Pub., 1916), 173.
99 S[amuel] Cohon, Response to "Report of the Committee on Revision of the Haggadah," Proceedings of the Central Conference of American Rabbis, Cincinnati, Ohio, 2–7 April 1919, *CCAR Yearbook*, vol. 29 (Cincinnati: C. J. Krehbiel, 1919), 57.

Jewry. In addition, the CCAR rabbinate was concerned about the lack of interest among American Reform Jews in celebrating the Seder.[100]

Changes in the Reform Movement

Rosenau was also convinced that "Reform, as launched by the fathers of *Die Wissenschaft des Judenthums*, is undoubtedly no longer acceptable."[101] What he does is call for "a clear Declaration of Principles. [Because] the Pittsburgh platform is Reform's last *pronunciamento*."[102] This suggestion of a new set of principles that would respond to "radical changes which have ensued in the world of thought"[103] was in response to the massive influx of Eastern European Jews who were anxious to throw off the traditional *shtetl* (village) Judaism, but did not like German Reform Judaism.[104] The suggestions for a new set of Reform principles tacitly acknowledges that without these immigrants the Reform Movement could fail because Reform synagogues were losing membership due to low birth rates and high intermarriage rates.[105] The impetus for a new set of Reform principles would be the same as for a new Haggadah – a new demographic of American Jews.

The following year, Rosenau reminded his colleagues that they must make "a whole-hearted effort to make Judaism a living faith."[106] He called his colleagues to task for not being "self-assertive" in representing and defining Reform Judaism.[107] The reprimand continued that Reform Judaism "must be thoroughly historical. It must be founded on Jewish principle and make for Jewish aim."[108] The contemporary Jewish lack of knowledge of Hebrew and Jewish literature was

---

100 Leo M. Franklin, et al., "Report of the Committee on Publications," Proceedings of the Central Conference of American Rabbis, Cincinnati, Ohio, 2–7 April 1919, *CCAR Yearbook*, vol. 29 (Cincinnati: C. J. Krehbiel, 1919), 45.
101 Rosenau, "A Message of the President to the Twenty-Seventh," 173.
102 Ibid.
103 Ibid., 172–173.
104 Gartner, "American Judaism," 51.
105 David Rudavsky, *Modern Jewish Religious Movements: A History of Emancipation and Adjustment* (New York: Behrman House, 1967), 310–311.
106 William Rosenau, "A Message of the President to the Twenty-Eighth Annual Convention of the Central Conference of American Rabbis" (presented at the Central Conference of American Rabbis Annual Convention, Buffalo, New York, 28 June 1917) *Year Book of the Central Conference of American Rabbis*, vol. 27 (Cincinnati: CJ Krehbiel & Co., 1917), 198.
107 Ibid., 202.
108 Ibid., 203.

not ignored and rabbis were asked to consider more demanding religious school curricula.[109] The founding of the Bureau of Jewish Education in New York City in 1916 by Alexander Dushkin,[110] Jewish educator, was in response to the ignorance of Jewish children concerning Judaism.[111] Rabbi Isaac E. Marcuson presented a lecture at the same Conference where he discussed the lack of spirituality among the younger generation, which he blamed on the older generation for not inculcating it in the younger generation and not presenting a good example.[112] We hear yet again the same complaint made 25 years earlier by Benjamin and Dushkin. If the concern is repeated, then there was some kind of problem. The new CCAR leadership, Samuel S. Cohon, Israel Bettan, and Solomon Freehof, were from Eastern European backgrounds and brought that group's desire for Jewish ritual with them.[113] Cohon especially wanted a return to a theistic Judaism and "mystery in prayer."[114]

At the 1918 convention, the Committee on Publication suggested that "the Haggada should in some respects be revised" and that "a new edition is imperative before next Pesach."[115] The committee did not see this as an arduous task, but a necessary one, especially as a number of rabbis had asked for such a revision.[116] The Executive Board concurred and suggested a committee be appointed.[117] By 1919, there was harsher criticism of the 1908 Haggadah[118] by the Committee on Revision of the Haggadah, whose members were clear that

---

[109] Ibid., 205.
[110] Alexander M. Dushkin, *Jewish Education in New York City* (New York: Bureau of Jewish Education, 1918), 100.
[111] Alexander M. Dushkin, "Editorial Statement." *The Jewish Teacher: A Quarterly Magazine for Jewish Religious School*, 1, no. 1 (1916): 1.
[112] Isaac E. Marcuson, "Conference Lecture—Judaism and Life" (presented at the Central Conference of American Rabbis Annual Convention, Buffalo, New York, 28 June – 4 July 1917) *Year Book of the Central Conference of American Rabbis*, vol. 27 (Cincinnati: CJ Krehbiel & Co., 1917), 218.
[113] Bronstein, "Platforms and Prayer Books," 32.
[114] Meyer, *A Response*, 320.
[115] Leo M. Franklin, Ephraim Frisch, Samuel Hirshberg, et al., "Report of the Committee on Publications," Central Conference of American Rabbis Annual Convention, Chicago, Illinois, 28 June – 4 July 1918. *Year Book of the Central Conference of American Rabbis*, vol. 28 (Cincinnati: CJ Krehbiel & Co., 1918), 49.
[116] Ibid.
[117] Louis Wolsey, to Samuel S. Cohon, 24 December 1918, 2. Jacob Rader Marcus Center of the American Jewish Archives, Cincinnati Campus, Hebrew Union College – Jewish Institute of Religion, MS coll. 276, 3/6.
[118] Note that the 1907 edition is completely ignored.

> The editors of the Union Haggadah must have been at least partly conscious of the fact that their work needed many improvements to render it acceptable to every modern Jewish home, and to endear it to every Jewish heart. Your Committee on Revision has, therefore, construed its task to consist mainly in supplying the Union Haggadah with those traditional elements that lend color to the service and that are in keeping with the sentiments of Reform.[119]

Their plan to bring back some of the "bursts of good humor" and "serious observations on Jewish life" was to return the Four Questions to the text, add some Hebrew passages, use the translations of the new Bible translation that the CCAR was endorsing, and remove some materials from the appendix.[120] The rabbis present agreed "that the Haggadah in its present form satisfies no one."[121] While the previous generation of Reform rabbis had appealed to that generation's Reform spirit of the Science of Judaism, the next Rabbinical generation was different. With a slowly growing Eastern European contingent who yearned for what they remembered and 1st- and 2nd-generation American German Jews seeking experiences similar to their Christian friends and neighbors, there was a growing desire for traditional Judaism without it being in conflict with assimilation. However, the committee came to no satisfactory conclusion as to whether or not the Haggadah could be revised.[122] At the beginning of 1919, Cohon, now chairman of the Committee for Revision of the Haggadah, requested suggestions for revisions from his fellow committee members.[123]

The admonitions at the annual CCAR conferences became more ardent about reforming Reform Judaism. For example, President Louis Grossman called for "constructive reform" that would "make Reform...more vital than mere opportun-

---

[119] Samuel S. Cohon, Samuel N. Deinard, Maurice Lefkovitz, et al., "Report of Committee on Revision of the Haggadah," Central Conference of American Rabbis Annual Convention, Cincinnati, Ohio, 2–7 April 1919. *Year Book of the Central Conference of American Rabbis*, vol. 29 (Cincinnati: CJ Krehbiel & Co., 1919), 55.
[120] Ibid., 55–56.
[121] Jonah B. Wise, Response to "Report of Committee on Revision of the Haggadah," Central Conference of American Rabbis Annual Convention, Cincinnati, Ohio, 2–7 April 1919. *Year Book of the Central Conference of American Rabbis*, vol. 29 (Cincinnati: CJ Krehbiel & Co., 1919), 58.
[122] [??] Schulman, Response to "Report of Committee on Revision of the Haggadah," Central Conference of American Rabbis Annual Convention, Cincinnati, Ohio, 2–7 April 1919. *Year Book of the Central Conference of American Rabbis*, vol. 29 (Cincinnati: CJ Krehbiel & Co., 1919), 57–58.
[123] Samuel S. Cohon, to Rabbi – –. 2 January 1919. Jacob Rader Marcus Center of the American Jewish Archives, Cincinnati Campus, Hebrew Union College – Jewish Institute of Religion, MS coll. 276, 3/6.

ism and prudence."¹²⁴ He called for a Reform Judaism that "also produce[d] new life." A major platform was "the reorganization of education"¹²⁵ including Sunday School. The flaw he found in the religious education programming is "that religion and its pieties are detached and isolated facts;" they are not part of life.¹²⁶ Grossman articulated the disconnection that the rabbis had begun addressing in the then deliberations concerning the Haggadah. Formal education was important, but it did not substitute for informal domestic religion. One had to have a mix of practice and knowledge in order to make Judaism effective.

The Committee on Revision of the Haggadah returned to the 1921 conference to report that they were focusing on "making the work at once modern in spirit and rich in those traditional elements that lend color to the service."¹²⁷ They added "much that is distinctly Jewish in form and spirit."¹²⁸ Near the end of 1921, Cohon asked for feedback concerning the manuscript from members of the CCAR. Most of the comments were in regard to the liturgy. However, some rabbis did discuss the non-liturgical material.

Rabbi David Rosenbaum at Congregation Beth Israel in Austin, Texas, requested that "some of the selections from Passover in History and Tradition, and Passover in Literature [from the existing manuscript]...be retained."¹²⁹ Rabbi Ephraim Frisch, of the New Synagogue in New York City, suggested "a miscellany or an appendix in two parts, one entitled 'Passover in History and Tradition', retaining the...selections of those we now have....The second section, the Passover in literature, I advise can be retained entirely as we have it in the pres-

---

124 Louis Grossman, "A Message of the President to the Thirtieth Annual Convention of the Central Conference of American Rabbis" (presented at the Central Conference of American Rabbis Annual Convention, Cincinnati, Ohio, 2 April 1919) *Year Book of the Central Conference of American Rabbis*, vol. 26 (Cincinnati: CJ Krehbiel & Co., 1919), 113.
125 Ibid., 116.
126 Ibid., 118.
127 Samuel S. Cohon, Samuel N. Deinard, Solomon B. Freehof, and Samuel Schwartz, "Report of Committee on Revision of the Haggadah," Central Conference of American Rabbis Annual Convention, Washington, D.C., 13–17 April 1921. *Year Book of the Central Conference of American Rabbis*, vol. 31 (Cincinnati: CJ Krehbiel & Co., 192), 38.
128 Ibid.
129 David Rosenbaum, to Samuel Cohon, 15 January 1922. Jacob Rader Marcus Center of the American Jewish Archives, Cincinnati Campus, Hebrew Union College – Jewish Institute of Religion, MS coll. 276, 3/6.

ent book."[130] Rabbi Leon Fram also wanted the "Passover in History and Traditions" "retained."[131]

Rabbi Julian Morgenstern, president of HUC, was "more than pleased with" the manuscript.[132] He believed "that people will read the introduction with almost as much pleasure and profit as they will experience in participating in the Seder itself."[133] He must have felt that Reform congregations needed such material to fulfill their Passover experience. His major concern was "that a paragraph or two dealing with the specific subject of the history of the Seder...would be interesting and stimulating" and "there should also be...full directions for preparing and conducting the Seder" because some people don't know how to.[134] Morgenstern had a prime example of what Marcuson had lectured about in 1916. The classroom education was not providing practical Jewish skills. Additionally, the complaints of Dushkin and Benjamin now nearly a generation earlier had come to fruition – the lack of parental concern about creating a Jewish home would and did result in a generation of domestically ignorant Jews who needed instructional material to create their Jewish homes. Rabbi Louis J. Haas of Ohev Shalom Temple in Harrisburg, Pennsylvania felt that "a suitable Haggadah for Reform Congs. [sic] has been a long-felt want. As a result of your labors the Seder Service is about to be presented in a very...Jewish manner."[135]

On the other hand, Rabbi Isaac Landman, editor of the Jewish weekly *The American Hebrew*, felt that the Haggadah manuscript was another example of "pussyfooting instead of striking out in accordance with our own ideas and ideals."[136] That the *Dayēnû* ends with: "Had he sent us prophets of truth, and not

---

[130] Ephraim Frisch, to Samuel S. Cohon, 4 March 1922. Jacob Rader Marcus Center of the American Jewish Archives, Cincinnati Campus, Hebrew Union College – Jewish Institute of Religion, MS coll. 276, 3/6.
[131] Leon Fram, to Samuel S. Cohon, 12 May 1922. Jacob Rader Marcus Center of the American Jewish Archives, Cincinnati Campus, Hebrew Union College – Jewish Institute of Religion, MS coll. 276, 3/6.
[132] Julian Morgenstern, to Samuel S. Cohon, 19 December 1922. Jacob Rader Marcus Center of the American Jewish Archives, Cincinnati Campus, Hebrew Union College – Jewish Institute of Religion, MS coll. 276, 3/6.
[133] Ibid.
[134] Ibid.
[135] Louis J. Haas, to Samuel Cohon, 1 January 1922. Jacob Rader Marcus Center of the American Jewish Archives, Cincinnati Campus, Hebrew Union College – Jewish Institute of Religion, MS coll. 276, 3/6.
[136] Isaac Landman, to Kohon [sic], 2 February 1922. Jacob Rader Marcus Center of the American Jewish Archives, Cincinnati Campus, Hebrew Union College – Jewish Institute of Religion, MS coll. 276, 3/6.

made us a holy people, Dayenu!"[137] Landman believed did not follow the Reform Movement's theology but rather that of Rabbinic Judaism. The Haggadah's authors had not gone far enough and asked "why not carry the blessings of G-d on Israel through beyond the Prophets down to modern times?"[138] He criticized the Committee for not "creat[ing] a modern Haggadah for a modern people under modern conditions, but crib[bing] the old Haggadah."[139] According to Landman, the Committee had relied on "quotations from the Bible in the old Mishnaic and Talmudic sense" to tell the story of Egyptian oppression.[140] Such phrases as "the Torah tells us"[141] he found offensive, as well as, the style of the story that is not presented "in a way that the parent can tell his children... and understand the story of the Passover."[142] For example, "And Joseph died, and all his brethren, and all that generation. Now there arose a new king over Egypt, who knew not Joseph. And he said unto his people: 'Behold, the people of the children of Israel are too many and too mighty for us."[143]

Berkowitz, who chaired the committee that produced the 1907 Haggadah, was initially not pleased by this new draft. While he concurred that both committees had faced the same problem of balancing "the contents of the ancient Haggadah...[with the] consideration of the actual needs of the American Jewish people," he accused the new committee of being more concerned with the former than the latter, although he did believe they have "carried out the promise made in the same Report to the Conference from which I have quoted above, when you say: – 'we have been guided by the desire to make the work at once modern in spirit and rich in the traditional elements that lend color to the service.'"[144]

Berkowitz protested the removal of parts of his "Forward" that explain the differences between modern Judaism and ancient Judaism:

> The attitude of mind of the modern man has completely changed in reference to such matters as these. He can no longer regard rites and symbols with the awe that vested them with mystic meaning, or super-natural sanction. To him they are, in truth, potent object-lessons of great events and of sublime principles hallowed and intensified in meaning by ages of devout usage. This fact has been honestly reckoned with in this reconstruction of the Hag-

---

137 CCAR, *Union* (1923), 30.
138 Landman, to Kohon.
139 Ibid.
140 Ibid.
141 CCAR, *Union* (1923), 24.
142 Landman, to Kohon.
143 CCAR, *Union* (1923), 24.
144 Berkowitz, to Committee, 1.

gadah. Furthermore, it was necessary candidly to recognize that to the present generation, much of the old Pesach Haggadah is obsolete. This is due to the commingling of religious sentiments with much that is purely didactic; of scholastic discussions, with the pronouncement of lofty precepts; the humorous with the tragic; psalms with folk-songs; universal truths with national concepts, and the like.[145]

Additionally, he disliked the re-insertion of various "devotional exercises, some of the old folk songs and Rabbinical references which are barren of present day significance."[146] Here is the first real statement of the changes taking place within the Reform Movement that would result in a new platform in the 1930s.

Thus, in 1937 a new set of principles, the Columbus Platform, was issued to reflect the needs of the Reform Jewish community and desires of its leadership. The platform affirmed that "Judaism is the historical religious experience of the Jewish people," G-d is central to Judaism, revelation continues, and "prayer is the voice of religion," among other doctrines.[147] The platforms is a response to the changes in Reform theology, which "had a direct impact on the role of liturgy, ritual, ethics, and observances."[148] There was a return to G-d, Torah, and Israel in the Platform. The shapers of this document admitted that Judaism is "a living force depend[ing] upon religious knowledge and upon the education of each new generation in our rich cultural and spiritual heritage."[149] This document, as Jacob B. Agus, a leading scholar of Jewish liturgy, explains, "fits the total body of Jewish tradition."[150]

The platform of 1937 explained Berkowitz's concerns thusly: "Reform Judaism recognizes the principle of progressive development in religion and consciously applies this principle to spiritual as well as to cultural and social life."[151] He acknowledges that the Haggadah addresses that "a degree of previous knowledge is presumed which does not exist."[152] This statement is based on the

---

145 CCAR, *Union* (1908), vi.
146 Ibid., 2.
147 Columbus Platform. CCAR. 1937.
148 Byron Sherwin, "Thinking Judaism through: Jewish theology in America," in *The Cambridge Companion to American Judaism*, ed. Dana Evan Kaplan (New York: Cambridge Univ. Press, 2005), 120.
149 The Guiding Principles of Reform Judaism Columbus, CCAR Annual Meeting, Columbus, Ohio, 1937, sec. C.9, accessed 26 July 2000, http://www.ccarnet.org/platforms/columbys.html.
150 Jacob B. Agus, "The Reform Movement," in *Understanding American Judaism: Toward the Description of a Modern Religion*, vol. 2, ed. Jacob Neusner (New York: KTAV Pub. House, 1975), 22.
151 The Guiding Principles of Reform Judaism.
152 CCAR, *Union* (1908), 2.

feedback he received from Elsi Pfaslzer with whom he shared the draft of the Haggadah, despite the fact that it was not to be released to the public. Pfaslzer explained that "this Haggadah lacks some of the explanations and statements which I felt essential to a seder given children and to adults who have not had a real Jewish training."[153] Her concern was that "knowledge even of the bible [cannot be taken] for granted."[154]

What we see with Berkowitz's and Pfaslzer's comments is not only a Reform rabbi who is beginning to understand that the constituency is changing, but also a congregant acknowledging that there has been a lack of Jewish education, both formal and informal. Pfaslzer wants "a more modern translation of the four questions" because the ones presented "are not natural questions to his [the modern child's] mind,"[155] and "the explanation of 'Pesach' on page 53 is unsatisfactory according to my teachings."[156] Berkowitz's solution was to "insert at appropriate places the proper excerpts from the Book Exodus."[157]

Cohon responded that the paragraph in question:

> The attitude of mind of the modern man has completely changed in reference to such matters as these. He can no longer regard rites and symbols with the awe that vested them with mystic meaning or supernatural sanction. To him they are, in truth, potent object–lessons of great events and of sublime principles hallowed and intensified in meaning by ages of devout usage. This fact has been honestly reckoned with in this reconstruction of the Haggadah. Furthermore, it was necessary candidly to recognize that to the present generation, much of the old Pesach Haggadah is obsolete. This is due to the commingling of religious sentiments with much that is purely didactic; of scholastic discussions, with the pronouncement of lofty precepts; the humorous with the tragic; psalms with folk–songs; universal truths with national concepts, and the like[158]

had a "polemical tone. Its spirit, however, was adequately embodied in the section entitled 'Union Haggadah',"[159] where "the moral and spiritual worth of the

---

153 Elsi Pfaslzer, to Henry Berkowitz, 6 February 1922, 1–2. Jacob Rader Marcus Center of the American Jewish Archives, Cincinnati Campus, Hebrew Union College – Jewish Institute of Religion, MS coll. 25, 1/26.
154 Ibid., 2.
155 Ibid., 5.
156 Ibid., 7.
157 Berkowitz, to Committee, 2.
158 Ibid.; CCAR, *Union* (1908), vi.
159 Samuel S. Cohon to Henry Berkowitz, 9 May 1922, 1. Jacob Rader Marcus Center of the American Jewish Archives, Cincinnati Campus, Hebrew Union College – Jewish Institute of Religion, MS coll. 276, 3/6.

hallowed institution of the Seder"[160] is explained. In this suggested edition the reader is reminded that "the Seder service was never purely devotional. Its intensely spiritual tone mingled with bursts of good humor, its serious observations on Jewish life and destiny with comments in a lighter vein, and its lofty poetry with playful ditties for the entertainment of the children."[161] The Committee on the Revision of the Haggadah was also concerned about reaching the knowledgeable Jew, because not all American Jews were ignorant.[162]

Berkowitz' response was sharp, reminding Cohon that "the very act of revising the Haggadah" is polemical and is concerned that the Conference committing "violence...to the theology of Reform Judaism."[163] Cohon put to various members of the Conference concerning Berkowitz' concerns, most specifically "that we retain in our introduction, the Passover of the old Union Haggadah setting forth the attitude of the modern man towards ceremonies. Do you think that the place for such polemics is in a Haggadah?"[164] Both Rabbis Solomon B. Freehof and William Rosenau responded negatively.[165]

The divide between 2 generations of Reform rabbis is articulated well here. Berkowitz, a member of the earlier generation, was not only an adherent to the Science of Judaism, but also felt a need to strongly oppose any sentiments that touched on superstition and traditional Judaism. Cohon, Freehof, and Rosenau understood the changes in American Jewish demographics and attitudes these change had brought about by traditionally Jewish Eastern European Jewish immigrant parents. If the Reform Rabbinate wished to reach out to the growing number of Eastern European Jews, they had to include more traditional elements in the purposed Haggadah. They had to include these new American Jews, if possible, because the Reform Movement needed new membership to stay alive. A strongly-worded Reform polemic would only turn these potential readers away.

---

160 CCAR, *The Union Haggadah: Home Service for the Passover* (New York: Central Conference of American Rabbis, 1923), viii.
161 Ibid., viii–ix.
162 Ibid.
163 Henry Berkowitz, to Samuel S. Cohon, May 1922. Jacob Rader Marcus Center of the American Jewish Archives, Cincinnati Campus, Hebrew Union College – Jewish Institute of Religion, MS coll. 25, 1/5.
164 Samuel S. Cohon, to Sol. B. Freehof, 9 June 1922, 1–2. Jacob Rader Marcus Center of the American Jewish Archives, Cincinnati Campus, Hebrew Union College – Jewish Institute of Religion, MS coll. 276, 3/6.
165 Ibid., 1; Samuel S. Cohon, to William Rosenau, 14 June 1922, 1. Jacob Rader Marcus Center of the American Jewish Archives, Cincinnati Campus, Hebrew Union College – Jewish Institute of Religion, MS coll. 276, 3/6.

A New Haggadah

The Committee submitted the manuscript for the revised Haggadah at the 1922 conference.[166] The conference accepted the manuscript, disbanded the committee,[167] and published the Haggadah.[168] They added "in accordance with your [the Conference's] sentiments...a miscellany of historical nature to the text."[169] The new generation of rabbis won the argument because the majority of the Conference understood the changing nature of the American Jewish community and that a *Minhag America* would only become accepted if Reform Judaism adjusted to the new American Jewish demographic.

The first section of the 1923 *Union Haggadah* "The Seder – A Forword" is a single page explaining "the ceremony grows out of the several injunctions in the Pentateuch for the Israelite TO RELATE to his children the story of the Exodus from Egypt."[170] Two pages of the section "The Union Haggadah" contain a rewrite of Berkowtiz's favorite paragraph. The Committee inserted:

> In "carrying on the chain of piety which links the generations to each", it is necessary frankly to face and honestly to meet the needs of our own day. The old Haggadah while full of poetic charm, contains passages and sentiments wholly out of harmony with the spirit of the present time. Hence the proper editing of the old material demanded much care and attention on the part of the editors of the first edition of the Union Haggadah. Benefiting by their labors, those entrusted with the task of its revision are able to represent a work at once modern in spirit and rich in those traditional elements that lend color to the service.[171]

Berkowitz praised this edition as "a real achievement in every way."[172] Perhaps the acknowledgment of his thinking in this paragraph pacified him.

---

166 Solomon B. Freehof, Samuel N. Deinard, Samuel Schwartz, and Samuel S. Cohon to the CCAR, ©1922. Jacob Rader Marcus Center of the American Jewish Archives, Cincinnati Campus, Hebrew Union College – Jewish Institute of Religion, MS coll. 276, 3/7.
167 Isaac E. Marcuson to Samuel S. Cohon, 1 January 1922. Jacob Rader Marcus Center of the American Jewish Archives, Cincinnati Campus, Hebrew Union College – Jewish Institute of Religion, MS coll. 276, 3/6.
168 CCAR, *Union* (1923).
169 Samuel S. Cohon, Solomon B. Freehof, Gerson B. Levi, and William Rosenau, "Report of Committee on Revision of Union Haggadah," Central Conference of American Rabbis Annual Convention, Cape May, New Jersey, 27 June – 2 July 1923. *Year Book of the Central Conference of American Rabbis*, vol. 33 (Cincinnati: CJ Krehbiel & Co., 1923), 41.
170 CCAR, *Union* (1923), vii.
171 Ibid., viii.
172 Henry Berkowitz to Samuel Cohon, 9 April 1923, p. 1; reprint in Samuel S. Cohon, Solomon B. Freehof, Gerson B. Levi, and William Rosenau, "Report of Committee on Revision of Union

The 3 pages of "Rites and Symbols of the Seder" include explanations of the various ceremonial objects and foods.[173] For example:

> ḤAROSES. This mixture of apples, blanched almonds, and raisins, finely chopped and flavored with cinnamon and wine, was probably originally a condiment. Owing to its appearance, it came to be regarded as representing the clay with which the Israelites made bricks, or the mortar used in the great structures erected by the bondmen of Egypt.[174]

Finally, before "Order of the Service" is a page and a half of "Directions for Setting the Table."[175] Following the service, there are 11 pages of "History of the Passover" that begins with "The Festival of the Shepherds" discussing ḥag haPesaḥ and the development of *Pesaḥ*.[176] Then this section moves to "The Farmer's Spring Festival,"[177] "The Feast of Israel's Birth,"[178] "The National Celebration" explaining how Passover changed with the destruction of the Second Temple and the loss of the sacrifice,[179] and "The Feast of Freedom" covering the Roman period.[180] The title of the section "The National Celebration"[181] presents an interesting comment on the changing understanding of Reform Judaism and nationalism. While the early Reformers denied Jewish nationalism in an effort to affirm their connection to the country in which they lived,[182] the Reform leaders of the early 1900s realized "the negative dogma of anti-nationalism"[183] was focusing on Zionism rather than on how Jews as a nation could create a "positive Jewish organization for self–help as a people" to combat anti-Semitism.[184]

Haggadah," Central Conference of American Rabbis Annual Convention. Cape May, New Jersey, 27 June – 2 July 1923. *Year Book of the Central Conference of American Rabbis*, vol. 33 (Cincinnati: CJ Krehbiel& Co., 1923), 43. A more complete explanation of the conflict between Berkowitz and Cohon concerning this Haggadah can be found in Mara W. Cohen Ioannides, "H. Berkowitz and S.S. Cohon: Two Men Battle Over One Haggadah." *American Jewish Archives Journal* 58 (2008): 103–119.

173 CCAR, *Union* (1923), xi-xii.
174 Ibid., xiii.
175 Ibid., xiv–xv.
176 Ibid., 125–126.
177 Ibid., 127–129.
178 Ibid., 129–130.
179 Ibid., 130–133.
180 Ibid., 133–136.
181 Ibid., 130–133.
182 Leon Fram, "Reform Judaism and Zionism," in *Reform Judaism: Essays by Hebrew Union College Alumni*, ed. by Abraham J. Feldman, et al. (Cincinnati: HUC Press, 1949), 182–183.
183 Ibid., 193.
184 Ibid., 192.

The next section, entitled "Moses," has 2 passages by thinkers Heinrich Heine and Henry George about the central figure of the Exodus story.[185] Following this is "Preparations for the Passover" divided into "Time of the Feast" about when the festival falls and why,[186] "Matzo–Baking" about the intricacies of baking the unleavened bread,[187] "Removing the Leaven" concerns the "quaint ceremony of 'b'dikas ḥometz – searching for leavening', still observed by orthodox Jews."[188] This is clearly a comment that Reform Jews did not participate in such antiquated ceremonies. This section ends with one paragraph and a sentence on "'Kashering' the Utensils." Again, this "is also customary among orthodox Jews," but "Reform Judaism does not consider these practices essential to the proper observance of the Passover."[189] With the growing number of Eastern European Jews who felt the need to stay connected to Jewish traditions and the acceptance by the Reform Movement that these Jews needed to be recruited to keep the Movement alive and relevant, an acknowledgement of the traditions and the Reform response to was seemed important.

In accordance with the growing understanding that Eastern European traditional Judaism is not the only Judaism, the next chapters in the Haggadah address Passover in various Jewish cultures. "Survivals of the Ancient Passover" covers two different cultures: "The Samaritan Passover" and "The Passover as Observed by the Falashas."[190] The rabbis were attempting to draw a parallel between these two non-mainstream Jewish communities and Reform Judaism, as Samaritan and Falasha religious outlooks were becoming accepted as part of the Jewish continuum, so too the Reform Movement. This was another attempt to include the Eastern European Jew in the Reform community. If the Eastern European could conceive the Samaritan and Falasha as a alternatives, especially as they exist in different parts of the world, than by moving to the New World, a new way of being Jewish should be acceptable. "Passover and Christendom" explains the relationship between Passover and Easter and how the Blood Accusations developed.[191] This section, especially that part titled "Passover and Easter,"[192] was a polemic against those Jews who had started calling Passover Easter. After all, the first paragraph ends with: "it is incorrect to speak of

---

[185] CCAR, *Union* (1923), 137–138.
[186] Ibid., 139.
[187] Ibid., 140–141.
[188] Ibid., 141.
[189] Ibid., 142.
[190] Ibid., 143–146.
[191] Ibid., 147–150.
[192] Ibid., 147–148.

Pesaḥ as the Jewish Easter for while Pesaḥ celebrates the deliverance of Israel from slavery, Easter commemorates the death and the legendary resurrection of the Christ."[193] The chapter on "Reform Judaism and Passover" contains passages by various Reform leaders including Claude Montefiore, David Einhorn, Samuel Hirsch, Isaac Mayer Wise, Kaufman Kohler, and Morris Joseph.[194]

The final chapter, "The Haggadah," begins with examples of parts of the Haggadah from the Hebrew Bible, moves to Medieval additions, and addresses the differences between Ashkenazic and Sephardic Haggadot.[195] Again, the emphasis on that there are multiple ways of being Jewish. Both communities accepted the other's Jewish practices as different, but acceptable. Thus, the underlying suggestion that American Reform Judaism is acceptable. There is a section on "Reform Judaism and the Haggadah" that reviews the history of Reform Haggadot from Leopold Stein's to the current edition. Of the previous *Union Haggadah* edition, it says:

> the work was executed in modern spirit, no longer regarding 'rites and symbols with the awe that vested them with mystic meaning, or supernatural sanction', but treating them rather as 'potent object-lessons of great events and of sublime principles hallowed and intensified in meaning by ages of devout usage.[196]

Then it moves to "the aim of the present edition of the Union Haggadah [which] is stated in the introduction"[197] and quoted previously. The final section is on "Illuminated Haggadahs."[198]

Cohon and his committee were clearly as devoted to reaching their audience as Berkowitz and his committee had been reaching theirs. They succeeded based on the declaration of the Committee on Publications at the 1924 conference: "the new Haggadah has met with instant success and the whole edition of 4,500 copies was sold."[199] Rabbi Harvey E. Wessel, of Har Sinai Congregation in Baltimore,

---

193 Ibid., 147.
194 Ibid., 151–154.
195 Ibid., 155–157.
196 Ibid., 158.
197 Ibid., 158.
198 Ibid., 159–162.
199 Isaac E. Marcuson, Clifton Harby Levy, Morris Newfield, and Julian Morgenstern, "Report of Committee on Publications," Central Conference of American Rabbis Annual Convention. Cedar Point, Ohio, 16–30 June 1924. *Year Book of the Central Conference of American Rabbis*, vol. 34 (Richmond, Virginia: Old Dominion Press, 1925), 78.

Maryland, congratulated Cohon immediately upon the receipt of his copy.[200] Rabbi Louis Wolsey believed this edition to be "very much superior to the old one,"[201] as did Rabbi Horace J. Wolf of Rochester, New York.[202] Rabbi Louis L. Mann, of New Haven, Connecticut, found that "it has stressed the imperishable elements in our tradition" and "there will be little need for a revision of such an Haggadah for generations to come."[203] Freehof found it to be "Jewish without sacrificing a single Reform principle." For him, this Haggadah was "the first fruits of the newer tendency [sic] in our American Reform Judaism towards *Jewishness* [emphasis his] & away from *mere* [emphasis his] ethical monotheism."[204] David Lefkowitz, of Temple Emanu-El in Dallas, Texas, agreed and commented that it "held the interest of the entire group [his congregation] throughout the entire service" and complimented Cohon of "perform[ing] a real service to Judaism."[205] Frisch found "the directions and the explanatory material before and after the Haggadah proper...very valuable."[206] Temple newsletter advertisements touted it as having "an interesting account of the origin of many of the Passover customs."[207] A new edition was published and the supply was "completely ex-

---

[200] Harvey E. Wessel, to Samuel S. Cohon, 24 March 1923. Jacob Rader Marcus Center of the American Jewish Archives, Cincinnati Campus, Hebrew Union College – Jewish Institute of Religion, MS coll. 276, 3/7.

[201] Louis Wolsey, to Edward N. Calisch, 27 March 1923. Jacob Rader Marcus Center of the American Jewish Archives, Cincinnati Campus, Hebrew Union College – Jewish Institute of Religion, MS coll. 34, 13/7.

[202] Horace J. Wolf, to Samuel S. Cohon, 29 March 1923. Jacob Rader Marcus Center of the American Jewish Archives, Cincinnati Campus, Hebrew Union College – Jewish Institute of Religion, MS coll. 276, 3/7.

[203] Louis L. Mann, to Samuel S. Cohon, 28 March 1923. Jacob Rader Marcus Center of the American Jewish Archives, Cincinnati Campus, Hebrew Union College – Jewish Institute of Religion, MS coll. 276, 3/7.

[204] Solomon B. Freehof, to Samuel S. Cohon, 2 April 1923. Jacob Rader Marcus Center of the American Jewish Archives, Cincinnati Campus, Hebrew Union College – Jewish Institute of Religion, MS coll. 276, 3/7.

[205] David Lefkowtiz, to Samuel S. Cohon, 3 April 1923. Jacob Rader Marcus Center of the American Jewish Archives, Cincinnati Campus, Hebrew Union College – Jewish Institute of Religion, MS coll. 276, 3/7.

[206] Ephraim Frisch, to Samuel S. Cohon, 4 April 1923. Jacob Rader Marcus Center of the American Jewish Archives, Cincinnati Campus, Hebrew Union College – Jewish Institute of Religion, MS coll. 276, 3/7.

[207] "Haggadahs." *Euclid Ave. Temple Bulletin* 4 April 1930, 3, accessed 28 July 2014, http://americanjewisharchives.org/collections/ms0882/00257/ms0882.00257.1930-04-04.pdf. Jacob Rader Marcus Center of the American Jewish Archives, Cincinnati Campus, Hebrew Union College – Jewish Institute of Religion, MS coll. 882.

hausted" the following year.[208] This supported Rabbi Edward N. Calisch's, president of the CCAR, assertion it "has been received with universal acclaim."[209] The non-liturgical materials continued to receive positive comments for another 20 years. Salman Schocken, of Greenwich, Connecticut, said in 1944 that "I was especially interested in the last part of your Haggadah [referring to "The Passover in History, Literature and Art"], surely a stimulus to many readers and of great service to them."[210] Thus, the need for more historical material for the community that grew from an understanding of the Science of Judaism and still touted many of its beliefs well past the Second World War.

The Great Depression and American Jewry

The Third Great Wave ebbed with the start of the First World War and, while it began again after the war until the limitations on immigration in 1922 and the Johnson Act of 1924, this post-war wave of immigration never had the same numbers as before the Great War.[211] The rise of anti-German sentiment during World War I in the United States affected both the Christian and Jewish German communities. German ceased to be spoken publicly by anyone as well as, in Christian houses of worship.[212] The Reform Movement had discarded German almost a generation earlier in a push towards Americanization. Because of anti–Germanism and the demise of many original German speakers, their descendants were English-speaking American congregants.[213] With the rise of non-German members, Reform Judaism once again began to change. The Reform leadership realized it had to address these issues of anti–Germanism and a growing non-German Jewish American population.

---

[208] Isaac E. Marcuson, Julian Morgenstern, Morris Newfield, and Nathan Stern, "Report of Committee on Publications," Central Conference of American Rabbis Annual Convention, Cincinnati, 20–23 October 1925. *Year Book of the Central Conference of American Rabbis*, vol. 35 (Richmond, Virginia: Old Dominion Press, 1925), 35.
[209] Edward N. Calisch, to Samuel S. Cohon, 6 May 1923. Jacob Rader Marcus Center of the American Jewish Archives, Cincinnati Campus, Hebrew Union College – Jewish Institute of Religion, MS coll. 276, 3/7.
[210] Salman Schocken, to Samuel A. [sic] Cohon, 18 April 1944. Jacob Rader Marcus Center of the American Jewish Archives, Cincinnati Campus, Hebrew Union College – Jewish Institute of Religion, MS coll. 276, 3/7.
[211] Gartner, "American Judaism," 45.
[212] Niel M. Johnson, "The Missouri Synod Lutherans and the War Against the German Language, 1917–1923." *Nebraska History* 56 (1975): 143.
[213] Ibid.

The Great Depression hindered the Movement's desire to expand. Membership rates dropped because congregants could not afford dues. For example, Emanu-El in New York City lost 44 percent of its membership during the Depression.[214] In 1930, the Union of American Hebrew Congregations (UAHC) had 61,000 members, but in 1932 that number dropped to 53,000. The UAHC provided sample letters to synagogues that encouraged members to stay even if they couldn't pay dues.[215] Reform leaders also understood that the lack of uniform practice were detrimental. Reform Judaism had to create a set of principles to appeal to the new generation. The Pittsburgh Platform reflected the views of the original German immigrant rabbis and their congregations, not the new Eastern European immigrants and their rabbis.[216]

A series of surveys between 1928 and 1930 showed that ritual was making a slow, but steady return in Reform families. Almost a quarter of Reform Jews lit Sabbath candles, $1/3^{rd}$ celebrated Seder, over $1/3^{rd}$ lit candles for Hannukah, and over 1/2 fasted on Yom Kippur.[217] Between 1928 and 1933, sales of the *Union Haggadah* stayed above 1,700 per year with 1928 being the highest at nearly 4,000.[218] Only during 1933, the heart of the Great Depression, did the sales

---

[214] Dana Evan Kaplan, "Reform Jewish Theology and the Sociology of Liberal Religion in America: The Platforms as response to the perception of socioreligious crisis." *Modern Judaism* 20 (2000): 66.

[215] Michael A. Meyer, "Thank You, Moritz Loth: A 125-Year UAHC Retrospective." *Reform Judaism* (fall 1998): 33.

[216] Ibid., 67.

[217] Unfortunately, there seems to be no earlier statistics on American Jewish practice with which to compare this.

[218] Isaac E. Marcuson, Max C. Currick, Clifton H. Levy, and Nathan Stern, "Report of Committee on Publications," Central Conference of American Rabbis Annual Convention, Chicago, Illinois, 27 June – 1 July 1928. *Year Book of the Central Conference of American Rabbis*, vol. 38 (n.p.: n.p., 1928), 47; Isaac E. Marcuson, Max C. Currick, Barnett A. Elzas, et al., "Report of Committee on Publications," Central Conference of American Rabbis Annual Convention, Detroit, Michigan, 27 June – 30 June 1929. *Year Book of the Central Conference of American Rabbis*, vol. 39 (n.p.: n.p., 1929), 55; Isaac E. Marcuson, Sol. L. Kory, Clifton Harby Levy, Harry A. Merfeld, et al., "Report of Committee on Publications," Central Conference of American Rabbis Annual Convention, Providence, Rhode Island, 25 June – 29 June 1930. *Year Book of the Central Conference of American Rabbis*, vol. 40 (n.p.: n.p., 1930), 42; Isaac E. Marcuson, Sol. L. Kory, Clifton Harby Levy, Norris Newfield, and Nathan Stern, "Report of Committee on Publications," Central Conference of American Rabbis Annual Convention, Wawasee, Indiana, 17 June – 21 June 1931. *Year Book of the Central Conference of American Rabbis*, vol. 41 (n.p.: n.p., 1931), 39; Isaac E. Marcuson, L. Elliot Grafman, Clifton Harby Levy, Harry A. Merfeld, and Nathan Stern, "Report of Committee on Publications," Central Conference of American Rabbis Annual Convention, Cincinnati, Ohio, 2 – 6 November 1932. *Year Book of the Central Conference of American Rabbis*, vol. 42 (n.p.: n.p., 1932), 44.

drop below 1,000.[219] The following year the sales picked up to over 1,700[220] and steadily grew until 1941 peaking at just over 3,500.[221]

It took nearly a decade until this desire for ritual was addressed by the Reform Movement. During the 1930s, the American Jewish population began to age as the birthrate declined and American–born Jews, as opposed to foreign–born Jews, began to dominate the American Jewish population. In 1937 there were 290 Reform congregations in the United States.[222]

The sales of the new *The Union Haggadah* continued to rise. The Haggadah exemplified the Platform's "call for faithful participation in the life of the Jewish

---

[219] Isaac E. Marcuson, L. Elliot Grafman, and Solomon Landman, "Report of Committee on Publications," Central Conference of American Rabbis Annual Convention, Milwaukee, Wisconsin, 22–24 June 1933. *Year Book of the Central Conference of American Rabbis*, vol. 43 (n.p.: n.p., 1933), 37.

[220] Isaac E. Marcuson, L. Elliot Grafman, Solomon Landman, Clifton Harby Levy, and Harry A. Merfeld, "Report of Committee on Publications," Central Conference of American Rabbis Annual Convention, Wernersville, Pennsylvania, 14–18 June 1934. *Year Book of the Central Conference of American Rabbis*, vol. 44 (n.p.: n.p., 1934), 37.

[221] Isaac E. Marcuson, L. Elliot Grafman, Solomon Landman, Clifton Harby Levy, and Harry A. Merfeld, "Report of Committee on Publications," Central Conference of American Rabbis Annual Convention, Chicago, Illinios, 25–30 June 1935. *Year Book of the Central Conference of American Rabbis*, vol. 45 (n.p.: n.p., 1935), 37; Isaac E. Marcuson, Benjamin Kelson, Solomon Landman, Clifton Harby Levy, and Harry A. Merfeld, "Report of Committee on Publications," Central Conference of American Rabbis Annual Convention, Cape May, New Jersey, 23–27 June 1936. *Year Book of the Central Conference of American Rabbis*, vol. 46 (n.p.: n.p., 1936), 54; Isaac E. Marcuson, Benjamin Kelson, Solomon Landman, Clifton Harby Levy, and Harry A. Merfeld, "Report of Committee on Publications," Central Conference of American Rabbis Annual Convention, Columbus, Ohio, 25–30 May 1937. *Year Book of the Central Conference of American Rabbis*, vol. 47 (Philadelphia.: JPS, 1937), 41; Isaac E. Marcuson, Benjamin Kelson, Solomon Landman, Clifton Harby Levy, and Harry A. Merfeld, "Report of Committee on Publications," Central Conference of American Rabbis Annual Convention, Atlantic City, New Jersey, 21–26 June 1938. *Year Book of the Central Conference of American Rabbis*, vol. 48 (Philadelphia: JPS, 1938), 37; Isaac E. Marcuson, Benjamin Kelson, Solomon Landman, Clifton Harby Levy, and Harry A. Merfeld, "Report of Committee on Publications," Central Conference of American Rabbis Annual Convention, Washington, D.C., 13 – 18 June 1939. *Year Book of the Central Conference of American Rabbis*, vol. 49 (Philadelphia: JPS, 1938), 50; Isaac E. Marcuson, Solomon N. Bazell, et al., "Report of Committee on Publications," Central Conference of American Rabbis Annual Convention, Charlevoix, Michigan, 18–23 June 1940. *Year Book of the Central Conference of American Rabbis*, vol. 50 (Philadelphia: JPS, 1938), 52.

[222] Jack Wertheimer, "The American synagogue: recent issues and trends." *American Jewish Yearbook* (2005), 7, accessed 31 January 2014, http://%3A%2F%2Fresearch.policyarchive.org%2F10414.pdf&ei=MCzsUr2EHsupsATTx4CoBg&usg=AFQjCNGnpmyyci2vvx1f9R9ACorSQ17Hjw&sig2=RbcqaxyzPoJH7iWCYv1PMg&bvm=bv.60444564,d.cWc.

community as it finds expression in home, synagogue and school."²²³ The prayers "direct[ed] man's heart and mind Godward,...which invest life with supreme value."²²⁴ The *Union Haggadah* was published before the Platform, yet it mirrored the Platform's orientation. For decades it "preserved...[the] festival, [and aided] the retention and development of such customs, symbols and ceremonies as possess inspirational value"²²⁵ as promised by the committee led by Cohon and enunciated in the Columbus Platform. The change in the demographics of the Reform Movement from a German Jewish to an Eastern European and American Jewish community increased the popularity and appropriateness of the revised *The Union Haggadah* because it was a true American product.

With the new platform came a new liturgy. While the updated *Union Prayer Book* published in 1918 included a bit more Hebrew and a new translation of Biblical passages, a major revision was not released until 1940, most likely because of the Depression that resulted in a lack of funds. Cohon called the 1918 edition "inadequate" because "Jewish people...cannot get accustomed to the Protestant manner of worship in which the minister prays for the congregations."²²⁶ Cohon saw the 1940 *Union Prayer Book* as a "continu[ation of] the traditions of our classical liturgy" that "manifests more clearly the fundamental departures of Reform from Orthodoxy" than any other item.²²⁷ However, he also believed it "unconsciously reflects the present apathy and skepticism toward prayer."²²⁸ He derided the move of prayer from communion with G-d to a lesson on moral improvement.²²⁹ Rabbi Louis Mann of Temple Sinai of Chicago called Reform Judaism a "religious mail-order business" and demanded that the Movement recruit non-German Jews.²³⁰ His call for a new prayerbook was not left unanswered, but due to his pressure and other motivations, the rabbis resolved to only respond to complaints, such as monotony in the liturgy.

---

223 The Guiding.
224 Ibid.
225 Ibid.
226 Samuel S. Cohon, "The Theology of the Union Prayer Book," in *Reform Judaism: A Historical Perspective: Essays from the Yearbook of the Central Conference of American Rabbis*, ed. Joseph L. Blau (New York: KTAV Pub., 1973), 283.
227 Ibid., 259.
228 Ibid., 261.
229 Ibid., 263.
230 Daniel Freelander, "Birth of a Synagogue Movement." *Reform Judaism* (summer 2011): 59–60.

Rabbi Solomon Freehof took charge as the new chair of the Liturgy Committee. He helped create 2 experimental pamphlets that were positively received.[231] Freehof saw the abandonment of Judaism as tied to "the neglect of worship." To him, the task of the Liturgy Committee and his fellow rabbis was "to restore the personal relationship to G-d through prayer."[232] He saw the achievement of making the "Jewish service interesting and often...inspiring...not inconsiderable," but certainly "not enough." The return to prayer at home was to him the next step.[233] As Judith Z. Abrams, founder of *Maqom: A School for Adult Talmud Study*, notes, "If a system of prayer is living, then it will grow and change to meet the needs of the times and the people who look to it for solace, hope, and inspiration."[234]

In the 1940 *Union Prayer Book* edition, a Zionist service was added to appeal to the resurgence of Zionism. Michael A. Meyer, professor of Jewish History at Hebrew Union College, is clear "the new volumes represent clear evidence of return to tradition...with passages from Ashkenazi and Sephardi traditions."[235] They also maintained the liturgical format resolved at the Frankfurt Conference in that communal prayer is in Hebrew and individual prayers in English.[236] What rabbis were discovering during the interwar period was that "it was American, not Jewish civilization...in which they lived."[237] This realization had to be addressed both by the theology and the liturgy. The new prayerbook also reflected the new post-World War I understanding that assimilation was not equivalent to acceptance.[238] The rise of fascism in the 1930s, along with economic chaos, brought rising anti-Semitism.

---

231 Bernard J. Bamberger, "Solomon B. Freehof in the Central Conference of American Rabbis," in *Essays in Honor of Solomon B. Freehof*, ed. Walter Jacob, Frederick C. Schwartz, and Vigdor W. Kavalier (Pittsburgh: Rodef Shalom Congregation, 1964), 98–99.
232 Solomon B. Freehof, "Reform Judaism and Payer," in *Reform Judaism: Essays by Hebrew Union College Alumni*, ed. Abraham J. Feldman, et al. (Cincinnati: HUC Press, 1949), 103.
233 Ibid., 105.
234 Judith Z. Abrams, "The Continuity of Change in Jewish Liturgy," in *Platforms and Prayer Books: Theological and Liturgical Perspectives on Reform Judaism*, ed. Dana Evan Kaplan (Lanham, Maryland: Rowman & Littlefield, 2002), 119–120.
235 Michael A. Meyer, *A Response to Modernity: A History of the Reform Movement in Judaism* (New York: Oxford Univ. Press, 1988), 320–322.
236 Leonard S. Kravitz, "A Response" (paper presented at the UAHC 48th Biennial), *The Theological Foundations of Prayer: A Reform Jewish Perspective*, ed. Jack Bemporad (New York: UAHC, 1967), 88–89.
237 Dreyfus, "The *Gates* Liturgies," 145.
238 Mel Scult, "Americanism and Judaism in the Through of Mordecai M. Kaplan," in *The Americanization of the Jews*, ed. Robert M. Seltzer and Norman J. Cohen (New York: New York Univ. Press, 1995), 341.

The return to Jewish rituals supported Jews' desires to again be distinctive.[239] The studies on ritual observance also encouraged the CCAR and UAHC to create the Committee on Ceremonies in 1938. Its task was to revitalize traditional rituals and create new ones. A UAHC staff member, Jacob D. Schwarz, wrote *Ceremonies in Modern Jewish Life* that explained traditional and modern observances.[240] In many respects, this was a response to the rising nativistic fundamentalism of the 1920s, when conservative Protestants were attempting to maintain the revivalist Protestant establishment. These conservatives were fighting the growing secularism that was affecting all Americans, not just the Jews.[241]

During the Second World War, the paper shortage did hamper publications of the new *The Union Haggadah* a bit,[242] but the sales remained "about normal."[243] They picked up again in 1945 with sales reaching nearly 7,900.[244] These numbers clearly show how popular the new *Union Haggadah* remained for over 20 years. Even when publishers had no paper to print books on in 1947[245] because of shortages during World War II, over 8,500 copies of *The Union Haggadah* were sold.[246] Again, the numbers continued to rise, with almost 12,000 sold in 1948.[247]

---

[239] Ibid.

[240] Meyer, *A Response*, 323.

[241] George M. Marsden, *Religion and American Culture* (Fort Worth: Harcourt Brace College Pub., 1990), 182–183.

[242] Isaac E. Marcuson, Solomon N. Bazell, et al., "Report of Committee on Publications," Central Conference of American Rabbis Annual Convention, Cincinatti, Ohio, 24 February – 1 March 1942. *Year Book of the Central Conference of American Rabbis*, vol. 52 (Philadelphia: JPS, 1942), 52.

[243] Isaac E. Marcuson, "Report of Committee on Publications," Central Conference of American Rabbis Annual Convention, New York, New York, 22–27 June 1943. *Year Book of the Central Conference of American Rabbis*, vol. 53 (Philadelphia: JPS, 1943), 47.

[244] Isaac E. Marcuson, Ernst Appel, et al., "Report of Committee on Publications," Central Conference of American Rabbis Annual Convention, Atlantic City, New Jersey, 25–27 June 1945. *Year Book of the Central Conference of American Rabbis*, vol. 55 (Philadelphia: JPS, 1946), 49.

[245] Simon Cohen, et al., "Report of Committee on Publications," Central Conference of American Rabbis Annual Convention, Montreal, Canada, 24–28 June 1947. *Year Book of the Central Conference of American Rabbis*, vol. 57 (Philadelphia: JPS, 1948), 43–44.

[246] Ibid., 45.

[247] Isaac E. Marcuson, Aryeh Lev, et al., "Report of Committee on Publications," Central Conference of American Rabbis Annual Convention, Montreal, Canada, 22–26 June 1948. *Year Book of the Central Conference of American Rabbis*, vol. 57 (Philadelphia: JPS, 1948), 60.

Conclusion

The further American Jews became from their immigrant past, the more explanation of how to be Jewish was needed, especially in the Haggadah. It is during this time, then, that we see more than just a list of what is needed to be on the Seder table. Additionally, as the Reform Movement defined its theology and how it was different, and more modern, than its Orthodox counterpart, we find the addition of introductory matter that explains Reform theology. With the closing of the Second World War, a change in the American Jewish population's understanding of who they were in relation to the rest of the world, both Jewish and Gentile, happened.

Chapter 6:
Evolution of the Reform Movement and Its Liturgies Including the Non-Liturgical Elements in CCAR Haggadot – The Modern Period

> "The content of the Haggadah, as revealed especially by alterations in American Haggadot in nearly every one of its aspects, including wording, layout, language, and sponsorship, indicates that it is a significant site of cultural negotiations and Jewish acts of self-definition."
>
> Joel Gereboff[1]

The Holocaust and birth of the State of Israel changed how American Jews thought of themselves. Gone were the cultural divisions between the Ashkenazim and the Sephardim that kept them from interacting. However, a greater appreciation for the problem of Jewish continuity also developed. The Reform Movement began to reflect this in changes in its liturgies. The Haggadah is no exception.

Impact of the Holocaust on Reform Judaism

American Jewry took the rise of Nazism seriously, although it could not at first conceive of the radical impact this political movement would have on European Jewry. The destruction of European Jewry resulted in American Jewry becoming the largest Jewish community in the world, thus, the "Holocaust-era of American Jewish life represented both a defensive response to adversity and a form of cultural resistance, a resolve to maintain Judaism in the face of opposition and danger."[2]

The divide between German and Eastern European Jews in America almost disappeared. German and Eastern European Jews socialized and intermarried, resulting in a postwar Jewish baby boom that helped to raise the Jewish population to 5 million in 1955.[3] In addition, now that these American Jews, Orthodox and Reform, German and Russian, had served together in the military against a

---

[1] Joel Gereboff, "One Nation, with Liberty and Haggadahs for All," in *Key Texts in American Jewish Culture*, ed. Jack Kugelmass (New Brunswick: Rutgers Univ. Press, 2003), 275.
[2] Jonathan D. Sarna, Marshall Sklare Memorial Lecture (paper presented at the Association for Jewish Studies annual conference, 2002). Transcript, 16.
[3] Alvin Chenkin, "Socio-Economic Data: Jewish Population of the United States, 1955." *Jewish American Year Book*, vol. 57 (1956), 119, accessed 4 June 2014, http://www.ajcarchives.org/AJC_DATA/Files/1956_4_USSocioEcnomic.pdf.

common enemy, they realized the distinctions were not boundaries.[4] No longer were the Eastern European Jews of the immigrant generation; they were 2nd-generation Americans and had become overwhelmingly middle class.[5] By the outbreak of the Second World War, there were estimated to be 4,831,180 Jews, 3–4 percent of the total population, in the United States.[6] There were 4,500,000 Jews in the United States in 1947,[7] about 2/3rds of who were American born.[8] This was the height of the American Jewish population as a percentage of the larger American population; Jews constituted over 3.6 percent of the American population.[9]

Reform Jews became even more involved with ritual than before the war. During World War II, army chaplains noted that Reform Jewish soldiers were more apt to attend services than their Orthodox counterparts, despite the fact Orthodox services were available. This apparently points to the need among Reform Jewish soldiers to identify as Jews, find solace in prayer and ritual, and gain support from other like-minded soldiers. A 1947 poll showed that 18 percent of Jews attended services at least monthly and by the mid–1950s that had risen to 33 percent.[10] In fact, the United American Hebrew Congregations (UAHC) member congregations grew to 536 and the member unit numbers rose to 161,000.[11] Some of these new Reform Jews came from the Conservative Movement and some from the Orthodox.[12] There are a number of reasons for this shift. Some Conservative Jews as they Americanized found the Reform Movement more appealing. Some Jews chose their synagogue in their new suburban neighborhoods because it

---

[4] Daniel Freelander, "Birth of a Synagogue Movement." *Reform Judaism* (summer 2011): 60.
[5] Arthur Hertzberg, *The Jews in America: Four Centuries of an Uneasy Encounter: A History* (New York: Simon and Schuster, 1989), 316.
[6] "Statistics of Jews." *American Jewish Yearbook*, vol. 41 (1939–1940), 588, accessed 31 January 2014, http://www.ajcarchives.org/main.php?GroupingId=10074.
[7] Ben B. Seligman and Harvey Swados, "Jewish Population in the United States." *American Jewish Year Book* (1949), 652, accessed 3 June 2014, http://www.jewishdatabank.org/Studies/american_jewish_year_book_articles.cfm.
[8] Ben Seligman, "Socio-Economic Data: Recent Demographic changes in some Jewish Communities." *American Jewish Year Book*, vol. 54 (Philadelphia: JPS of America, 1953), 21, accessed 4 June 2014, http://www.jewishdatabank.org/Studies/downloadFil.cfm?FileID=2965.
[9] Ira Sheskin and Arnold Dashefsky, *Jewish Population in the United States, 2010*, ed. Arnold Dashefsky, Sergio DellaPergola, and Ira Sheskin (Storrs, Connecticut: North American Jewish Databank, 2011), 3.
[10] Chenkin, "Socio-Economic Data," 113.
[11] Hertzberg, *The Jews*, 316.
[12] Jacob Sloan, "Communal Affairs: Religion." *American Jewish Year Book*, vol. 57 (1956), 189, accessed 5 June 2014, http://www.ajcarchives.org/AJC_DATA/Files/1956_6_USCommunal.pdf.

was the nearest or the only one, and the largest number of synagogues in suburbia were aligned with the Reform Movement.

Despite the high percentage of Jews in suburban neighborhoods—sometimes as high as 50 percent—it didn't equal the nearly 90 percent Jewish population of the neighborhoods of the 1st settlement they had left.[13] Jews also fled the urban areas faster than many of their Gentile neighbors because they had the economic ability to do so, they were not attached to a particular location, and they had no religious hierarchy (like the Catholic parish) to hold them.[14] The G.I. Bill provided Jewish veterans with home loans and the opportunity to flee the cities. Thus, the identification with Judaism through ethnicity reinforced by being near other Jews decreased. Other ethnic groups had to be considered as part of the neighborhood and contact with them had to be managed. Jews embraced the opportunity to join American society, but still limited their close friendships to co-religionists. This too added to the growth of the Reform Movement. Jews in the suburbs realized that to maintain their Judaism, they needed a community of Jews. Thus, the surge in membership, which did not necessarily imply greater observance.

The number of Reform congregations was 698 by 1950.[15] While the numbers of new synagogues in New York City were overwhelmingly Orthodox between 1948 and 1962, the numbers of new synagogues in suburban communities of New York City and elsewhere were more often Reform.[16] Suburban communities were not conducive to Orthodox and Conservative Jewish practice. Because there was no downtown or central square, to get to a synagogue required a car and both of these more traditional movements forbade the use of vehicles on the Sabbath. Therefore, the design of suburbia was more conducive to the Reform Movement. Additionally, half of the existing Reform congregations were expanding or contemplating expanding their facilities. Of more than 1,700 Jewish congregations in North America in 1952, 520 of them belonged to the UAHC,

---

13 Glazer, *American Judaism*, 117.
14 Nathan Glazer, "Jews and the Urban Experience: A Historical Assessment." Keynote (presented at Jews and the Urban Experience, Cohn-Haddow Center for Judaic Studies, Temple Beth El, Bloomfield Hills, Michigan, 7 March1999) (Bloomfield Hills, Michigan: Wayne State University, 1999), 9.
15 Jack Wertheimer, "The American synagogue: recent issues and trends." *American Jewish Yearbook* (2005), 7, accessed 31 January 2014, http://%3A%2F%2Fresearch.policyarchive.org%2F10414.pdf&ei=MCzsUr2EHsupsATTx4CoBg&usg=AFQjCNGnpmyyci2vvx1f9R9 ACorSQ17Hjw&sig2=RbcqaxyzPoJH7iWCYv1PMg&bvm=bv.60444564,d.cWc.
16 Leibman, "Changing Social Characteristics," 214, 217; Sloan, "Communal Affairs: Religion," 191.

which translated to 255,000 member families.[17] By 1967, there were close to 650 UAHC congregations.[18]

Religious affiliation was generally declining between 1965 and 1975.[19] Thirty percent of middle-aged Reform Jews claimed their parents had been Reform, and 40 percent of young adult Reform Jews claimed their parents were Reform Jews.[20] This reflected the demographics of immigrant Jews preferring the Orthodox congregations, but native-born Jews preferred Reform or Conservative congregations.[21] Conservative Judaism appealed mostly to 2nd-generation Jews who were seeking a bridge between the Orthodoxy of their parents and the bi-cultural American life.

By 1960, almost 60 percent of American Jews belonged to a synagogue, 3 times the percentage of 30 years earlier.[22] Studies also show a continuation of the rise of ritual observance. In the 1950s, Bernard C. Rosen discovered that 64 percent of teen Jews attended services at least monthly.[23] Other studies showed during the 1950s, that 61 percent of Jewish teens enjoyed attending services,[24] and 15 percent of Reform Jewish teens planned on being more observant than their parents.[25]

Part of this return to religion was "Americans priding themselves that their belief in G-d set them apart from atheistic communism."[26] This was a double-edged sword because the trend brought religion into schools and places of employment where it hadn't been before and weakened the separation of church and state.[27] The founding of the State of Israel is a partial contribution to this

---

[17] Ibid.
[18] David Rudavsky, *Modern Jewish Religious Movements: A History of Emancipation and Adjustment* (New York: Behrman House, 1967), 314.
[19] Ibid., 29.
[20] Ibid., 189.
[21] Ibid.
[22] Dana Evan Kaplan, "Trends in American Judaism from 1945 to the present," in *The Cambridge Companion to American Judaism*, ed. Dana Evan Kaplan (New York: Cambridge Univ. Press, 2005), 63–64.
[23] Bernard C. Rosen, "Minority Group in Transition: A Study of Adolescent Religious Conviction and Conduct," in *The Jews: Social Patterns of an American Group*, ed. Marshall Sklare (Glenco: The Free Press, 1958), 339.
[24] Sloan, "Communal Affairs," 190.
[25] Ibid., 193.
[26] Michael A. Meyer, *A Response to Modernity: A History of the Reform Movement in Judaism* (New York: Oxford Univ. Press, 1988), 353.
[27] Ibid., 365.

revival of religious practice among Jews.[28] There was also, at this time, a growth in the number of Jews who defined themselves as secular Jews. They were proud to be Jewish because of the power of the Israeli army, but they were not interested in the spiritual aspects of the religion. American Jews were now more powerful and freer than Jews had been anywhere before them. No longer was America a strictly Western Judeo–Christian country; immigrants from the Far and Mid East were changing that. Nationally, $2/3^{rds}$ of Americans attended a house of worship monthly in the 1950s. However, the extent of this new-found religiosity was questioned by scholars. Researchers were unsure worshippers were truly committed or understood what their faiths espoused.[29]

This return to religion also inspired conversion to Judaism. Marrying a Jew no longer meant an immediate exclusion from the larger Christian society and family. Even though intermarriage during the Colonial through the Reconstruction Periods was tolerated, the expectation was that the household would be Christian. If this did not happen, then there were certain social clubs, and hence business contacts and transactions, one was excluded from. However, now it was more acceptable to have a Jewish household when one intermarried. In 1953, 2,000 Americans converted to Judaism and the numbers increased for the next two decades.[30] Half of these converts were converted by a Reform rabbi.[31] Because of the lack of absorption of Judaism through immediate and regular contact with other Jews and the growing Christian influence in society, suburban synagogues began educational programming. These educational programs were created to also provide "enlightenment" for those who "meet the threat of discrimination" and were coupled with "Jewish organizations ... laboring to further the process of intergroup understanding."[32] This was not the only way to educate the children of converts, but also 3rd-generation Jewish children as well.

Beginning in the mid-1950s, the Civil Rights Movement gained importance and power. The CCAR and UAHC formed a Social Action Committee in 1948 after the CCAR had released the statement "Judaism and Race Relations" in

---

28 A. Stanley Dreyfus, "The *Gates* Liturgies: Reform Judaism Reforms Its Worship," in *The Changing Face of Jewish and Christian Worship in North America*, ed. Paul F. Bradshow and Lawrence A. Hoffman (Notre Dame: Univ. of Notre Dame Press, 1991), 146.
29 George M. Marsden, *Religion and American Culture* (Fort Worth: Harcourt Brace College Pub., 1990), 213.
30 Meyer, *A Response*, 380.
31 Sloan, "Communal Affairs," 190.
32 Jacob Rader Marcus, *The Future of American Jewry* (Presented at Dropsie College for Hebrew and Cognate Learning, Philadelphia, Pennsylvania, 2 June 1955) (Cincinnati: American Jewish Archives, 1956), 2.

1946 that called for an end to racial segregation and discrimination.[33] However, the black community's anti-white sentiments and the anti-Semitic sentiments among a number of African Americans made ongoing support difficult to maintain.[34]

With all of these changes came the realization that by the late 1960s American Jews were nearly 6 million in number and 1/2 of world Jewry.[35] The Jewish community was no longer awash in new immigrants. Americanized Jews were 2nd- and 3rd-generation American-born and increasingly suburban. When the Jewish suburban communities were established, they constituted only 22 percent of the Jewish population in 1951, but by 1970 they were 36 percent of the Jewish population.[36] Nationally, there were 703 UAHC member congregations in 1973.[37] In addition, even though the New York City metropolitan region still had the largest Jewish population in the country, there was a definite westward shift of the population. Plus, Jews were becoming more publicly proud of their Jewishness because of the rise in ethnic pride among Americans generally and the victory of the Israeli military in the 1967 Six-Day War. Involvement in the Civil Rights Movement led Jews to join the anti-Viet Nam War protests and other social justice grass-roots programs. All of these factors influenced the mentality and psychology of the Jewish American population. The need for comfort in liturgy became apparent.

At the end of the Second World War, American Jewish attitudes changed. American Jews had assumed a new place in the world of Judaism as the largest Jewish community in the world. Jewish theology after the Holocaust also changed as Jews questioned their relationship with G-d. Finally, the founding of the State of Israel altered how Jews perceived themselves. The first inkling of how this would affect the liturgy under discussion in this dissertation came from Salman Schocken, the publisher, who in 1944 wanted to have "a personal conversation" with Cohon about how his "view as a Palestinian and Zionist"

---

33 Meyer, *A Response*, 364–365.
34 Kaplan, "Trends," 66.
35 Sidney Goldstein, "American Jewry, 1970: A Demographic Profile." *Jewish American Year Book* (1971), 5, accessed June 4, 2014, http://www.jewishdatabank.org/Studies/downloadFile.cfm?FileID=2983.
36 Ibid., 42.
37 Temkin, Sefton D. "A Century of Reform Judaism in America." *American Jewish Year Book* vol. 74 (1973), 66, accessed 12 August 2014, http://www.ajcarchives.org/AJC_DATA/Files/1973_3_SpecialArticles.pdf.

contrasts with material in the *Union Haggadah*.³⁸ Then in 1948 the State of Israel was founded and Jews developed a new sense of pride.

Cries for a new Union Haggadah

In 1949, the UAHC was displeased enough with the CCAR *Union Haggadah* that it issued 2 leaflets. It affirmed that "the Union Haggadah was a marvelous achievement, but it is not the last word," and the supplements that "replace[s] nothing and changes nothing in the Haggadah itself."³⁹ *The Union Haggadah* was now almost 25 years old and had been produced when the Movement was just beginning to accept Eastern European members. A 1/4 of a century later, there was a much larger Eastern European contingent than the German contingent in the Reform Movement. One supplement, the *Ceremonial for Opening the Door for Elijah* is a responsive reading that elucidates for those gathered, specifically for children, who Elijah is and what he represents to the Reform Jew.⁴⁰ It contrasts strongly with Psalms 117 and 118 that are presented in *The Union Haggadah* for the ceremony of opening the door for Elijah.⁴¹ These say nothing about Elijah. Rather, they praise G-d for "His mercy."⁴² Even in the section "Rites and Symbols of the Seder" in the 1923 *The Union Haggadah* explains that the ceremony of opening the door to Elijah "helped, in times of darkness and persecution, to keep in mind the Messianic era of freedom, justice, and good-will" for our ancestors, but in the current edition he has been "stripped of [his] legendary form, [he] is still the hope for the realization of which Israel ever yearns and strives."⁴³ With the supplement, the CCAR rabbis understood that in order to interest children in Judaism they had to be addressed in ways that intrigued them. Additionally, the Eastern European constituency valued the more traditional concept of Elijah as precursor to the arrival of the messiah, rather than a superstitious notion.

---

38 Salman Schocken, to Samuel A. [sic] Cohon, 18 April 1944. Jacob Rader Marcus Center of the American Jewish Archives, Cincinnati Campus, Hebrew Union College – Jewish Institute of Religion, MS coll. 276, 3/7.
39 Jacob D. Schwarz, to Friend, 11 March 1949. Rodef Shalom Congregational Archives, BA 70, FF 34.
40 Joint Committee on Ceremonies, UAHC and CCAR, *Ceremonial for Opening the Door for Elijah* (New York: CCAR, 1942).Rodef Shalom Congregational Archives, BA 70, FF 34.
41 CCAR, *The Union Haggadah: Home Service for the Passover* (New York: Central Conference of American Rabbis, 1923), 62–63.
42 Ibid., 62.
43 Ibid., xii.

Passover and the Contemporary Scene offers a more modern interpretation of the Four Sons. Instead of the Wise, Wicked, Simple, and Unable to Inquire, the UAHC and CCAR Joint Committee on Ceremonies' new offering was "the Jew who is at one with Israel," "The Jew who would flee from his G-d and his people," "The Jew who esteems all knowledge except that of his own people," and "The Jew who has been adrift and seeks the way back to Israel."[44] The conclusion of this double-sided document explains the meaning of the Seder as "the unity of Israel" and answers the question about the continuation of the celebration of Passover.[45] This language is in response to the Jewish post–Holocaust need to understand why one should stay connected to Judaism and the American Jews' growing belief in individualism and connection with Judaism not through belief but through religious ceremony. There were 32,000 copies of this distributed to UAHC congregation members.[46]

Despite sales in 1953 of 11,561,[47] 1954 of 13,713,[48] and 14,421 in 1955[49] of the *Union Haggadah*, in 1955, the CCAR recognized that "since the Jewish community of America is becoming more homogeneous and stabilized, and since Israel has become an independent, sovereign state, we must continue a process which the founding fathers of Reform initiated; that is, shaping Judaism for the Western World into a living faith."[50] At this time, CCAR President Barnett Brickner called for the revision of *The Union Haggadah* and *Prayer Book* "in the light of the history-making events of the twenty-five years."[51] He saw this as part of the evolution of Reform Judaism to meet the needs of a "more homogeneous and stabilized" community and in keeping with the "process which the founding fathers of Reform initiated; that is, shaping Judaism for the Western World

---

44 Joint Committee on Ceremonies, UAHC and CCAR, *Passover and the Contemporary Scene* (New York: CCAR, 1942), side one. Rodef Shalom Congregational Archives, BA 70, FF 34.
45 Ibid., side two.
46 Martha L. Berg, to author, 3 August 2010.
47 Sidney L. Regner, "Report of Committee on Publications," Central Conference of American Rabbis Annual Convention, Estes Park, Colorado, 23–28 June 1953. *Year Book of the Central Conference of American Rabbis*, vol. 63 (Philadelphia: Maurice Jacobs, 1957), 145.
48 Sidney L. Regner, "Report of Committee on Publications." Central Conference of American Rabbis Annual Convention, Pike, New Hampshire, 22–27 June 1954. *Year Book of the Central Conference of American Rabbis*, vol. 64 (Philadelphia: Maurice Jacobs, 1957), 66.
49 Ely E. Philchik, "Report of Committee on Publications," Central Conference of American Rabbis Annual Convention, Asbury Park, New Jersey, 20–23 June 1955. *Year Book of the Central Conference of American Rabbis*, vol. 65 (Philadelphia: Maurice Jacobs, 1957), 79.
50 Barnett Brickner, "President's Message," Proceedings of the Central Conference of American Rabbis, Asbury Park, New Jersey, 20–23 June 1955. *Central Conference of American Rabbis Yearbook*, vol. 65 (Philadelphia: Maurice Jacobs, 1955), 11.
51 Ibid.

into a living faith."⁵² This move may also have been motivated by the earlier mentioned UAHC leaflets.⁵³ The request was passed by the convention.⁵⁴ At this same convention, the Committee on Marriage, Family and the Home, reminded its constituents that "the family...has had to adapt itself to this condition of rapid social change [suburbanization is most likely to what it is referring]," but "the family is our principal character-building institution. Religious and educational institutions are at best supplementary."⁵⁵

Between 1952 and 1960, the Committee on Liturgy studied the *Union Haggadah* with the idea of revision⁵⁶ while sales continued to rise to around 20,000.⁵⁷ The Committee understood that it had to "produce relatively durable materials which are recommended for general use."⁵⁸ The Liturgy Committee decided in 1956 "that the sub-committee appointed to work on [the Haggadah revision is] requested to supply additional material to the present Haggadah but that the

---

52 Ibid.

53 Solomon B. Freehof to Abraham J. Feldman, 18 March 1949. Rodef Shalom Congregational Archives, BA 70, FF 34.

54 Note following Joseph L. Fink, "Report of the Committee on President's Message," Central Conference of American Rabbis Annual Convention, Asbury Park, New Jersey, 20–23 June 1955. *Year Book of the Central Conference of American Rabbis*, vol. 65 (Philadelphia: Maurice Jacobs, 1957), 112.

55 Morton M. Berman, "Report of the Committee on Marriage, Family and the Home," Central Conference of American Rabbis Annual Convention, Asbury Park, New Jersey, 20–23 June1955. *Year Book of the Central Conference of American Rabbis*, vol. 65 (Philadelphia: Maurice Jacobs, 1957), 69.

56 Bernard J. Bamberger, "Report of the Committee on Liturgy," Central Conference of American Rabbis Annual Convention, Atlantic City, New Jersey, 25–28 June1956. *Year Book of the Central Conference of American Rabbis*, vol. 64 (Philadelphia: Maurice Jacobs, 1957), 83; Bernard J. Bamberger, "Report of the Committee on Liturgy," Central Conference of American Rabbis Annual Convention, Buffalo, New York, 10–15 June 1952. *Year Book of the Central Conference of American Rabbis*, vol. 62 (Philadelphia: Maurice Jacobs, 1957), 258–259; Bernard J. Bamberger, "Report of the Committee on Liturgy," Central Conference of American Rabbis Annual Convention., Chicago, Illinois, 24–29 June 1958. *Year Book of the Central Conference of American Rabbis*, vol. 68 (Philadelphia: Maurice Jacobs, 1958), 102.

57 Ely E. Philchik, "Report of Committee on Publications," Central Conference of American Rabbis Annual Convention, Miami Beach, Florida, 24–27 June 1957. *Year Book of the Central Conference of American Rabbis*, vol. 67 (Philadelphia: Maurice Jacobs, 1958), 74; Ely E. Philchik, "Report of Committee on Publications," Central Conference of American Rabbis Annual Convention, Chicago, Illinois, 24–29 June 1958. *Year Book of the Central Conference of American Rabbis*, vol. 68 (Philadelphia: Maurice Jacobs, 1959), 112; Eugene J. Sack, "Report of Committee on Publications," Central Conference of American Rabbis Annual Convention. Bretton Woods, New Hampshire, 23–28 June 1958. *Year Book of the Central Conference of American Rabbis*, vol. 69 (Philadelphia: Maurice Jacobs, 1960), 110.

58 Bamberger, "Report," vol. 62, 259.

present body of the Haggadah be retained."[59] The sub-committee, consisting of Rabbi Ahron Opher and Rabbi David Polish, was "somewhat dissatisfied with the limitations imposed on them at a previous meeting of the Committee – namely that only verbal changes should be made in the present text....Both would prefer a more drastic revision of the Haggadah," but the Liturgy Committee refused permission.[60] In 1959, the Committee reviewed "what a revision would involve" and concluded that "it might include dramatic elements, that there by stylistic revision, insertions of a contemporary nature, restoration of traditional materials, [and] other music."[61] Here the conflict between the followers of the Classical Reform Movement, who really wanted to maintain what was, and those in the Reform Movement, at the time who wanted more rituals and more material to help their fellow Reform Jews enrich their middle-class suburban lives, is illustrated.

In 1960, Polish submitted a subcommittee report explaining why a new Haggadah was necessary, rather than "minor patch-work changes."[62] The subcommittee believed "that the new times and new conditions which now obtain, the modern history of the Jew, with its dramatic tragedies and triumphs, call for an added contribution to our Passover literature." This was the same rationale for the revisions for the *Union Prayer Books* and *Rabbi's Manual*.[63] Among other changes, committee members suggested a "new brief forward, short directions for setting table... [and] all rituals explained more fully with possibility of their being read out loud."[64] The Liturgy Committee unanimously approved the suggestions and "urged" the Executive Board to do so as well.[65] The Liturgy Committee understood the nature of their constituency: Jews interested in practice, but unschooled in how to practice and uneducated concerning the meanings behind the practice.

---

59 Sidney L. Regner, Bernard J. Bamberger, et al., Minutes of the Liturgy Committee Meeting, Hotel Sheraton–Gibson, Cincinnati, Ohio, 24 January 1956.
60 Sidney L. Regner, Minutes of the Liturgy Committee Meeting, New York, New York, 29 May 1956. Jacob Rader Marcus Center of the American Jewish Archives, Cincinnati Campus, Hebrew Union College – Jewish Institute of Religion, MS coll. 34.
61 Sidney L. Regner, Minutes of Liturgy Committee Meeting, 23–29 December 1959, p. 2. Jacob Rader Marcus Center of the American Jewish Archives, Cincinnati Campus, Hebrew Union College – Jewish Institute of Religion, MS coll. 34.
62 David Polish, Albert Goldstein, and Hyman J. Schachtel, Subcommittee on Haggadah, ©1960, p. 1. Jacob Rader Marcus Center of the American Jewish Archives, Cincinnati Campus, Hebrew Union College – Jewish Institute of Religion, MS coll. 24, 20/11.
63 Ibid.
64 Ibid., 2.
65 Ibid., 3.

As the 3 members of the subcommittee, consisting of Rabbi David Polish, Rabbi Hyman J. Schachtel, and Rabbi Albert Goldstein, continued their work,[66] congregants were writing to the CCAR requesting a new Haggadah.[67] Sales began to show a growing dissatisfaction with the *Union Haggadah*. Rabbi Alvan D. Rubin, chairman of the Committee on Publications, at the 1963 conference was "concern[ed]...[in] the drop in sales of the Union Haggadah [in 1963], which seems to indicate that the Haggadah is in need of revision."[68] The drop was significant; less than 6,000 had been sold in 1963,[69] in contrast to the rising sales during the previous 3 years.[70] The people were calling for a change in the liturgy. In addition, there was now serious competition with a growing number of food companies providing free Haggadot with the purchase of their products and an explosion of the editions published by various publishing houses (1,100 new editions between 1960 and 1974).[71] Thus, Jews now had a large number of Haggadot from which to choose and if the CCAR wished to keep their audience, they had to re-evaluate their product.

Polish explained to the 1965 meeting of the Liturgy Committee that "the most important issue is that of timeliness vs. timelessness. The people don't understand our liturgy; they don't care. There is a massic [sic] lack of awareness of Jew-

---

[66] Beryl D. Cohon, to the Central Conference of American Rabbis, 1964. Jacob Rader Marcus Center of the American Jewish Archives, Cincinnati Campus, Hebrew Union College – Jewish Institute of Religion, MS coll. 34, 20/8.

[67] Leon I. Feuer to Albert M. Schaler, 26 April 1965. Jacob Rader Marcus Center of the American Jewish Archives, Cincinnati Campus, Hebrew Union College – Jewish Institute of Religion, MS coll. 34, 22/10.

[68] Alvan D. Rubin, "Report of Committee on Publications," Central Conference of American Rabbis Annual Convention, Philadelphia, Pennsylvania, 17–20 June 1963. *Year Book of the Central Conference of American Rabbis*, vol. 73 (Philadelphia: Maurice Jacobs, 1963), 79.

[69] Ibid., 80.

[70] Eugene J. Sack, "Report of Committee on Publications," Central Conference of American Rabbis Annual Convention, Detroit, Michigan, 21–26 June 1960. *Year Book of the Central Conference of American Rabbis*, vol. 70 (Philadelphia: Maurice Jacobs, 1961), 88; Eugene J. Sack, "Report of Committee on Publications," Central Conference of American Rabbis Annual Convention, New York, New York, 20–24 June 1961. *Year Book of the Central Conference of American Rabbis*, vol. 71 (Philadelphia: Maurice Jacobs, 1962), 108; Alvan D. Rubin, "Report of Committee on Publications," Central Conference of American Rabbis Annual Convention, Minneapolis–St. Paul, Minnesota, 19–23 June 1962. *Year Book of the Central Conference of American Rabbis*, vol. 72 (Philadelphia: Maurice Jacobs, 1963), 108–109.

[71] Yosef Hayim Yerushalmi, *Haggadah and History: A Panorama in Facsimile of Five Centuries of the Printed Haggadah from the Collections of Harvard University and Jewish Theological Seminary of American* (Philadelphia: JPS of American, 1975), 26.

ish symbolism....The people want to know about symbolism."[72] Rabbi Eugene Mihaly reminded those in attendance at that Liturgy Committee Meeting in April 1965 that "we are not creating the Haggadah for the already alienated, but for the serious though uninformed."[73]

However, Rabbi Herbert Bronstein, creator of the 1974 *A Passover Haggadah*, believed that part of the problem of the revisions being proposed was that they had not "caught up with the Movement," nor had they "caught up with the Columbus Platform" of the 1930s.[74] In fact, Reform Jews were turning mostly to the Conservative Haggadah because they wanted more ritual. The CCAR realized it needed to address this loss of readership as well as membership due to the rise in desire for ritual and spirituality coupled with the social changes in America.

At the 1966 convention, the Report of the Committee on Liturgy and Music included a request for more feedback from the Convention before the Committee committed itself to an entirely new Haggadah.[75] The Committee was concerned about meeting "the needs of the masses who are alienated from the synagogue and who no longer feel the need for prayer, [they felt they] must do what [they] can for the saving remnant."[76] The question was asked if there is "any longer a homogeneous Reform Judaism."[77] After a year of surveys and study groups, the Committee concluded that "we are now in a period of transition, as Reform Judaism was in the nineteenth century and as our fathers were prior to the Gaonic age."[78] The Committee also observed the Movement was no longer homogeneous. There were conflicts regarding the usage of Hebrew in the liturgy and the question of maintaining traditionally recited prayers or more relevant prayers for the "contemporary human experience, knowledge, and thought."[79] In an effort to help Reform Jews learn Jewish practice, the UAHC published *Liberal Juda-*

---

[72] Joseph Narot, Minutes of the Liturgy Committee Meeting, New York City, 13–14 April 1965, 2. Jacob Rader Marcus Center of the American Jewish Archives, Cincinnati Campus, Hebrew Union College – Jewish Institute of Religion, MS coll. 34.
[73] Ibid.
[74] Herbert Bronstein, Interview by author, 13 December 1996.
[75] Joseph R. Narot, "Report of Committee on Liturgy and Music," Central Conference of American Rabbis Annual Convention, Toronto, Canada, 21–25 June 1966. *Year Book of the Central Conference of American Rabbis*, vol. 76 (Philadelphia: Maurice Jacobs, 1967), 63.
[76] Ibid., 64.
[77] Ibid.
[78] Joseph R. Narot, "Report of Committee on Liturgy and Music," Central Conference of American Rabbis Annual Convention, Los Angeles, California, 19–22 June 1967. *Year Book of the Central Conference of American Rabbis*, vol. 77 (New York: CCAR, 1968), 54.
[79] Ibid.

ism at Home: The Practices of Modern Reform Judaism* in 1967 as a source of "practical answers...[and] traditional Jewish customs."[80] Sentiment leaned toward "a new Haggadah" rather than a revision of the existing one.[81]

Creating a New Haggadah

Liturgical revisions began in 1967, when both the *Union Prayer Book* and *The Union Haggadah* were sent to committee for changes to address the new postwar constituency including the desire for social justice.[82] The prayerbook committee had to consider "a balance between the conflicting claims of tradition and modernity," a way to bring Hebrew to the Hebraically illiterate, as well as, modern English translations, gender-inclusive language, and a return of traditional liturgies. The new generation of Reform Jews wanted a Sabbath service that was religious and spiritually meaningful. They wanted the congregations to be worshippers, not observers. American Jewish children spent summers at Jewish camps where services were innovative and, now as teens and adults, they wanted this innovation in their synagogue services. Rabbi Joseph R. Narot, chairman of the Committee on Liturgy and Music, recognized in 1967 that "new worship services attuned to the sixties rather than to the thirties are needed."[83] He understood that the new liturgies must address the issue that there was no "longer a homogeneous Reform Judaism" or "any consensus...as to what constitutes piety" and the Liturgy Committee must address this in their revisions.[84]

In 1969, Rabbis Polish and Bronstein began working together to devise a complete revision of the Haggadah,[85] although Bronstein had been given "the task of preparing a manuscript for a revised Haggadah which combines the best features of all previous work [manuscripts submitted] in response" to the surveys conducted by the Committee.[86] Bronstein had joined the Committee in 1962 or 1963 and was one of the few members of the Committee who had not

---

80 Morrison David Bial, *Liberal Judaism at Home: The Practices of Modern Reform Judaism* (New York: UAHC, 1971), back cover.
81 Committee on Liturgy and Music Minutes, 2 March 1966, 1.
82 Dreyfus, "Reform Judaism's Worship," 147.
83 Narot, "Report of the Committee on Liturgy and Music," 1967, 54.
84 Narot, "Report on the Committee on Liturgy and Music," 1966, 64–65.
85 Robert I. Kahn, "Report of Committee on Liturgy," Central Conference of American Rabbis Annual Convention, Boston, Massachusetts, 17–20 June 1968. *Year Book of the Central Conference of American Rabbis*, vol. 78 (New York: CCAR, 1969), 90.
86 Herbert Bronstein, Minutes of Liturgy Committee Meeting, 29 November 1967, 2.

worked on the 1923 *The Union Haggadah*, although Cohon was a friend of the family and one of Bronstein's professors. Thus, Bronstein felt he was continuing in Cohon's footsteps.[87] Rabbi Robert I. Kahn, chairman of the Committee on Liturgy and Music, told the 1970 CCAR convention that "the [new] Haggadah has been tried out in both home and congregational *Seders* and is being revised in accordance with suggestions developed by these groups."[88] Kahn suggested to the Committee that after a final review of the text of the proposed Haggadah in the fall of 1971, it should be passed on the Executive Committee.[89]

This did not happen as planned. The revised Haggadah was given to the Conference at the 1972 convention.[90] Bronstein, who completed the edition, pointed out to the CCAR members that "we want our Haggadah to be one of the finest published in our period," "we must guard against anxious pursuit of whatever is current (and always remaining two steps behind) so an authentic Jewish text does not mean slavish adherence to the present order or text of the traditional or othodox [sic] Haggadah."[91]

Bronstein took his job as editor, or creator, seriously. He understood that all Haggadot "reveal the wrenches, skewings and marks of historic needs and outlooks," and so purposely "resist[ed] using the Haggadah as current propaganda or teaching of ideology."[92] His goal was for this Haggadah to be "a teaching Haggadah...not in the way of lecturing," but by showing the reader what is significant and having the translations be more than interpretations.[93] Additionally, he tried to get some feminist prayers included. This was the beginning of the feminist movement and Bronstein saw gender inclusiveness as the future of Reform Judaism. He wanted this to reach more than the immediate generation, just

---

[87] Bronstein, Interview.
[88] Robert I. Kahn, "Report of Committee on Liturgy," Central Conference of American Rabbis Annual Convention, Jerusalem, Israel, 6–10 March 1970. *Year Book of the Central Conference of American Rabbis*, vol. 80 (New York: CCAR, 1971), 45.
[89] Robert I. Kahn, Memo to CCAR Liturgy Commmittee, ©1970. Jacob Rader Marcus Center of the American Jewish Archives, Cincinnati Campus, Hebrew Union College – Jewish Institute of Religion, MS coll. Miscellaneous Correspondence from April 17, 1970 through 1972.
[90] Herbert Bronstein, to Members of the Central Conference of American Rabbis, 1 March 1972. Jacob Rader Marcus Center of the American Jewish Archives, Cincinnati Campus, Hebrew Union College – Jewish Institute of Religion, MS coll. Bronstein, copy new Haggadah.
[91] Ibid., back.
[92] Herbert Bronstein, "Re: Ltr. To Mara W. Cohen Ioannides – CORRECTED VERSION 8/22 BRONSTEIN," Message to the author, 24 August 24, 2000.
[93] Bronstein, Interview.

as he had admonished the convention. However, these suggestions were rejected by the various committees.⁹⁴

Bronstein was well aware of his audience's lack of Jewish education and exemplary secular education, but rather than being pedantic or discursive, he wanted to "convey…information…within the dimension of the transcendent, the sacred, and the poetic, as the teaching had to take place under the auspice of liturgy."⁹⁵ Thus, the intent was not a revision of the 1923 *The Union Haggadah*, but one that went "back to the original sources."⁹⁶ This is clearly stated in the "Preface:" "This Haggadah is not a revision of the previous Union Haggadah. It is an attempt at *renovation ab origine*: a return to the creative beginning so as to bring forth what is utterly new from what was present in the old."⁹⁷

A salient idea in the Bronstein Haggadah is that the leader should be able to start easily with a Seder, even without much previous knowledge. Thus, the Passover's history was moved from the end of the Haggadah to the beginning so that the leader and the participant could understand why they were involved in this ceremony before they began. Another key point of the Haggadah was to meet the needs of the people who wished for more tradition.⁹⁸ In fact, the "Preface" states that "most of the rubrics of the traditional Haggadah are retained."⁹⁹ This is a text that "represents an attempt to eliminate what does not seem to appeal to our generation while adding elements which are new and contemporary."¹⁰⁰

In 1973, the Executive Board "approved with enthusiasm" the Haggadah by Bronstein and requested members' comments of show their support or displeasure with the text.¹⁰¹ The majority of responses were "in high favor of the text."¹⁰² The 4 page "Historical Introduction," by Lawrence Hoffman, renowned scholar of Jewish liturgy, begins with the 1ˢᵗ Century C.E. and the beginning of the Haggadah. It concludes with the statement that this edition "can be seen as a con-

---

94 Sue Levi Elwell, Interview by author, 14 February 2014.
95 Bronstein, "Re: Ltr."
96 Bronstein, Interview.
97 Bronstein, הגדה של פסח, 5.
98 Bronstein, Interview.
99 Bronstein, הגדה של פסח, 6.
100 Jacob, "70," 112.
101 J. B. G., to Colleague, 31 May 31 1973. Jacob Rader Marcus Center of the American Jewish Archives, Cincinnati Campus, Hebrew Union College – Jewish Institute of Religion. MS coll. Passover nearprint, 1.
102 Robert I. Kahn, "Report of Committee on Liturgy and Music," Central Conference of American Rabbis Annual Convention, Grossinger, New York, 12–15 June 1972. *Year Book of the Central Conference of American Rabbis*, vol. 82 (New York: CCAR, 1973), 47.

tinuation of its predecessors."[103] Hoffman, and Bronstein, are placing this Haggadah, and Reform Judaism, in the chronology of Jewish development. This could only help with recruitment of new members to Reform congregations and more purchases of the CCAR Haggadah since it was presented as a more viable option than previous Haggadot.

The section "Preparing for the Seder" was expanded to 4 pages and written by W. Gunther Plaut, the acclaimed Reform rabbinic scholar. The Haggadah included a discussion of "בדיקת חמץ" that begins with a mention of "spring cleaning" and continues with a focus on "different foods, dishes, and utensils that should be set aside and used only during Passover, [which] will recall the special sanctity of the time."[104] This is a departure from the previous edition that considered this to be an Orthodox practice. It shows the return to traditional practices that the Reform Movement accepted as a norm in their theology.

Then the way to clean the house and blessing are provided. The instructions are an example of the lost knowledge of the practice among Reform Jews. Participants are urged to "arrange to leave your place of work a little earlier than usual, so that you may properly prepare yourself for the arrival of the holy day."[105] Each ceremonial food is presented with a short description. The festival is presented as a weeklong holiday with a paragraph concerning "food during the Passover week."[106] Finally, there is a paragraph by Anthony Hecht, American Jewish poet, reminding participants that "this is a joyful but serious religious service."[107] Rabbi Harvey J. Fields, who sat on the Liturgy Committee that oversaw this manuscript, explained that:

> the inclusion of ...[this section] is altogether practical. Since the Haggadah is intended for use in the home, many of those who might be preparing the celebration around the seder table are seeking some kind of guide, and appreciate the detailed explanations of the symbols. It helps them not only set the table appropriately, but to open the gates of understanding and appreciation for the ancient symbols of our tradition....Given the fact there are so many who are distant today from the tradition, having such ready accessibility into the wisdom of their tradition, is a great enabler of participation and involvement.[108]

---

103 Bronstein, הגדה של פסח, 12.
104 Ibid., 13.
105 Ibid., 14.
106 Ibid., 16.
107 Ibid., 17.
108 Harvey J. Fields, to author, 14 October 1999.

This follows the demands of the constituency who were looking for a more spiritual experience than in the past.[109] The explanations of how to conduct the Seder and the importance of the festival and the ceremony were shortened because during the 1970s there was an explosion of materials published on how to be Jewish and to conduct the celebrations, both by the CCAR and by others.[110]

The Haggadah was released in 1974, and the 1975 sales report shows how welcome the text was: 50,000 1st editions were sold, 60,182 2nd editions were sold,[111] 3,732 deluxe editions[112] were sold, as well as 95 limited editions[113].[114] This makes a total of over 144,000 copies sold in 2 years. Dreyfus commented that "the surprisingly large distribution...reflects the hunger of American Jewry for meaningful liturgy."[115] Rabbi Peter Knobel, president of the CCAR, called it "revolutionary."[116] Three years later, the Committee reported 210,000 Haggadot had been sold.[117]

Reviews of the Haggadah were positive. *Hadassah Magazine* commended it for the "blend[ing of] the traditions with commentary written throughout Jewish history – from the Bible to the writings of lay authors, including Elie Wiesel and Martin Buber."[118] Lily Edelman of *The National Jewish Monthly* found the text "relevant" with "splendid lines [by] Erich Fromm, Elie Wiesel, Abraham Heschel and other modern writers."[119] Jack Reimer in *Conservative Judaism* found that "the new readings are woven into the text like a *midrash*. We feel that enslavement and exodus are not just things that occurred long ago in Egypt; they are

---

[109] Arnold Jacob Wolf, "A More Traditional and Radical Prayer Book" (paper presented at the UAHC 48th Biennial.), in *The Theological Foundations of Prayer: A Reform Jewish Perspective.* ed. Jack Bemporad (New York: UAHC, 1967), 93, 95.
[110] Peter Knobel, Interview by author, 7 August 2013.
[111] This edition had gender neutral language.
[112] This edition had signed lithographs by the illustrator Leonard Baskin.
[113] This edition had signed lithographs by the illustrator Leonard Baskin and a slipcase.
[114] A. Stanley Dreyfus, "Report of the Liturgy Committee," Central Conference of American Rabbis Annual Convention, Cincinnati, Ohio, 15–19 June 1975. *Year Book of the Central Conference of American Rabbis*, vol. 85 (New York: CCAR, 1975), 41.
[115] Ibid.
[116] Knobel, Interview.
[117] A. Stanley Dreyfus, "Report of the Liturgy Committee," Central Conference of American Rabbis Annual Convention, Toronto, Canada, 26–29 June 1978. *Year Book of the Central Conference of American Rabbis*, vol. 88 (New York: CCAR, 1979), 39.
[118] Review of *A Passover Haggadah*, by Herbert Bronstein, *Hadassah Magazine* (March 1974), 27.
[119] Lily Edelman, "Leonard Baskin's New Haggadah: The Artist Celebrates the Movement 'from the green gloom of slavery to the hot orange of freedom,'" review of *A Passover Haggadah*, by Herbert Bronstein, *The National Jewish Monthly* (April 1974), 6.

themes that occur and reoccur all through our history, as well as in our own time."[120] He commended the CCAR for a Haggadah that

> is an example of a movement that has thought again. The influence of Israel and the Holocaust...has caused the Reform movement to undergo a metamorphosis that makes it almost unrecognizable. Anyone who looks at these books [the 1923 and 1974 Union Haggadah] can see that the movement may bear the same name, but it is no longer the same in spirit or in style as it was half a century ago.[121]

Reimer articulated what the Movement had attempted to do: grow with its audience.

Gates of Prayer was issued in 1975. Dreyfus, who chaired the Liturgy Committee, remarked:

> We have made Reform worship recognizably Jewish in style and mood....The new liturgy has enabled at least some Reform Jews to experience firsthand something of the numinous, to come into the presence of the holy, as former generations were privileged to do.[122]

The 1975 edition contained references to the *Shoah* and the founding of Israel; the two seminal mid-century events impacting world Jewry. The desire to be inclusive resulted in a compendium of 10 different possible Friday night services and 6 for Saturday morning.[123] This resulted in many complaints that the book was too heavy for use.[124]

A New Platform

The postwar migration of American Jews within the United States was significant and bares mentioning. By 1979, the South's share of the American Jewish population had doubled since 1930 and the West's had tripled.[125] Considering that the majority of Southern and Midwestern congregations were Reform, this was a

---

[120] Jack Reimer, review of *A Passover Haggadah*, by Herbert Bronstein, *Conservative Judaism* (spring 1974), 89.
[121] Ibid.
[122] Dreyfus, "The *Gates* Liturgies," 153.
[123] Peter S. Knobel, "The Challenge of a Single Prayer Book," in *Platforms and Prayer Books: Theological and Liturgical Perspectives on Reform Judaism*, ed. Dana Evan Kaplan (Lanham, Maryland: Rowman & Littlefield, 2002), 158.
[124] Dreyfus, "The *Gates* Liturgies," 152.
[125] Goldstein, "Jews in the United States," 30.

boon to the Movement. In fact, during the 1970s, another 150 congregations joined the UAHC and memberships of third- and fourth-generation Americans rose significantly in all Reform congregations.[126] By 1975, Boston Jews preferred Reform Jewish affiliation over either Orthodox or Conservative, and the children of Conservative Jews preferred Reform to Conservative affiliation.[127] Conservative Judaism, while appealing to the children of Eastern European Orthodox Jewish immigrants, did not hold quite the same draw for the following generations who were more willing to assimilate further than their parents. During the late 1960s and 1970s, the Lubavitch Hassidim began outreach to bring unaffiliated Jews back into Judaism. They opened Habad Houses on university campus and sent young men to do missionary work among other Jewish communities.[128]

Reform Jews also began to see ritual as a way to creating a community. Lighting Hanukkah candles or celebrating Seder was as much, to them, about expressing Jewish identity as it was being religious.[129] The Reform leadership began to see that "the greater the separation from the immigrant experience, the less likely one is to engage in ritual," and so encouraged ritual as a way of identification.[130] Because ritual practice continued to rise and Jews had become more comfortable being publicly Jewish sociologists were hopeful that Jews were not assimilating and disappearing despite intermarriage topping 30 percent in the 1970's.[131] One factor accounting for the growing numbers of Reform members was the acceptance of patrilineal descent, which permitted interfaith couples, where the mother is Christian, the opportunity to join a synagogue, rather than being forced to Christianity, not affiliating with any religious group, or not converting to Judaism.

In 1976, the Centenary Platform was passed by the CCAR.[132] In this new platform, the CCAR recognized the diversity within the Movement, understanding that though "we may differ in our interpretation and application of the ideas enunciated here, we accept such differences as precious and see in them Juda-

---

[126] Michael A. Meyer, "Thank You, Moritz Loth: A 125-Year UAHC Retrospective." *Reform Judaism* (fall 1998), 37.
[127] Meyer, *A Response*, 382.
[128] Marc Lee Raphael, *Profiles in American Judaism: The Reform, Conservative, Orthodox, and Reconstructionist Traditions in Historical Perspective* (San Fransciso: Harper & Row, 1984), 174.
[129] Hertzberg, *The Jews*, 382–383.
[130] Peter J. Rubinstein, "The Next Century," in *Tanu Rabbanan: Our Rabbis Taught: Essays on the Occasion of the Centennial of the Central Conference of American Rabbis*, ed. Joseph B. Glaser (New York: CCAR, 1990), 136.
[131] Hertzberg, *The Jews*, 382–383.
[132] "Reform Judaism: A Centenary Perspective." *Central Conference of American Rabbis* (1976), accessed 26 July 2000, http://www.ccarnet.org/platforms/centenary.html.

ism's best hope for confronting whatever the future holds for us."[133] The Platform also emphasized the need for "creating a Jewish home centered on family devotion,... [and] keeping the Sabbath and the holy days."[134]

Feminism and Other Social Changes and the Reform Movement

During the 1970s, women began to explore their religious experience after the "gradual awakening to the fact that theology is very much rooted in the experience – generally, male experience."[135] The movement from women being on the periphery to the center of the Jewish religion began at the end of the 19th Century when women became the "spiritual exemplars" in their families.[136] Jewish women began preaching in synagogues during the early part of the 20th Century, and in 1921 Martha Neumark petitioned the HUC for ordination. The faculty approved it, on a close vote, but the board of governors turned down the petition.[137] From 1951–1953, Paula Ackerman, a widowed *rebbitzin*, served as the *de facto* rabbi for her deceased husband's congregation.[138] By 1956, 72 percent of Reform congregations had had women presidents; by 1970 that number had risen to 96 percent, showing the growing acceptance of women leaders in the Reform house of worship and the influence of the growing feminist movement. In 1972, Sally Preisand became the first woman ordained by HUC. The CCAR had over 300 women members by 2001.[139] *Gates of Prayer* had addressed some gender issues by removing male language, though G-d was still referred to as a male.[140]

In the 1980s, the CCAR had to readdress gender-neutral language because Reform congregations were rewriting the services themselves. The 1982 edition of *Gates of Prayer* shows "a growing sensitivity to the need for liturgy which is sexually neutral"[141] as promulgated by the increasingly powerful feminist move-

---

133 Ibid., "Diversity Within Unity."
134 Ibid.
135 Carol P. Christ, and Judith Plaskow. "Preface," in *Womanspirit Rising: A Feminist Reader in Religion*, ed. by Carol P. Christ and Judith Plaskow (New York: Harper &Row, Pub., 1979), x.
136 Ellen M. Umansky, "Spiritual Expressions; Jewish Women's Religious Lives in the Twentieth Century United States," in *Jewish Women in Historical Perspective*, ed. by Judith R. Baskin (Detroit: Wayne State Univ. Press, 1991), 266.
137 Ibid., 278–279.
138 Ibid., 280.
139 Levy, *A Vision*, 197.
140 Meyer, *A Response*, 380.
141 Wollheim, "Reform Passover," 1.

ment that expanded the number of women rabbis. Rabbi Elyse Goldstein proposed a gender-neutral language edition of *Gates of Repentance* in 1988, but the Committee on Liturgy turned it down because "the large number of volumes in circulation at the present time would not make a revision helpful."[142]

A decade after its publication, Bronstein's Haggadah was still very popular. Rabbi Elliot L. Stevens, director of publications at the CCAR, praised it: "with nearly 400,000 copies in print after nine printings, our Haggadah has achieved...undisputed status as a modern classic of the genre."[143] This in turn encouraged the Executive Board's statement in 1990 that "all new publications will need to reflect gender-neutral language."[144] Bronstein finally got his gender-neutral language, but he had to wait for the Movement to catch up with his fore thinking. The CCAR revised *Gates of Prayer*[145] to include gender-neutral references to G-d to meet the new guidelines set out by the CCAR Executive Board in 1990 that required "all new publications...to reflect gender-neutral language."[146]

Another influx of Jewish immigrants who arrived between 1975 and 1979 influenced American Jewry. Over 58,000 Russian Jews came to American shores, followed by a steady flow of Israelis during the 1970s.[147] Neither of these groups was knowledgeable or interested in Jewish ritual. The Reform Movement did not appeal to these new arrivals because Russian Jewish immigrants did not appreciate public religious practice, nor did they identify the non-Orthodox movements as Jewish.[148]

---

142 H. Leonard Poller, "Report of the Committee on Liturgy." Proceedings of the Central Conference of American Rabbis, Jerusalem, Israel, 7–13 March 1988. *Central Conference of American Rabbis Yearbook*, vol. 98 (New York: CCAR, 1989), 137.
143 Elliot L. Stevens, to Colleague, 20 January 1984. Jacob Rader Marcus Center of the American Jewish Archives, Cincinnati Campus, Hebrew Union College – Jewish Institute of Religion, MS coll. CCAR Nearprint, special topics/CCAR 1984.
144 "Actions of the Executive Board 1989–1990," Central Conference of American Rabbis Annual Convention, Seattle, Washington, 22–28 June 22–28, 1990. *Year Book of the Central Conference of American Rabbis*, vol. 100 (New York: CCAR, 1991), 253.
145 Chaim Stern, *Gates of Prayer for Shabbat and Weekdays* שערי תפלה לשבת ויום חול: *A Gender Sensitive Prayerbook* (New York: CCAR, 1994).
146 CCAR Executive Board, "Actions of the Executive Board 1989–1990," Proceedings of the Central Conference of American Rabbis, Seattle, Washington, 22–29 June 1990. *Central Conference of American Rabbis Yearbook*, vol. 100 (New York: CCAR, 1991), 253.
147 Ibid., 8.
148 Sam Klinger, "Russian–Jewish Immigrants in the U.S.: Social Portrait Challenges, and AJC Involvement," *American Jewish Committee Commission on Contemporary Jewish Life*, accessed 5 August 2014, http://www.ajcrussion.org/site/nlet/content2.aspx?c=chLMK3PKsF&b-7718799&ct=11713359.

In 1992, after discussions during 1990 and 1991,[149] a Russian-Hebrew edition of the Haggadah was produced to meet the needs of the Russian Jewish immigration to the United States and Israel, "along with a parallel (and equally gratifying) re-awakening of opportunities for and interest in Jewish observances in Russian itself."[150] The liturgy was in demand immediately and the CCAR sought donations to help ship the books to Moscow in time for Seder.[151] Soviet Jews had no Jewish education formal or informal, and this non-liturgical material was most important to reconnect the Soviet Jews with Judaism and Passover.

In some respects, the CCAR was still working on creating a *Minhag America*, Rabbi Isaac Meyer Wise's dream. This Haggadah was the second most popular in the United States, 2nd only to the Manischewitz Haggadah. In addition, with a Russian language version, they were reaching out to large portion of the Jewishly unaffiliated and providing them with a Seder. The volume of number of people who were using this Haggadah made it the standard – the *Haggadah America* if you will.

However, Reform rabbis understood that they had to continue to be innovative in order to keep their congregations vibrant.[152] The ability to take part in social justice programs and the Israeli victory of the 1967 Six Day War, which gave Jews worldwide a feeling of pride, also brought about a need for a new Reform platform. The centenary of the UAHC was also a factor. Rabbi Eugene Borowitz, who chaired the committee that created the Century Platform, noted that the CCAR appreciated that the Reform Movement had "become the model for other Jewish movements in this country [America]...so the centenary of the Union would say a good deal about American Jewry as a whole."[153] The CCAR

---

149 "Summary of Committee Activity 1990–91," Committees and Members. Central Conference of American Rabbis Annual Convention, Fort Lauderdale, Florida, 23–27 June 1991 and San Antonio, Texas, 6–9 April 1992. *Year Book of the Central Conference of American Rabbis*, vol. 101–102 (New York: CCAR, 1993), 75.
150 Elliot L. Stevens, to Colleagues and Friends, February 1992. Jacob Rader Marcus Center of the American Jewish Archives, Cincinnati Campus, Hebrew Union College – Jewish Institute of Religion, MS coll. CCAR 4/CCAR 1992.
151 "Haggadahs to Moscow." *News Letter: Central Conference of American Rabbis* (February 1992), 1. Jacob Rader Marcus Center of the American Jewish Archives, Cincinnati Campus, Hebrew Union College – Jewish Institute of Religion, MS coll. CCAR Nearprint, special topics/CCAR 1984.
152 Leon I. Feur, "Summary and Prospect." In *Retrospect and Prospect: Essays in Commemoration of the Seventy-fifth Anniversary of the Founding of The Central Conference of American Rabbis: 1889–1864*. Edited by Bertram Wallace Korn (New York: CCAR, 1965), 266.
153 Eugene Borowitz, "How a Document Came to be Written," in *Reform Judaism Today: Book Two What we Believe* (New York: Behrman House, 1977), 160–161.

had become divided over the issue of intermarriage and President Robert Kahn pushed for a "definition of our movement which can pull together its disparate factions."[154] This was reinforced by lay members and leaders who felt that the "movement no longer had a clear sense of direction."[155] The committee realized that trying to address such diversity could end up with a statement so "bland to the point of being contentless." An original draft was rejected for just that reason.[156]

The "Reform Judaism: A Centenary Perspective" "reflected the state of the movement,"[157] especially as American Jews were struggling with a new post-Holocaust theology and counter-cultural spokespersons made problematic references about G-d.[158] It was only in the 1960s that serious reflection on and study of the Holocaust had begun.[159] The new platform addressed the fragmentation of the Movement[160] in the introduction: "Our Sense of the Unity of our Movement Today."[161] The Reform Movement had been struggling to maintain the membership of 3rd- and 4th-generation Reform Jews who liked the Classical Reform traditions they had grown up with. Therefore, the Movement sought to reconcile the desire to maintain these traditions with a growing number of Jews by choice, an increase in the number of formerly Conservative and Orthodox members who liked traditional Judaism's customs, as well as, the views of members from a broad array of socio-economic backgrounds. The platform instructed the community to engage in "private prayer and public worship; [and] daily religious observance." While there is an affirmation of "individual autonomy" in the Platform, Reform Judaism now officially recognized the importance of Jewish tradition,[162] while appreciating there was a diversity of practice. Charles A. Kroloff, past CCAR president, warned that the platform should not be viewed as the

---

154 Ibid., 167.
155 Ibid., 162.
156 Ibid., 178.
157 Meyer, *A Response*, 383.
158 Dana Evan Kaplan, "Reform Jewish Theology and the Sociology of Liberal Religion in America: The Platforms as response to the perception of socioreligious crisis." *Modern Judaism* 20 (2000): 68.
159 Levy, *A Vision*, 183.
160 Meyer, *A Response*, 383.
161 *Reform Judaism: A Centenary Perspective* (Central Conference of American Rabbis, 1976), accessed 5 December 2010, http://www.ccarnet.org/platforms/rabbis-speak/platforms/reform-judaism-centary-perspective/.
162 Ibid., sec. 4.

ultimate one because "there must be an evolving standard for Reform Jews from which we can sense that we have been commanded to fulfill *mitzvot*."[163]

Modernity and the Reform Movement

The rise of feminism also influenced gender roles and the CCAR addressed this through the 1983 resolution accepting patrilineal descent. The push for acceptance of children born to Jewish fathers was because religious leaders understood that "the Jewish group faces demographic losses both through the assimilation of the Jewish partner in the marriage and through the loss of children born to such marriages,"[164] as well as a desire on the part of the Jewish spouses in religiously mixed marriages who wanted to raise their children as Jews.[165] After all, in the 1960s, only 63 percent of Jewish fathers raised the children of intermarriage Jewishly versus the 98 percent of Jewish mothers in the same situation.[166]

Rabbi Peter J. Rubinstein, Senior Rabbi of Central Synagogue in Manhattan, predicted that as the 21st Century approached, American Jews would be less and less Jewishly educated. Thus they would demand rabbis to explain Jewish practices more and aid the worshipper in obtaining an intimate relationship with G-d, rather than leading a performance.[167] Alan M. Dershowitz, professor at Harvard Law School, published *The Vanishing American Jew* in 1997 articulating a fear that had begun to be discussed in the 1960s: "American Jewish life is in danger of disappearing."[168] He was reiterating what Sidney Goldstein, demographer, had said in his 1981 study: "The growth rate [of American Jews] is likely to continue to decline, and may even become negative in the not too distant future."[169] Goldstein based his statement on the "low Jewish birthrate, the losses sustained through intermarriage and assimiliation,... [and] higher levels of mortality due to

---

163 Charles A. Kroloff, "Unity within Diversity," in *Tanu Rabbanan: Our Rabbis Taught: Essays on the Occasion of the Centennial of the Central Conference of American Rabbis*, ed. Joseph B. Glaser (New York: CCAR, 1990), 102.
164 Sidney Goldstein, "Jews in the United States: Perspectives from Demography." *Jewish American Year Book* (1981), 21, accessed 5 June 2014, http://www.acjarchives.org/AJC_DATA/Files/1981_3_SpecialArticles.pdf.
165 Bernard Susser and Charles S. Liebman, "American Jews: New Images," in *Choosing Survival: Strategies for a Jewish Future* (New York: Oxford Univ. Press, 1999), 84.
166 Goldstein, "Jews in the United States," 25.
167 Ibid., 142–143.
168 Alan M. Dershowitz, *The Vanishing American Jew* (New York: Touchstone, 1997), 1.
169 Goldstein, "Jews in the United States," 9.

the aging of the population,"[170] and, thus, predicted in 1970 a loss of Jewish identity,[171] but softened that prediction in his 1981 report. He saw "the potential for continued vitality."[172] Part of the fear that assimilation was the future was because no longer did Jews have to be Jewish because of outside pressure. Social conformity did not include religious affiliation. Institutional anti-Semitism had been eliminated, as well. Jews no longer lived in Jewish neighborhoods and, so, found locating Jewish spouses problematic. Social conformity, anti-Semitism, and residence in Jewish neighborhoods had kept Jews within Judaism. Arnold M. Eisen, professor in the Department of Religious Studies at Stanford University, predicted that without separation, which Jews at the time were unwilling to do, Judaism would change drastically. However, he also did not believe Judaism would disappear.[173]

By the 1990s, "Jews have become," as Goldstein explained, "part of the very fabric of American life."[174] Over the 20 years since the last population survey, the most conservative estimate was only a 1 million person increase to 6,840,000 Jews in the United States;[175] however, Jews had proportionally shrunk to under 2.4 percent of the overall population.[176] Their dispersion around the country had also changed dramatically. By 1990, only 43.6 percent were in the Northeast, with 45.1 percent equally divided between the South and the West, and 11.3 percent in the Midwest.[177] According to the North American Jewish Data Bank, Southern Jews were affiliated with synagogues at a higher rate than their northern counterparts.[178] While 23 percent of American Jews were children of immigrants in 1970, definitely lower than the numbers 50 year earlier, by 1990 that number had dropped to 9 percent.[179] Intermarriage rates rose to over 60 percent

---

170 Sidney Goldstein, "Profile of American Jewry: Insights from the 1990 National Population Survey." *Jewish American Year Book* (1992), 77, accessed 5 June 2014, http://www.jewishdatabank.org/Studies/downloadFile.cfm?FileID=3004.
171 Ibid., 93.
172 Ibid., 59.
173 Arnold Eisen, "The American Jewish Experience." *The Jerusalem Quarterly* 38 (1986): 85.
174 Goldstein, "Profile of American Jewry," 77.
175 Ibid., 93.
176 Sheskin and Dashefsky, *Jewish Population in the United States, 2010*, 3.
177 Ibid., 97.
178 Peter B. Friedman, Sidney Goldstein, and Mark Alan Zober, "Factors Influencing Synagogue Affiliation: A Multi-Community Analysis," 11–24. *Building an Awareness of a Continental Jewish Community*, North American Jewish Data Bank, Occasional Paper No. 3, May 1987.
179 Goldstein, "Profile of American Jewry," 108.

and only 25 percent of these couples were raising their children Jewish.[180] Of American Jews, 38 percent defined themselves as Reform Jews.[181]

The Jewish community continued to age, as well. The median age of the Jewish core was 37.3 years, by 1990.[182] Reform Judaism was still a religion for younger Jews because only 31 percent of the elderly Jews claimed to belong to the Reform Movement, while 50 percent of those between 25 and 44 belonged and 35 percent of those under 25 defined themselves as Reform.[183] By 1998, there were almost 820 Reform congregations and over 300,000 member units.[184] Ritual observance continued to grow in importance for all Jews: over 38 percent of American Jews lit Sabbath candles at least sometimes over the course of a year, over 80 percent attended a Seder at least sometimes, and nearly 75 percent lit Hanukkah candles.[185] Close to 38 percent of Jews who lit Hanukkah candles also had, at least on occasion, a Christmas tree.[186]

A Reinvention of the Reform Movement

Despite the admonition of the Committee on Liturgy in 1988 "that the large number of volumes [of Haggadah] in circulation at the present time would not make a revision helpful,"[187] committee members changed their minds in time for the 1989 Convention and explained that they "discussed proposals for either a new CCAR *Haggadah* or a children's *Haggadah*."[188] In 1995, "it was moved and seconded that the CCAR revised the current Haggadah, including guidance for users."[189] This was defeated. The Summary of Committee Activity did not say

---

180 Ibid., 126–127.
181 Ibid., 129.
182 Ibid., 105.
183 Ibid., 130.
184 Meyer, "Thank You," 39.
185 Goldstein, "Profile of American Jewry," 172.
186 Ibid., 138.
187 H. Leonard Poller, "Report of the Committee on Liturgy," Central Conference of American Rabbis Annual Convention, Jerusalem, Israel, 7–13 March 1988. *Year Book of the Central Conference of American Rabbis*, vol. 98 (New York: CCAR, 1989), 137.
188 H. Leonard Poller, "Report of the Committee on Liturgy," Central Conference of American Rabbis Annual Convention, Cincinnati, Ohio, 21–26 June 1989. *Year Book of the Central Conference of American Rabbis*, vol. 99 (New York: CCAR, 1990), 202.
189 "Summary of Committee Activity 1995–96," Committees and Members. Central Conference of American Rabbis Annual Convention, Jerusalem, Israel, 8–13 March 1995 and Philadelphia, Pennsylvania, 24–28 March 1996. *Year Book of the Central Conference of American Rabbis*, vol. 106–107 (New York: CCAR, 1997), 346.

why though one could suppose that this was because the discussion had begun with the idea of a new Haggadah, rather than a revision. Even the idea of a supplement "with a guide on how to conduct a seder" did not succeed.[190] However, Steven's move "for a totally new Haggadah" with optional readings, more accessible language, and simplicity for beginners, among other criteria was adopted.[191] Knobel saw the need for "a Haggadah that really reflected the voices of women...[that would represent] a commitment to the role of women."[192]

Both Knobel and Hoffman explained to the conference that one of the main considerations for new liturgies should be to meet the needs and expectations of the laity, a new concept of grassroots liturgy development.[193] American Jews were returning to tradition and ritual[194] even with intermarriage above 30 percent.[195]

In 1997, Rabbi Richard Levy, CCAR president, suggested it was time for a new Reform platform because it was "time to chart a new course for our movement in the twenty-first century."[196] This would be, as the previous 3 platforms were, a response to "a perceived crisis in American Judaism."[197] He advocated for a return to *kedushah* through traditional practices.[198] While critics appreciated that Levy was responding to the call of many Reform Jews to become more traditional, they criticized him for "obscuring the essence of Reform Judaism."[199] Such leaders as Rabbi Robert Seltzer, professor of Jewish History at Hunter College of the City of New York, called for a re-examination of the 1885 Pittsburgh Platform.[200] He and others berated Levy for falling prey to current trends[201] despite Kroloff's contention that Reform Judaism must continue to evolve[202] and suggest-

---

190 Ibid.
191 Ibid.
192 Knobel, Interview.
193 Elliot L. Stevens, "The Prayer Books, They Are A'Changin'." *Reform Judaism* (summer 2006), accessed 17 November 2008, http://urj.org//worship/mishkan/current//?syspage=article&item_id=3588.
194 Peter J. Rubinstein, "The Next Century," in *Tanu Rabbanan: Our Rabbis Taught: Essays on the Occasion of the Centennial of the Central Conference of American Rabbis*, ed. Joseph B. Glaser (New York: CCAR, 1990), 136, 144.
195 Ibid., 144.
196 Richard N. Levy, "Is It Time to Chart a New Course for Reform Judaism?" *Reform Judaism* (winter 1998), 12.
197 Levy, *A Vision*, 2.
198 Levy, "Is It Time," 18.
199 Robert Seltzer, "This is Not the Way." *Reform Judaism* (winter 1998), 24.
200 Ibid., 24.
201 Ibid., 26.
202 Kroloff, "Unity," 102.

ed more reflection before a new set of principles be decided.[203] However, at the same time, Rabbi Elliot Stevens, Director of Publications at the CCAR, called "for a totally new Haggadah...[that] should include guidelines on choreography... have more accessible language, and be readily usable by beginners,"[204] clearly a call to address the needs of the new Jews by choice and those who were returning to "traditional practices." The motion was accepted by the CCAR.[205]

Conclusion

Haggadot liturgies reflected the issues Jews in the second half of the 20th Century faced with additions of readings about the creation of Israel, poems remember the pain of the Holocaust, and the addition of gender-neutral language and the *Kos Miriam*. As the agenda changed in the Reform Movement to becoming a more international organization, with their outreach to Russian Jews, just as it had been in the past to Eastern European immigrants to the United States and women, so too did their liturgy. Bronstein's Haggadah was translated into Russian and both the prayerbook and Haggadah became gender-neutral. The non-liturgical material reflected the further removal of Reform American Jews from their immigrant past that had focused on traditional practices. Additionally, as the theology shifted to become more spiritual and more accepting of what had been considered superstitious and extraneous because of the overwhelming number of Easter European Jews who joined the Reform Movement, the non-liturgical parts of the Haggadah reflected, sometimes quite obviously, these changes, for example, by addressing the reason why Elijah has been returned to the Seder.

---

[203] Seltzer, "This is," 80.
[204] "Summary of Committee Activity 1995–1996," 346.
[205] Ibid.

Chapter 7:
The Reform Movement and the Non Liturgical Elements in the CCAR Haggadot in the New Millennium

> "We shall turn towards the open, secular society not despite our faith but because of it, and we shall achieve great things for ourselves and our fellow-men."
>
> Jacob Neusner[1]

As the world moved towards a new century, the Central Conference of American Rabbis (CCAR) realized that it had to address the new century and new millennium. The Conference had moved from a strict Science of Judaism approach to a more accepting, and at times, traditional view of Judaism. Some Americans, including Jewish Americans, were becoming more engaged with religious traditions and wanted ritual returned to their lives. Various groups within the Movement called for change.

A New Platform

At the 1999 CCAR Convention, a new "Statement of Principles" was accepted. It acknowledged the two Platforms and Centenary Perspective that had come before, "reaffirm[ed] the central tenets of Judaism – G-d, Torah and Israel," and reminded everyone of the "the diversity of Reform Jewish beliefs and practices."[2] One can clearly see Rabbi Richard Levy's, past President of the CCAR, mark on this document as the introduction refers to "transform[ing] our lives through *kedushah*" with a prayer as part of the conclusion.[3] The slight to women in the Centenary Perspective "that women have full rights to practice Judaism,"[4] rather

---

[1] Jacob Neusner, "Judaism in Freedom," in *Understanding American Judaism: Toward the description of a modern religion. vol. II: Sectors of American Judaism: Reform, Orthodoxy, Conservatism, and Reconstructionism*, ed. Jacob Neusner (New York: KTAV Pub. House, 1975), 314.
[2] "A Statement of Principles for Reform Judaism," Central Conference of American Rabbis, Annual Conference, Pittsburgh, Pennsylvania, May 1999.
[3] Ibid.
[4] "What We Have Taught." *Reform Judaism: A Centenary Perspective*. CCAR 1976. Accessed 5 December 2010, http://www.ccarnet.org/platforms/rabbis-speak/platforms/reform-judaism-centary-perspective/.

than "women are equal," which suggests "that there may be areas of Jewish practice in which men and women differ"[5] was corrected in "A Statement of Principles." This document was written when the full influence of the Feminist Movement was being felt. It promised "to fulfill Reform Judaism's historic commitment to the complete equality of women and men in Jewish life."[6]

Some criticism remained that the theological foundation found in previous documents as well as the emphasis on reason were missing, though Levy believed the emphasis on study and scholarship mitigated such complaints.[7] The hope of the Conference was that "the Pittsburgh Principles will prove to be an important force shaping the Reform Movement's perception of itself and other people's understanding of us…and…prove to be a guide to assist Reform Jews…to resist the trends in the common culture that so often degrade us."[8] Rabbi Dana Evan Kaplan, scholar of American Judaism, however, warned that this new platform, while being gender inclusive, also has no solid theological basis, making it "very difficult for them [Reform Jews] to pass on those beliefs to their children and grandchildren. As ethnicity continues to wane, this lack of theological clarity will become a more and more serious problem."[9]

Rabbi Paul J. Menitoff, Executive Vice-President of the CCAR, saw the Platform entirely differently. He believed it "provides our laypeople with a simple statement of what it means to be a Reform Jew" that individuality in approach to Judaism is acceptable.[10] While Kaplan is concerned with the intellectual elite, the community that had founded the Reform Movement, Menitoff understood the needs of the folk, those who live the Movement.

During this time of change in the United States' Reform Movement, Reform Judaism also grew in Europe. Already in 1956 the Leo Baeck Institute was opened in London. It offered, along with other programs in Judaica, ordination for Progressive (Reform) rabbis,[11] but it was not until 1999 that the Abraham Geiger College in Potsdam was opened, thus returning a Reform Jewish seminary to the

---

5 Richard N. Levy, *A Vision of Holiness: The Future of Reform Judaism* (New York: URJ Press, 2005), 197.
6 "A Statement of Principles for Reform Judaism." Central Conference of American Rabbis Annual Conference, Pittsburgh, Pennsylvania, May 1999, "Israel."
7 Levy, *A Vision*, 9.
8 Ibid., 13.
9 Dana Evan Kaplan, "Reform Jewish Theology and the Sociology of Liberal Religion in America: The Platforms as response to the perception of socioreligious crisis." *Modern Judaism* 20 (2000): 73.
10 Paul J. Menitoff, "Pittsburgh Principles: A Continuing Process." *CCAR Journal* (winter 2000): 13.
11 *2014–2015 Prospectus* (London: Leo Beck Institute, 2014), 4.

Movement's founding country. The CCAR saw this as the "catalyst for the rejuvenation of European Judaism."[12] The 3 institutions that ordain Reform rabbis pledged to work together to "strengthen their sense of Progressive Judaism as a World Movement."[13] The CCAR, the largest Reform rabbinic organization in the world, had to address this changing world.

A New Haggadah for a New Century

In 1997 the *Criteria for a New Haggadah* was set down in writing by Rabbi Peter Knobel and the Ad Hoc Committee for Haggadah Development. It included such stipulations as it "will be for adults, written in contemporary, gender-inclusive language with an explicit mission to be more representative of women's contributions;" it "will contain all of the traditional rubrics, in sequence, with as much of the traditional material as would be acceptable to a mainstream Reform audience." The criteria also stipulated that supplemental materials will include historical notes, alternative prayers, and the like; this Haggadah will be intellectual, but not inaccessible; and "recognize that newcomers to Judaism or those newly participating in a Passover Seder are every bit as educated and sophisticated as those who have been participating in Seders for some time."[14] This inclusion was in response to the rising intermarriage rates[15] and continued rising participation in Jewish holiday celebrations.[16] For these reasons Rabbi Sue Levi Elwell was chosen as author of the new CCAR Haggadah because she is "bright, talented, has a PhD, [is] a leader in Jewish feminism, [and has a] track record in leadership."[17] Elwell had published two Haggadot already, one with the Jewish Center in Los Angeles, and had consulted on a number of feminist Haggadot, as well.[18]

---

12 Ralf Melzner and Stefanie Flamm, "New Rabbinical School Praised." *Abraham Geiger Kolleg*, 14 November 2000, accessed 17 September 2011, http://abraham-geiger-kolleg.de.
13 Kim Zeitman, "Leadership and Jewish Peoplehood North American and European Rabbinical Students Join Together at HUC-JIR/Jerusalem." *Chronicle* [HUC–JIR] 70 (2007): 8–9.
14 Peter Knobel, et al., Criteria for a New Haggadah. Ad Hoc Committee for Haggadah Development, 2 April 1997.
15 Peter B. Friedman, Sidney Goldstein, and Mark Alan Zober, "Factors Influencing Synagogue Affiliation: A Multi-Community Analysis." In *Building an Awareness of a Continental Jewish Community* (North American Jewish Data Bank, Occasional Paper No. 3, May 1987), 126.
16 Laurence Kotler-Berkowitz, et al., *The National Jewish Population Survey 2000–01 Strength, Challenge and Diversity in the American Jewish Population* (New Haven: Berman Institute – North American Jewish Databank, Updated January 2004), "Errata," accessed 6 June 2014, http://jewishfederations.org/local_includes/downloads/4606.pdf.
17 Peter Knobel, Interview by author, 7 August 2013.

In 1999, A Statement of Principles for Reform Judaism was adopted by the CCAR. In it, the CCAR affirms that "Jews have remained firmly rooted in Jewish tradition, even as we have learned much from our encounters with other cultures."[19] Reform Judaism supports "the creation of homes rich in Jewish learning and observance" and "inclusive communities" that include converts and the intermarried.[20]

Elwell was quite aware of the international reach of Reform Judaism and wanted her Haggadah to appeal to the entire English speaking world, at least. She "didn't see it as a limited audience, but a potentially enormous audience."[21] This was not an unrealistic goal as the World Union for Progressive Judaism (WUPJ) has grown stupendously in the last two decades with over 100 new congregations to a total of 1,176 Reform Jewish congregations around the world in 2014.[22] Plus, the CCAR had a partnership with the Abraham Geiger Institute and the Leo Baeck Institute to promote international Reform Judaism outreach. The project took years to complete and during that time Elwell shared various sections of the text with people who used them during Seders and then provided feedback. Her great disappointment was that the CCAR members were not able to provide creative prayers or interpretations for her to use.[23]

As part of the "Introduction" she included material on "The Haggadah in History"[24] and "Haggadot in the Reform Tradition."[25] Elwell felt that her Haggadah "reflects the historic commitment of Reform Judaism to consider tradition in the light of historical and contemporary scholarship and experience."[26] As the CCAR was over 100 years old at this point, there was tradition to follow in the Reform Movement. Even though the thrust of the movement is to respond to the changing needs of its constituents, humans by nature like tradition. She drew on feminist texts and international Jewish culture developments to draw in the next generation.[27] Additionally, there was a public acknowledgement of inter-religious families, Jews by choice, and non-European Jewries.

---

[18] Sue Levi Elwell, Interview by author, 14 February 2014.
[19] "A Statement."
[20] Ibid., "Israel."
[21] Elwell, Interview.
[22] Joel Oseran, "Reform Judaism Worldwide." *Reform Judaism* (spring 2014), 32–33.
[23] Ibid.
[24] Sue Levi Elwell, כל-דכפין *The Open Door: A Passover Haggadah* (New York: CCAR, 2002), viii.
[25] Ibid., ix–x.
[26] Ibid., ix.
[27] Hara Person, "RE: CCAR Yearbook inquiry." Email to author, 7 August 2013.

In the greeting, "An Abundance of Blessings – New and Old," she explained the difference between using את, the feminine you, and אתה, the masculine you, in prayers.[28] Here Elwell's devotion to feminism comes forth along with a response to the growing desire for more Hebrew in Jewish prayers among Reform Jews.[29] As she explained, "once you realize you've been exclusive, you can't go back without apologizing along the way. I don't want my children, boys or girls, thinking that G-d is male, or a Jewish leader has to be, or a Jew has to have a beard."[30]

The purpose of "Preparing for Passover"[31] and "Setting the Table,"[32] which includes explanations of "בדיק חמץ" and the symbols of the Seder, was because

> there are lots of people who have never been to a Seder and now they are making a Seder. It is about empowering people to claim Judaism as their own and to get a teacher. And so I the writer, get to be the teacher. The door is open, come in and learn, and I'll help you. This is not about mastering a skill and doing it perfectly. It is about inviting people to have an experience that you are facilitating. So I want to give some guidelines in the book so that you can feel empowered and open-hearted about this. How blessed am I that I can sing at my Seder. It is really to be a guide.[33]

In "Preparing for Passover," Elwell reminds her readers that "Jews clean our homes and examine our hearts to prepare for Passover."[34] She refrains from dividing Jews into movements, instead using "many Jews"[35] to explain who cleans their homes of leavening. This clearly addresses the *Criteria*'s call for containing traditional rubrics and belief that individuality is what makes Judaism powerful. The inclusiveness that the Mvoement was addressing in the new century is key to Elwell's avoidance of words that would divide the members. Thus, by offering instruction for traditional rubrics, there is the opportunity for the Jewishly uneducated to learn about practice and then choose to do it or not. She described the meaning of the symbolic foods, such as *charoset*:

> Charoset is a mixture of fruits, nuts, and wine that reminds us of the clay or the mortar that the Israelites used to build the palaces and pyramids of Egypt. The fruits and nuts serve as

---

28 Ibid., xi–xiii.
29 Jeffery Wildstein, "Hebrew in the Reform Movement." *CCAR Journal: A Reform Jewish Quarterly* (winter 2005): 82–84.
30 Elwell, Interview.
31 Elwell, כל-דכפין, xiii–xiv.
32 Ibid., xiv–xix.
33 Elwell, Interview.
34 Elwell, כל-דכפין, xiii.
35 Ibid.

a reminder of the trees under which Israelite women gave birth in an attempt to keep secret the arrival of their imperiled infants.[36]

Such an interpretation speaks of her feminist leaning and a modern interpretation of texts in Reform Judaismm, yet it does not belittle the traditional interpretation as earlier editions had.

She noted in the "Introduction," in keeping with her feminist leanings, that *Kos Miryam* is included[37] and a vegetarian substitute for the פסח.[38] The latter substitution supports the 1999 Statement of multiculturalism. The closing of the initial section of the Haggadah included an explanation of the modern feminist tradition of placing an orange on the Seder Plate. This description was placed here, apart from the liturgy, because putting the explanation in the liturgy would interrupt the flow of the service.[39] For Elwell, the "Introduction" "was not about cleaning your home. It was about preparing your heart....It never occurred in our Observant Reform home that breakfast cereal isn't appropriate for Passover. I wanted people to think about and acknowledge the chametz in our hearts. It will be different for everyone. Putting it in gives people more options."[40]

Again, the CCAR's Haggadah received praise. *Publisher's Weekly* said that it "fulfills its own stated goal of being 'the essential Jewish travel guide,' using the seder to transport readers from the past through the present to the future. A product of Reform Judaism, the book seeks to embrace and celebrate the 'expanded' Jewish community, drawing upon the writings of female rabbis and relating Passover customs from all over the world."[41] *The Mothers Circle* complimented it for "provid[ing] both technical and spiritual instructions for Passover preparation and the steps of the *seder.*"[42] The reviewer believed that "this is a *haggadah* that can be accessible and enriching for participants with a range of prior experience."[43] Rabbi Mary L. Zamore, of the Jewish Center of Northwest New Jersey, called it "a heady ideological Haggadah."[44] Rabbi

---

36 Ibid., xvi.
37 Elwell, כל-דכפין, xiv–xv.
38 Ibid., xvi.
39 Elwell, Interview.
40 Ibid.
41 Review of "The Open Door: A Passover Haggadah," by Sue Levi Elwell. *Publisher's Weekly*, 18 February 2002, accessed 24 January 2013, http://www.publishersweekly.com/978-0-88123-079-6.
42 Review of "The Open Door: A Passover Haggadah," by Sue Levi Elwell. *The Mothers Circle*, 2014, accessed 28 July 2014, http://www.joi.org/motherscircle/index.php?page=education-Passoverhaggadot.
43 Ibid.
44 Mary L. Zamore, Interview by author, 10 January 2014.

Laura Geller, of Temple Emmanuel in Beverly Hills and a partner in projects with Elwell, said, "*The Open Door* haggadah is revolutionary in its inclusiveness."[45] Elwell's goal was to "put this in the context of our [the CCAR] prayer books" and follow the current trends,[46] while the goal of the CCAR "was to create a haggadah for the next generation."[47]

Reform Judaism in the Twenty-First Century

The new century brings new challenges and new understandings. To start the millennium, new Jewish population surveys were undertaken because of the panic Alan M. Dershowitz, Harvard Law School professor, had spread with his book in 1997.[48] These surveys created another set of problems as there were questions concerning who was being counted as a Jew and how changes in this definition might affect comparisons with previous surveys. There were 6.1 million Jews counted by one survey[49] and 5.2 million by another,[50] placing Jews proportionally where they had been at the beginning of the previous century – hovering around 2 percent of the population.[51]

The variance is most likely due to the difference of who was counted as Jewish. In the former, Jewish organizations were asked to estimate the Jewish populations in their area.[52] For the latter, randomly selected people who defined themselves as Jewish, Jewishly-connected, or as having some Jewish background were interviewed and from those interviews a national population was extrapolated.[53] American Jews have continued to age and are older than the general

---

45 Ruth Andrew Ellenson, review of "The Open Door: A Passover Haggadah," by Sue Levi Elwell. *University of Southern California: Trojan Magazine* (winter 2003), accessed 28 July 2014, http://www.usc.edu/dept/pubrel/trojan_family/winter03/whats-new.html.
46 Elwell, Interview.
47 Person, Re: "CCAR Yearbook inquiry."
48 Alan M. Dershowitz, *The Vanishing American Jew* (New York: Touchstone, 1997).
49 Jim Schwartz and Jeffrey Scheckner, "Jewish Population in the United States, 2000." *Jewish American Year Book* (2000), 253, accessed 6 June 2014, http://wwwjewishdatabank.org/Studies/downloadFil.dfm?FileID=3013.
50 Kotler-Berkowitz, et al., *The National Jewish Population Survey 2000–01*, viii.
51 Sheskin and Dashefsky, *Jewish Population in the United States, 2010*, 3; Jim Schwartz, Vivian Klaff, and Frank Mott, *National Jewish Population Survey (NJPS) 2000–01* (New York: Jewish Federations of North America, 2001), accessed 31 January 2014, http://www.jewishdatabank.org/Studies/details.cfm?StudyID=307.
52 Schwartz and Scheckner, "Jewish Population in the United States, 2000," 1.
53 Kotler-Berkowitz, et al., *The National Jewish*.

United States population.⁵⁴ While the Northeast is still where the largest proportion of Jews resides, it hasn't been the area of residence for the majority of the American Jews for over a decade. Only 46 percent of American Jews are Northeasterners.⁵⁵ A decade later, that number had dropped again to 44 percent.⁵⁶ Over 30 years (between 1970 and 2012), the percentage of Jews who lived in the Northeast dropped by almost 22 percent, while the South and West had an almost 100 percent rise Jewish population.⁵⁷ The number of Jews in the United States rose even more to 5.3 million in 2013, making them 2.2 percent of the American population.⁵⁸ Thus, while the actual numbers of Jews in the United States rose, their proportion of the American population fell.

Synagogues are "arguably the most important institution in American Jewish life."⁵⁹ Forty-six percent of American Jews belong to a synagogue.⁶⁰ Thirty-eight percent of American Jews consider themselves Reform Jews and only 22 percent of American Jews define themselves as Orthodox.⁶¹ In 2001, there were a total of 3,727 in the United States: 26 percent were Reform, 40 percent Orthodox, and 23 percent Conservative. This works out to 976 Reform congregations, 879 of which belong to the Union of American Hebrew Congregations (UAHC).⁶² Of these, 339 are in major metropolitan areas.⁶³ However, the majority of Reform synagogues are not in metropolitan areas.⁶⁴ They "dominate in small communities and rural areas, especially in the South,"⁶⁵ a continued reflection of how the Reform Movement addresses the concerns and needs of the more isolated Jews. The ma-

---

54 Ibid.
55 Schwartz and Scheckner, "Jewish," 261.
56 Sheskin and Dashefsky, *Jewish Population in the United States, 2010*, Table 2.
57 Ira Sheskin and Arnold Dashefsky, *Jewish Population in the United States, 2012*, ed. Arnold Dashefsky, Sergio DellaPergola, and Ira Sheskin (Storrs, Connecticut: North American Jewish Databank, 2013), 29, accessed 6 June 2014, http://www.jewishdatabank.org/Studies/downloadFile.cfm?FileID=2917.
58 *A Portrait of Jewish Americans: Findings From A Pew Research Center Survey of U.S. Jews* (Washington, D.C.: Pew Research Center, 2013), 23, accessed 31 January 2014, http://www.jewishdatabank.org/Studies/downloadFile.cfm?FileID=3088.
59 Jim Schwartz, Jeffrey Scheckner, and Laurence Kotler-Berkowitz, "Census of U.S. Synagogues, 2001." *Jewish American Year Book* (2002), 112, accessed 6 June 2014, http://www.jewishdatabank.org/Studies/downloadFile.cfm?FileID=3022.
60 Kotler-Berkowitz, et al., *The National Jewish*, 7.
61 Kotler-Berkowitz et al., *The National Jewish*, "Errata."
62 Schwartz, Scheckner, and Kotler-Berkowitz, "Census of U.S. Synagogues," 117.
63 Ibid., 120.
64 Ibid., 122.
65 Ibid., 123.

jority of UAHC member synagogues have a maximum of 250 member families and the majority of these have a maximum of 50 member families.[66]

The importance of ritual has continued to grow in the new century. The 2000 National Jewish Population Survey tells us that 67 percent of American Jews participate in some way in a Passover Seder. This practice is only surpassed by lighting of Hanukah candles.[67] While the 2013 Pew Survey shows that over 33 percent of American Jews, regardless of affiliation or non-affiliation, attend Seders, nearly 3/4 light Hannukah candles, and over ¼ light Shabbat candles.[68] Additionally over 70 percent of Americans Jews perform at least one of these rituals regularly.[69] The idea of being publicly Jewish as acceptable was also very strong, because over 60 percent of American Jews hang a mezuzah by their front door.[70]

However, there was great concern that synagogue membership was not as high as it should be. Around the country, synagogue membership at the turn of the 21st Century was about 42 percent.[71] The National Jewish Population Survey of 2000 revealed that only 24 percent of American Jews attend services at least monthly[72] and 40 percent never go to synagogue.[73] Rabbi Rick Jacobs, Union for Reform Judaism (URJ) (the renamed UAHC) [74] president, published an opinion editorial in *JTA: The Global News Service of the Jewish People* calling for a "reorientation" of synagogues to reach out to "the fastest growing group in the Jewish community...what we too often call the 'the unaffiliated.'"[75] *Reform Judaism* and the URJ leadership, in the summer of 2011, started a think-tank dialogue about questions of concern to Reform and unaffiliated Jews in North Amer-

---

66 Allen S. Kaplan, "Small Congregations." *CCAR Journal* (summer 2000): 5.
67 Kotler-Berkowitz, et al., *The National Jewish Population*, 7.
68 Ibid., 7.
69 Ira Sheskin, *Religious Practices and Synagogue Attendance*, ed. Laurence Kotler-Berkowitz. (Storrs, Connecticut: North American Jewish Data Bank, 2013), 4, accessed 6 June 2014, http://www.jewishdatabank.org/Studies/downloadFile.cfm?FileID=2888.
70 Ibid., 6.
71 Ira Sheskin and Arnold Dashefsky, *Jewish Population in the United States, 2013*, ed. Arnold Dashefsky, Sergio DellaPergola, and Ira Sheskin (Storrs, CT: North American Jewish Databank, 2012), 27, accessed 6 June 2014, http://www.jewishdatabank.org/Studies/downloadFile.cfm?FileID=3111.
72 Sheskin, *Religious* Practices, 35.
73 Ibid., 36.
74 The UAHC changed its name in 2003 "to better reflect today's reality." ("History," Union for Reform Judaism (n.d.), accessed 6 June 2014, http://urj.org/about/union/history/.)
75 Rick Jacobs, "Op-ed: Synagogues must reach out to 'the uninspired,'" *JTA: The Global News Services of the Jewish People* 28 March 2012, accessed 28 March 2014, http://www.jta.org/news/article-print/2012/03/29/3092388/op-ed-synagogues-must-reach-out-to-the-uninspired.

ica to access what "we need to do to strengthen the Jewish future in North America."⁷⁶ The result was a "Proposed Vision Statement" that includes the following statement:

> In our sacred communities, Reform Jews make thoughtful and informed choices about how we put our values into action. We explore our spirituality, and we engage in reflection, critical study, and sacred acts in order to renew our living covenant with G-d and the Jewish people.⁷⁷

This in no way mitigates Kaplan's concerns that Reform Judaism has no central articulated theology. This may be a vision statement, not a theological one. Other than reinstating the importance of covenant, there is little guidance about what "our values" are.

A New Liturgy for a New Millennium

The Reform leadership realized it was time, yet again, to reach out to their membership and potential membership by creating a new liturgy. The effort began in earnest in 1985 with an emphasis on input from the laity. Rabbi Lawrence Hoffman, professor of Liturgy at HUC, remarked that the new prayerbook had to address such agenda items as a return to a need for sacredness, diverse constituencies, new ritual occasions, and feminist theology and language.⁷⁸

After two decades of research among its members to understand how the existing modes of worship actually reached their constituency,⁷⁹ Rabbi Peter Knobel was selected to chair the committee that would cull the survey material and create *Mishkan T'filah* – the new prayerbook. The leadership realized that with the advent of computers and inclusiveness, there was a plethora of congregationally-produced services that often crossed denominational lines.⁸⁰ Knobel made it clear that:

---

76 "Post Your Perspectives about the Jewish Future." *Reform Judaism Online* (summer 2011), accessed 6 June 2014, http://data.urj.org/rjmag/thinktank/.
77 "A New Vision for Reform Judaism." *Reform Judaism* (fall 2012), 5.
78 Elliot L. Stevens, "The Prayer Books, They Are A'Changin'." *Reform Judaism* (summer 2006), accessed 17 November 2008, http://urj.org//worship/mishkan/current//?syspage=article&item_id=3588.
79 Peter S. Knobel, "The Challenge of a Single Prayer Book," in *Platforms and Prayer Books: Theological and Liturgical Perspectives on Reform Judaism*, ed. Dana Evan Kaplan (Lanham, Maryland: Rowman & Littlefield, 2002), 155.
80 Ibid., 156.

the recommendations…suggest the following: "The new Central Conference of American Rabbis' prayer book should avoid 'theme' services, because most congregants fail to recognize the thematic messages as such, because theme services may fragment the congregation and not be relevant to all congregants. Multivocality is crucial to an effective congregational liturgy."[81]

The use of Hebrew had steadily risen since the publication of the last prayerbook because the clergy was more fluent and congregants saw it as more authentic, and so more Hebrew had to be included. In fact, 98 percent of Reform rabbis surveyed in 2001 believed Hebrew should be emphasized. An overwhelming majority also felt transliterations aided in congregational participation.[82] Transliterations, the rabbis felt, would assist congregants in becoming familiar and comfortable with the Hebrew; rather than keeping Hebrew as a language for the Jewishly educated, Hebrew could be learned through repetition.

All the prayers were faithfully translated and a traditional service was maintained with thematic alternatives, prayers and readings, offered. This permitted the leader and congregation to select a more traditional service or incorporate these alternative readings and prayers in an effort to make the service more appropriate for the moment and/or congregation. This *siddur*, in its return to traditional structure and Hebrew, was part of "addressing the needs of the Jewish people right now"[83] as Levy expressed, and a cue that "we need to remind ourselves that *Kenesset Yisrael* is not some *other* group of Jews. We are part of *Kenesset Yisrael*."[84] It does meet these needs, because as the 2013 Pew Study found that 52 percent of American Jews can pronounce Hebrew words, but that only 13 percent of Jews can understand what they are reading.[85] The CCAR's prayerbook was praised for addressing the younger generation that is comfortable with ritual, values, and inclusiveness, while helping the Hebraic illiterate with transliterations.[86] The excitement concerning the work from hundreds of UAHC congregation members garnered over 75,000 presale orders by 2006.[87]

---

81 Ibid., 160.
82 Jeffery Wildstein, "Hebrew in the Reform Movement." *CCAR Journal: A Reform Jewish Quarterly* (winter 2005): 83–85.
83 Levy, "Is It Time," 20.
84 Ibid., 21.
85 "A Portrait of Jewish Americans," *Pew Research: Religion and Public Life Project*, 1 October 2013, accessed 14 July 2013, http://www.pewforum.org/2013/10/01/jewish-american-beliefs-attitudes-culture-survey/.
86 Stuart Kelman, "Mishkan T'Filah: A reform Sidder." *Jewish Book Council* (n.d.), accessed 6 June 2014, http://www.jewishbookcouncil.org/book/mishkan-tfilah.
87 Steven, "Prayer Books."

The CCAR also published 3 new Haggadot in the new century: *The Open Door*,⁸⁸ which is "a haggadah for the next generation, one that drew on feminist text as well as Jewish history from around the Jewish world;"⁸⁹ *Sharing the Journey: The Haggadah for the Contemporary Family*,⁹⁰ which is "a haggadah ... accessible and welcoming for those with non-Jewish family members and friends around the table, and for those who might be new to leading a seder;"⁹¹ and *The New Union Haggadah*,⁹² a gender-neutral version of the Union Haggadah because "many people still have fond associations with this hagaddah."⁹³

With the ongoing acceptance of intermarriages and the Reform Movement's encouragement to interfaith families to raise their children Jewishly,⁹⁴ the CCAR publishing house realized it needed to produce a Haggadah "that was accessible and welcoming for those with non-Jewish family members and friends."⁹⁵ This is an effort to make "sure that most people can be a part of the community in an effort to encourage continuity."⁹⁶ In the new century, Rabbi Mary Zamore explained, "we [American Jews] are in an era where we are more comfortable with traditional ritual. We are happy to explore traditional ritual and find meaning in it, but not with the imperative of a halakhic mindset."⁹⁷ The UAHC, CCAR, and Hebrew Union College–Jewish Institute of Religion (HUC–JIR) understood that a new century required a new mission statement to help define the Movement. The Reform Leadership Council (RLC) Think Tank created "the first ever Vision Statement articulating what it means to be a Reform Jew."⁹⁸ It "welcomes all who seek Jewish connection," encourages members to "explore our spirituality," and urges Reform Jews to "make thoughtful and informed choices about how we put our values into action."⁹⁹

---

88 Sue Levi Elwell, כל-כפין.
89 Hara Person, "RE: CCAR Yearbook inquiry." Email to author, 7 August 2013.
90 Alan S. Yoffie *Sharing the Journey: The Haggadah for the Contemporary Family*, ill. Mark Podwal (New York: CCAR, 2012).
91 Person, "RE: CCAR."
92 Howard A. Berman, *The New Union Haggadah: Revised Edition* (New York: CCAR, 2014).
93 Person, "RE: CCAR."
94 Mara W. Cohen Ioannides, "Creating a Community: Who Can Belong to the Reform Syangogue," in *Who Is a Jew? Reflections on History, Religion, and Culture*, ed. Leonard Greenspoon (West Lafayette, Indiana: Purdue Univ. Press, 2014), 66.
95 Person, "RE: CCAR."
96 Cohen Ioannides, "Creating a Community," 73.
97 Zamore, Interview.
98 Reform Leadership Council Think Tank, "Proposed Vision Statement." *Reform Judaism* (fall 2012), 5.
99 "A New Vision for Reform Judaism."*Reform Judaism* (fall 2012), 5.

Rabbi Peter J. Rubinstein predicted in 1990, at the centenary of the CCAR, that the "movement is in a transitional stage...[and] will be different because our constituency and leadership is changing."[100] In keeping with this, Alan Yoffie developed *Sharing the Journey*. When his son started dating a Catholic woman, he had the opportunity to attend "an Outreach Training Institute seminar focused on people involved in interfaith relationships. I found it extraordinarily interesting. At one point the question of Passover came over. I asked if there was a Haggadah for the contemporary Jewish family that included non-Jews. That's how it began. That's why it is called the contemporary family."[101]

Yoffie composed such a Haggadah for his family, but felt that it could benefit others. At the time Yoffie, a lawyer by education, approached the CCAR Press, because "the CCAR wanted to publish a series of Haggadahs for different audiences."[102] Each of these would represent Reform practice. The press at that moment was looking for a Haggadah that was not overtly intellectual and addressed the needs of the current Reform Jewish constituency.[103] Zamore, who acted as a rabbinical guide for the project, discovered that her congregants who gave up participating in Seders did so because the Haggadot were not engaging, had too much Hebrew, or did not explain to the uninitiated what to do. Thus, the CCAR Press was anxious to provide an alternative for these people.[104] Rabbi Rick Jacobs, president of the CCAR, believed "interfaith families [to be] enriching [to] our congregational lives" and encouraged inclusion of these families.[105] Yoffie had two guiding thoughts as he composed this Haggdah: "Why do we celebrate Passover? Who is our target family?"[106]

Mark Podwal, the illustrator for *Sharing the Journey*, remarked that "this Haggadah is trying to draw in as many people as possible to participate in the service....There are wonderful explanations that are very inclusive, and so you can come to this seder not knowing anything."[107] Dr. Paula J. Brody, director of the

---

[100] Peter J. Rubinstein, "The Next Century," in <u>Tanu Rabbanan</u>: *Our Rabbis Taught: Essays on the Occasion of the Centennial of the Central Conference of American Rabbis*, ed. Joseph B. Glaser (New York: CCAR, 1990), 135.
[101] Alan Yoffie, Interview by author, 24 January 2014.
[102] Ibid.
[103] Zamore, Interview.
[104] Ibid.
[105] Rick Jacobs, "Keynote Address." (presented at the Union for Reform Judaism Biennial, San Francisco, California, 12 December 2013), accessed 4 January 2015, http://urj.org/biennial.
[106] Yoffie, Interview.
[107] Mark Podwel, "New Passover Seder Haggadah." *Religion & Ethics Newsweekly* 15 January 2013, accessed 30 March 2012, www.pbs.org/wnet/religionandethics/episodes/march-30-2012/new-passover-seder-haggadah/10622/.

Outreach Training Institute for the URJ, complimented Yoffie on "encourage[ing] us to be sensitive to the unique personal and religious background....[and] enabl[ing] everyone around the table to feel involved in the universal theme of the struggle for freedom, especially important for those having a first experience of attending or hosting a Passover seder."[108]

Yoffie included "A Passover Checklist,"[109] something Zamore found to be "trendy,"[110] that begins with the arranging the Seder Plate (including the options of the beet and orange), other Passover symbols, and setting the table. He was thoughtful enough to remind the reader to not only have candlesticks and candles, but also matches,[111] and that one needs a "napkin for wrapping and hiding the *afikoman*."[112] Because he "created for [him]self a checklist, what do I want to include. It became a working heading and fit appropriately and it stayed there."[113] The search for *ḥamets* is presented as a "family activity" with explanations on how to do this and the blessing for concluding the search and burning the leavening in the morning.[114] Because there are those who want to know more, Yoffie included "a moment for additional learning" where he presented Biblical and Talmudic passages to explain the eating of *ḥamets*.[115] Then the reader was presented with material on how to celebrate Passover for 7 days[116] and counting the Omer.[117]

As a service to the new Seder leaders, there is a page of helpful hints to facilitate a smooth running celebration.[118] Finally, there is a list further questions one could ask with page references to place them appropriately. For example, one might ask, after discussing matzah as a symbol of hope, what groups still suffer in some kind of servitude and "what are the responsibilities of free persons?"[119] Yoffie "thought it would be a very good thing to have a series of questions that the leader or group could choose from so that everyone could get in-

---

108 Paula J. Brody, "Forward," in *Sharing the Journey: The Haggadah for the Contemporary Family*, by Alan S. Yoffie, ill. Mark Podwal (New York: CCAR, 2012), xi.
109 Ibid., 1–4.
110 Zamore, Interview.
111 Yoffie, *Sharing the Journey*, 3.
112 Ibid., 4.
113 Yoffie, Interview.
114 Yoffie, *Sharing the Journey*, 5–6.
115 Ibid., 6.
116 Ibid., 6–7.
117 Ibid., 7.
118 Ibid., 8.
119 Ibid., 9.

volved in the conversation. You hope to get everyone involved at the beginning."[120] This is part of the desire to include the non-Jews in the event.

There is also *The Seder Leader's Guide to Sharing the Journey*, which the description claims "focuses on practical suggestions for an inclusive family seder... [and] includes explanations of seder traditions and suggests a few additional rituals."[121] No other Haggadah yet published has a separate document like this to assist the leader. In the leader's guide, Yoffie has offered explanations for numerous Seder traditions to enlighten the leader and, thus, the participants. For example, the opening section of *Sharing the Journey* is "Why Do We Celebrate Passover?" In it the leader reads a page of historical material about the holiday including: "Jewish tradition requires that each of us act as if we had personally gone forth from Egypt...By telling the story of freedom on Passover (in Hebrew: *Pesach*), we celebrate our Jewish history."[122] The section in *The Seder Leader's Guide* suggests that:

To help create a more inclusive experience, the seder leader may explain that everyone at the seder table has a responsibility to:
- Help create a joyful seder experience;
- Help each other better understand the story of the Exodus;
- Help each other to draw upon the story of our deliverance from Egypt for discovery (and rediscovery each year) of the spiritual foundation of Judaism; and
- Help each other to renew and strengthen our commitment to the pursuit of freedom, tolerance and justice.[123]

This 10 page book comes with 2 CDs of Seder songs and blessings "performed by Cantor Joshua Breitzer and Rabbi Sarah Reines" and others.[124]

Zamore believes that this Haggadah represents the Reform Movement well:

> It speaks to the importance of our tradition. It speaks to the importance of mixing modernity with our tradition. And with both the love of ritual and...modern ...with recognition that Judaism is evolving with that practical streak that Reform Judaism brings of acceptance of

---

120 Yoffie, Interview.
121 "Sharing the Journey: The Seder Leader's Guide." *Central Conference of American Rabbis* 2014, accessed 5 January 2015, http://www.ccarpress.org/shopping_product_detail.asp?pid=50236.
122 Yoffie, *Sharing the Journey*, 15.
123 Alan S. Yoffie, *The Seder Leader's Guide to Sharing the Journey: The Haggadah for the Contemporary Family* (New York: CCAR, 2012), 1.
124 Yoffie, *The Seder Leader's Guide*, back cover.

Jews of all levels. With recognition that the family that sits around the table is also evolving and changing. And we appreciate engagement with our non-Jewish family and friends.[125]

The reviews, however, were mixed. David A. M. Wilensky, of *The Times of Israel*, found it to be "terrific for its introductions and artwork, [but] bland in its content."[126] Zelda Shluker, of *Hadassah Magazine*, called it likeable.[127] Steve Lipman, of the *New York Jewish Week*, believed that "the Haggadah unambiguously speaks to readers not comfortable with classic approaches to Jewish tradition" and specially noted the introductory materials "of special value to the individual who comes to the seder with little Jewish education or none at all."[128] Benjamin Maron, of *interfaith family* a "resource supporting interfaith couples exploring Jewish life and inclusive Jewish communities,"[129] complimented the "naturally woven" telling of the Exodus story with the service and believed that Yoffie had succeeded in his desire to include the non-Jewish members of Jewish families in the service.[130]

By 2013 Bronstein's 1974 Haggadah had sold over 1 million copies.[131] "Article for Temple Bulletins," included with Stevens' letter of praise, describes the 1974 Haggadah "as embodying Reform's concern for continuity with tradition combined with latitude and scope for individual choice."[132] This new concept of choice, rather than understanding or emotion, is taken from the Statement of

---

125 Zamore, Interview.
126 David A. M. Wilensky, "Looking for a new haggada?" Review of *Sharing the Journey: The Haggadah for the Contemporary Family*, by Alan S. Yoffie, *The Times of Israel* 22 March 2012, accessed 24 January 2013, http://www.timesofisrael.com/looing-for-anew-haggada/.
127 Zelda Shluker, "Passover 2012: New Haggadot." *Hadassah Magazine* (January 2013), accessed 24 January 2013, www.hadassahmagazine.org.
128 Steve Lipman, "The Telling, And the Retelling." *The New York Jewish Week* 4 September 2012, accessed 24 January 2013, http://www.thejewishweek.com/special_sections/special_holiday_issues/telling_and_retelling.
129 *About InterfaithFamily.* n.d., accessed 7 August 2014, http://www.interfaithfamily.com/about_us_advocacy/about_us_advocacy.shtml.
130 Benjamin Moran, "Two New Haggadot for your Passover Seder." *interfaith family* (30 March 2012), accessed 24 January 2013, www.interfaithfamily.com/holidays/passover_and_easter/Two_New_Haggadot_For_Your_Passover_Seder.
131 Hara Person, Re: "CCAR Yearbook inquiry," email to author, 7 August 2013.
132 William Wollheim, "Reform Passover Haggadah Reaches Sales Milestone," Article for Temple Bulletins, 1. attached to Elliot L. Stevens to Colleague, 20 January 20, 1984. Jacob Rader Marcus Center of the American Jewish Archives, Cincinnati Campus, Hebrew Union College – Jewish Institute of Religion, MS coll. CCAR Nearprint, special topics/CCAR 1984.

Principles from 1999 that "embrace[s] religious and cultural pluralism."[133] It was described as having "introductory material and contemporary language that will contribute to any Seder."[134] The introduction was commended for "provid[ing] background on the history of the seder and there is detailed information on the practical and spiritual aspects of preparing for a seder."[135]

In 2013, the 1923 *Union Haggadah* was reprinted because "many people still have fond associations with this haggadah....Some people love the elegance and simplicity of the language. We [the CCAR Press] got many requests for it."[136] At the same time,[137] the Press was working with Rabbi Howard A. Berman, executive director of the Society for Classical Reform Judaism, on *The New Union Haggadah*, a revision of the 1923 edition. It was published in 2014. The Society for Classical Reform Judaism worked with the CCAR to produce this continuation of the Reform Movement's commitment to reaching all of its members. The Society for Classical Reform Judaism found the "reappraisal and embrace of traditional Jewish ritual observance" contrary to its desire for the more classical Reform Judaism and used the latest Platform's acceptance of multiple interpretations of Judaism to its advantage. Berman believed "this *New Union Haggadah* seeks to reflect this pluralism."[138]

Berman kept "the Classical Reform spirit...cherished by many Reform Jewish families," but made the language gender-neutral and added transliterations of the few Hebrew prayers offered. In addition, the Ten Plagues were returned to the liturgy, along with the welcoming of Elijah because he is "stubbornly ensconced in the hearts of most Reform Jews."[139] *Kos Miriam* and the orange were added, as well.[140] However, no new non-liturgical material was added.

---

133 "A Statement of Principles for Reform Judaism," Central Conference of American Rabbis Annual Conference, Pittsburgh, Pennsylvania, May 1999.
134 Carla Cohen, "Selecting Your Passover Haggadah," review of *A Passover Haggadah*, by Herbert Bronstein *Politics and Prose: Bookstore/Coffeehouse*, accessed 27 July 2014,
http://www.politics-prose.com/passover-haggadah.
135 Wollheim, "Reform Passover," 2.
136 Person, Re: "CCAR Yearbook inquiry."
137 Person, Re: "CCAR Yearbook inquiry."
138 Howard A. Berman, "Introducing the New Union Haggadah!" *Reform Judaism* (28 March 2014), accessed 28 July 2014, http://www.reformjudaism.org/blog/2014/03/28/introducing-new-union-haggadah.
139 Ibid.
140 Berman, *The New Union Haggadah*.

The reviews of this liturgy have been positive. Maron L. Waxman, of the Jewish Book Council, called it "elegant" and considers the language "elevated."[141] Jay Michaelson, of *The Jewish Daily Forward*, said it "is very old school...[but] it works....it is a Haggadah that can be used.... as the volume's introduction discusses, 'The New Union Haggadah' is also self-reflectively old school. Its editors have realized that there is value in the old-new forms of the Reform liturgy, and have embraced them."[142] The CCAR Press touted it as "blend[ing] the best of the old and the new! This thoughtful update of the beloved 1923 Haggadah preserves the elegance and beauty of the original version while making it relevant to 21st Century families."[143]

Looking Forward

The 2013 Pew Study on American Jews has raised some significant questions about Judaism in the United States and how Jews are surveyed. The 2013 Pew Survey of U.S. Jews "shows that Reform Judaism continues to be the largest Jewish denominational movement in the United States. One-third (35%) of all U.S. Jews identify with the Reform movement."[144] In addition, more Jews change their affiliation to the Reform Movement from Orthodoxy or Conservatism than move from Reform to the more orthodox movements.[145] That the Pew researchers compared their data to the questionable National Jewish Population Survey of 2000–20001 resulted in some questionable results, like a belief that Jews are abandoning Judaism. [146] Some scholars urged others to read the Pew Study results carefully because the survey did not follow expected methodological stand-

---

141 Maron L. Waxman, Review of *The New Union Haggadah, Revised Edition*, by Howard A. Berman and Benjamin Zeidman, *Jewish Book Council* (©2014), accessed 28 July 2014, http://www.jewishbookcouncil.org/book/the-new-union-haggadah-revised-edition.
142 Jay Michaelson, "All The 2014 Haggadah Info You'll Ever Need." *The Jewish Daily Forward* 3 April 2014, accessed 28 July 2014, http://forward.com/articles/195696/all-the–haggadah-info-youll-ever-need/#ixzz38nn40XN3.
143 "The New Union Haggadah." *Central Conference of American Rabbis Press* 2014, accessed 28 July 2014, http://www.ccarpress.org/shopping_product_detail.asp?pid=50125.
144 Luis Lugo, et al., *A Portrait of Jewish Americans: Findings from a Pew Research Center Survey of U.S. Jews* (Washington, D.C.: Pew Research Center, 2013), 10.
145 Ibid.
146 J. J. Goldberg, "Pew Survey About Jewish America Got It All Wrong: With Flawed Comparisons, Study Reached Faulty Conclusions." *The Jewish Daily Forward* 13 October 2013, accessed 14 July 2014, http://forward.com/articles/185461/pew-survey-about-jewish-america-got-it-all-wrong/?p=all#ixzz37TssioRu.

ards[147] and others want "some genuine, reality-grounded alarmism (I think it's justified)" concerning the results.[148]

The survey results show that "the percentage of U.S. adults who say they are Jewish when asked about their religion has declined by about half since the late 1950s and currently is a little less than 2%."[149] This is a trend throughout the United States, regardless of religious upbringing – Americans are turning away from traditional religion though they are still interested in spirituality. Sixty percent of American Jews have intermarried,[150] 50 percent of Reform couples are intermarried,[151] and only 20 percent of those are raising their children Jewish. Reform Judaism is still the largest movement in the United States with 35 percent of American Jews identifying with Reform, 18 percent with Conservative, and 10 percent with Orthodox Judaism. Over a 1/4 of Orthodox and Conservative former members have realigned with the Reform Movement. However, Orthodox Jews have the lowest median age and the highest fertility rates. Therefore, there is speculation that Orthodox Jewry will grow quickly over the next few decades. While certain ritual observance is high (70 percent of American Jews participate in a Seder), this is slightly lower than the 2000 National Jewish Population Survey results. Household membership in synagogues is about 40 percent. The American Jewish geographic distribution has stabilized at 43 percent in the Northeast, 23 percent in both the South and the West, and 11 percent in the Midwest with almost equal numbers in suburban and urban areas and only 4 percent of Jews in rural areas.[152]

The desire of the Reform Movement to have a place of power in American Judaism has been somewhat successful because the 2013 survey of American Jewry by the Pew Research Center revealed that the majority of American Jews who belong to a synagogue belong to a Reform congregation. The official figure is 35 percent,[153] which is not far off from the 38 percent reported in the 2000 National Jewish Population survey and the 1990 survey.[154] "The synagogue is the

---

[147] Bethami Horowitz, "Push-back about Cohen's Pew policy 'take-aways'." Email to NRJE, 14 December 2013.
[148] Steven M. Cohen, email to Judy Aronson, 13 December 2013.
[149] "A Portrait of Jewish Americans."
[150] Ibid.
[151] Schulson, "Mixed Blessings," 19.
[152] Ibid.
[153] *A Portrait*, 10.
[154] Laurence Kotler-Berkowitz, et al., *The National Jewish Population Survey 2000–01: Strength, Challenge and Diversity in the American Jewish Population* (New Haven: Berman Institute – North American Jewish Databank, Jan. 2004), 7; Sidney Goldstein, "Profile of American

most prevailing and arguably the most important institution in American Jewish life" because along with being a location for prayer and study, it offers its members identification with Judaism, education, and social networking.[155] However, that more contemporary American Jews belong to Reform congregations than any other branch of Judaism, did not console Rabbi Rick Jacobs, president of the URJ. In 2012, he called upon congregations to revitalize and inspire nonaffiliated Jews "to be part of something larger than just ourselves."[156]

American Jewish historian Jonathan Sarna is hopeful about the future. He sees the current generation of North American Jews as better educated Jewishly than the previous ones and more involved in causes.[157] Young adults are calling for programs that address their needs as single Jews in their 20s and 30s.[158] URJ Senior Vice President Rabbi Daniel Freelander sees "the Reform Movement [as] the change agent of North American Jewry...the Union...will be able to morph into the Movement that will best meet the needs of Jews in the next decade and beyond."[159] To do so, the CCAR, URJ, and HUC–JIR are working on a new vision of the Reform Movement,[160] because as Kaplan explains: "it is so pluralistic and diverse....we've hit the point where we have to decide...what we are."[161] There are many contradictions in Reform Judaism because of this diversity and so it becomes hard to motivate people to participate.[162] However, Jacobs sees these adjustments as "what is needed to strengthen Jewish life."[163]

Jewry: Insights from the 1990 National Jewish Population Survey." *American Jewish Yearbook* (Philadelphia: Jewish Pub. Society, 1992), 129.
155 Schwartz, Scheckner, and Kotler-Berkowitz, "Census of U.S. Synagogues," 112.
156 Rick Jacobs, "Op-Ed: Synagogues must reach out to 'the uninspired,'" *JTA: The Global News Services of the Jewish People* (28 March 2012), accessed 28 March 2012, http://www.jta.org/2012/03/28/news-opinion/opinion/op-ed-synagogues-must-reach-out-to-the-uninspired.
157 Sarna, "The Discontinuity," 25.
158 David Cygielman, "Home Shuling." *Reform Judaism* (winter 2012), 27; Yoav Schlesing, "Rebooting Judaism." *Reform Judaism* (winter 2012), 27–28.
159 Freelander, "Birth," 64.
160 Steve Fox and Lance Sussman, "Rabbinic Road Out of a Wilderness." *Reform Judaism* (summer 2011), 57.
161 Dana Evan Kaplan, Interview, *TCJ: Up Close*, The Jewish Channel, 17 March 2014, accessed 22 July 2014, http://newsdesk.tjctv.com/2014/03/up-close-march-17–2014/.
162 Ibid.
163 Jacobs, "Keynote."

Conclusion

American Reform Jews have gone from believing being American means a sloughing off of tradition, to realizing that being American can include religious difference and traditions. Reform Judaism has moved to a more traditional approach and a reincorporation of Hebrew in worship services. The CCAR reflects this multi-cultural and multi-spiritual acceptance by not having 1 Haggadah, but many, each of which focuses a specific segment of the Reform constituency. Each Haggadah's non-liturgical material responds to the needs of the constituency it is addressing, but including much material on how to prepare, or what is the holiday, or less.

Conclusion

"The Seder, the ceremonial feast of Passover, is an incomparable religious creation. It represents the unique artistry of the Jewish soul."

Rabbi Herbert Bronstein[1]

The evolution of the non-liturgical parts of the most published book in Jewish history, the Haggadah – produced by what is now the largest Jewish denomination in the world – the American Reform Movement, developed over time as a response to the needs of the users, the Jews of the period, and how they interpreted the story of freedom portrayed in the Exodus. This too is how the non-liturgical material was developed – in response to the needs of the users, the readers. As the American Jew became less Jewishly educated, the need for explanatory material became greater and so introductory material about how to prepare for Passover and what the festival means was created. As the communty's needs and interests changed, so did the interpretations of the meaning of the Festival of Freedom for the community.

The Reform Movement came into its own in the United States, adjusting its theology to its constituency. Early on it became an inclusive community. First it accepted the Russian immigrants, which changed Reform Judaism from a German Jewish experience to an American Jewish experience, then it included non-Jewish family members, and most recently same-sex couples have been wrapped into the Reform community. All of this reflects the larger American interpretations of inclusiveness. This reflection indicates the impact that American society has on the Reform Movement. It was begun as a grass-roots response to a situation, the inability of many Jews to connect spiritually with their religion, and continues to operate in that way.

Having created 8 Haggadot in more than 130 years, the Central Conference of American Rabbis (CCAR) has worked valiantly to meet the needs of its constituency. The response may not have been immediate, like the decade it took to make the 1974 edition gender-neutral, but they were carefully thought through. The earliest Haggadot had little non-liturgical material, the rabbinate was following the Haggadot already published and did not see a need in their constituency for any serious instruction. However, as American Jews sloughed off the traditional practices of their immigrant families and Reform Judaism had to define itself to make it different than the traditional Judaism that arrived with the immigrants,

---

1 Herbert Bronstein, הגדה של פסח: *A Passover Haggadah: A New Union Haggadah* (New York: Grossman Pub., 1974), 5.

the non-liturgical material grew to include not only how to set the table, but history lessons on the holiday and ceremonies, and theological discussions. When the Reform Movement accepted the Eastern European Jews, the theology changed to re-incorporate more superstition and tradition and the Haggadah began to reflect this. This resulted in a need of the rabbinate to explain this shift in the non-liturgical parts of the Haggadah. The 21st Century opened with a more accepting Reform Movement that accepted different ways of practicing Judaism. This in turn resulted in the shift of the Movement from publishing 1 Haggadah to publishing many hoping to meet the needs of everyone. Alan Yoffie addressed the non-Jewishly literate by including checklists and suggestions on how to make the Seder interactive and meaningful. Rabbi Sue Levi Elwell presented a more intellectual adaptation with explanations as to why one does what they do, to meet the needs of the educated, but not necessarily Jewishly educated. The Classical Reform sub-Movement pushed to republish the original stand-alone Haggadah and to update it, because they wanted a return to the Classical Reform of the early 1800s.

How then will the CCAR meet the needs of the future? Rabbi Rick Jacobs, Union for Reform Judaism (URJ) president, stated at the 2013 URJ Biennial Conference that "we will not expect the next generation to be just like us, because only the eternals [the truth in the Torah] are not negotiable, everything else is."[2] Alan M. Dershowitz, professor at Harvard Law School, warns us that "the Jewish community of 2076 will bear little resemblance to the vibrant, influential, mainstream one of today."[3] The CCAR leadership is well aware of this. They predict that shortly "the rabbis...will be almost entirely without personal knowledge of their familial immigrant generation" and without having grown up in a Jewish neighborhood.[4] These factors will influence their understanding of American Judaism both positively, in that they truly will understand the American Jewish experience, and negatively, in that they will not understand the immigrants who will arrive. They will be a likeness of the American Reform Movement constituency. No longer is American Judaism waves of large groups of immigrants. It is more 3rd- and 4th-generation Jews, or later, who know little of their Old World backgrounds and.

---

[2] Rick Jacobs, "Keynote Address" (presented at the Union for Reform Judaism Biennial, San Francisco, California. 12 December 2013), accessed 4 January 2015, http://urj.org/biennial.
[3] Alan M. Dershowitz, *The Vanishing American Jew* (New York: Touchstone, 1997), 25.
[4] Peter J. Rubinstein, "The Next Century," In *Tanu Rabbanan: Our Rabbis Taught: Essays on the Occasion of the Centennial of the Central Conference of American Rabbis*, ed. Joseph B. Glaser (New York: CCAR, 1990), 136.

The CCAR, URJ, and Hebrew Union College – Jewish Institute of Religion (HUC– JIR) are currently working on a joint vision for the next half-century.[5] Rabbi Eric Yoffie, past president of the URJ, sees this as necessary because

> the great majority of North American Jews will not choose a Judaism that is halakhically-based; they will not choose a narrow, ritually-obsessed Judaism; they will not choose an ethically-limited Judaism; and they will certainly not choose a fundamentalist, ghetto Judaism. The great majority will choose the modern, liberal, Torah-inspired Judaism that is Reform. And this will require College, Conference, Union and congregations working together to build a strong movement.[6]

They will have to address multi-ethnic Jews, as American Jews are developing interests in how non-Eastern European Jews practice Judaism, multi-gendered Jews, because Americans are becoming more accepting of a multi-gendered, not a dual-gendered, understanding of the world, and they have been working on being more ritually observant, since that's what their constituency desires.

Executive Vice President of the CCAR Rabbi Paul J. Menitoff is under no illusions that the Pittsburgh Principles of 1999, not the principles of the Pittsburgh Platform of 1885, will remain the ultimate set of principles for the Reform Movement. He declares that "the [1999] document is an accurate snapshot of where we are as a Movement and how we have changed in the past quarter century." However, he doesn't see these principles as reflecting what the Reform Movement will be 50 years from now.[7] In fact, Rabbi Daniel G. Zemel, of Temple Micah in Washington, D.C., calls on the leaders of the Reform Movement "to craft a compelling ideology for a new era of American Reform Judaism."[8] This new era, as Yoffie explains is "a fast-changing, unpredictable" one[9] and Jacobs supports the idea of reinvention of the Reform Movement.[10]

Haggadot are being reinvented as well. Already we have digital copies of Haggadot that are available to download to an e-reader, some like the ShopRite Haggadah, are available online to be printed on one's home printer. One need

---

[5] Steve Fox and Lance Sussman, "Rabbinic Road Out of a Wilderness." *Reform Judaism* (summer 2011), 57.
[6] Eric Yoffie, "Rabbi Yoffie's Remarks to the URJ Executive Committee March 2010" (presented at the URJ Executive Committee, New York, New York, 15 March 2010), accessed 30 July 2014, http://urj.org/about/union/leadership/yoffie/?syspage=article&item_id=37320.
[7] Paul J. Menitoff, "Pittsburgh Principles: A Continuing Process." *CCAR Journal* (winter 2000): 15.
[8] Daniel G. Zemel, "A Response to the Pittsburgh Principles." *CCAR Journal* (winter 2000): 51.
[9] Eric Yoffie, "Forward," in *The New Reform Judaism: Challenges and Reflections*, ed. Dana Evan Kaplan (Philadelphia: JPS, 2013), x.
[10] Jacobs, "Keynote."

not have a ShopRite in town to use their Haggadah. Hillel of Southwest Missouri for their interfaith Seder used a Haggadah in Powerpoint format to save on reproduction costs and create a stronger community atmosphere, because participants are looking up and around, rather than down at their laps. Thus, just as other publishers have had to reconsider how to sell their product, so will the CCAR.

There has also been a return to the art of illustrating Haggadot. Artist David Moss was commissioned to illustrate a Haggadah by Richard Levy, rare Jewish book collector. This was then reproduced in a limited edition of 500, one of which was given as an official gift by President Ronald Reagan to Israel's President Chaim Herzog on the occasion of the first state visit of an Israeli president to the U.S. in 1987.[11] Jacobs calls the 21st Century in the United States a Golden Age for Judaism with more art and music being created than at any other time or place in Jewish history[12] and Moss' Haggadah is an example.

While Rabbi Dana Evan Kaplan, renowned scholar regarding American Reform Judaism, is not optimistic about the future of Reform Judaism, because "the Reform movement seeks to be a theological 'big tent' into which almost everyone can fit,"[13] Rabbi Peter Knobel, past CCAR President, believes the CCAR Press to be "a publisher of Haggadot. Not THE Reform Haggadah."[14] Thus, the press produces Haggadot that are part of a "variety of theologies that enable growing numbers of individuals to deeply engage" in Jewish life. Jacobs understands this as an aspect of the positive outcomes of American Reform Judaism.[15] The last 3 Haggadot published by the CCAR Press are examples of the "big tent" in American Reform Judaism. The Classical Reformers' focus on Classical Reform theology[16] resulted in the reprint of the 1923 *Union Haggadah*[17] and the revision of it into *The New Union Haggadah*.[18] The "neo-Reform" Judaism (as Kaplan calls it) of ritual resulted in both *The Open Door*[19] and *Sharing the Journey* Haggadot.[20]

---

11 David Moss, "My Haggadah: The Book of Freedom." *David Moss Projects* 2015, accessed 5 January 2015, http://davidmoss.com/projects/moss-haggadah/.
12 Jacobs, "Keynote."
13 Dana Evan Kaplan, *The New Reform Judaism: Challenges and Reflections* (Philadelphia: JPS, 2013), 7.
14 Peter Knobel, Interview with author, 7 August 2013.
15 Rick Jacobs, "Afterword," in *The New Reform Judaism: Challenges and Reflections*, ed. Dana Evan Kaplan (Philadelphia: JPS, 2013), 320.
16 Ibid., 11.
17 Central Conference of American Rabbis, *The Union Haggadah: Home Service for the Passover* (New York: Central Conference of American Rabbis, 1923).
18 Howard A. Berman, *The New Union Haggadah*, Revised Edition (New York: CCAR Press, 2014).
19 Sue Levi Elwell, כל-דכפין *The Open Door: A Passover Haggadah* (New York: CCAR, 2002).

These Haggadot seek to provide examples of what Kaplan is calling for: "a liberal Judaism that can provide a personal experience that speaks directly to each individual."[21] However, with the multiple interpretations of Reform Judaism and the concept of "the big tent" comes the problem that there really is not unity. Rabbi Isaac Mayer Wise's dream of a *Minhag America* must fail. There really is not a *Minhag Reform* because of the options provided both by the multiple Haggadot and the *Mishkan T'filah* (prayerbook).

Knobel's view of the CCAR as a publisher of Haggadot highlights a few changes in the Reform Movement that Kaplan is concerned about. The multitude of theologies acceptable to the Reform Movement makes it both inclusive and difficult to define. A series of Haggadot addressing the religious viewpoints of different types of Reform Jews is a boon to book sales, but a problem in defining the beliefs of Reform Judaism. The Reform Movement has become adept at addressing different types of Jewish religious outlooks, but has lost its central focus. However, the number of Haggadot produced by the CCAR Press accurately define the Reform Movement – an inclusive one, a vibrant one, and one that fulfills the needs of numerous types of Jews.

The mission for HUC–JIR states that one of its goals "is to educate rabbis to... teach effectively people of all ages, across denominations and faiths."[22] The authors of each of the recent CCAR Haggadot attempted to address particular niches: interfaith families, neo-Reform, Classical Reform, etc. The mission of the CCAR continues to promote what its educational branch began: "The CCAR enriches and strengthens the Jewish community."[23] The CCAR Haggadot reach many people. In fact, it could be said that Haggadot are one of the most democratic prayerbooks in the world. They are created by people for people, and there is not necessarily a religious leader involved. The CCAR Press produced Elwell's Haggadah because it wanted "to create a haggadah for the next generation."[24] Rabbi Mary Zamore, a past editor of the *Central Conference of American Rabbis' Newsletter*, sees Sue Levi Elwell's כל-דכפין *The Open Door: A Passover Haggadah* as a "heady ideological haggadah."[25] However, Alan Yoffie's as "a more user friend-

---

20 Alan S. Yoffie, *Sharing the Journey: The Haggadah for the Contemporary* Family, ill. Mark Podwal (New York: CCAR, 2012).
21 Kaplan, *The New Reform Judaism*, 315.
22 "Mission." *Hebrew Union College—Jewish Institute of Religion* 2015, accessed 4 January 2015, http://huc.edu.
23 "Mission Statement." *Central Conference of American Rabbis* 17 January 2008, accessed 4 January 2015, http://ccarnet.org.
24 Hara Person, "RE: CCAR Yearbook inquiry." Email to author, 7 August 2013.
25 Mary L. Zamore, Interview by author, 10 January 2014.

ly Haggadah that didn't have a high level of knowledge. There was very much a need in the community for a Haggadah just like this."[26] The 1923 *The Union Haggadah* fulfilled a felt need. It was reprinted because there was a call for it; there was a sense of nostalgia for its clarity of language.[27]

Since Haggadot are the most-published Jewish text in the United States, we should not be surprised to see a continuation of this publishing trend. The celebration of Passover Seder has maintained a special place in the hearts of American Jews, even when other holidays have been ignored. Thus, with the increase in observance, we should see that Passover continues as a favorite festival. Knobel sees the Seder as the "quintessential opportunity for a family meal"[28] and, since Americans have lost that family time, Passover provides the opportunity to do so. Because American Jews have reinterpreted the symbols and traditions of Seder to intersect with their understandings of their world,[29] they will do so in the future. Joel Gereboff, professor of Religious Studies at Arizona State University, believes "the Haggadah is truly a key text for enacting the cultural and social negotiations of American Jews."[30] Therefore, as the CCAR's theology evolves, so will its Haggadot.

This work matched the iterations of the CCAR Haggadah with various events in American history so that we could see how the non-liturgical parts of the CCAR Haggadah addressed the needs of the American Reform Jew. What we have learned is that the CCAR responded to the demographic shifts in American Judaism, immigration of Eastern European Jews and later Russian and Israeli Jews, the changes in American Jewish social patterns, movement to the suburbs and acceptance of inter-Jewish cultural marriage, and the educational patterns of the American Jew. There has been no extensive study before that examined the non-liturgical material of Haggadot and how it is a reflection of the larger society in which Jews live. This opens new ground both in Jewish studies and rhetorical studies to understanding how religious groups, in this case specifically Jewish groups, address the changes of the larger society in their prayerbooks.

---

26 Ibid.
27 Person, "RE: CCAR."
28 Peter Knobel, Interview by author, 7 August 2013.
29 Joel Gereboff, "One Nation, with Liberty and Haggadahs for All," in *Key Texts in American Jewish Culture*, ed. by Jack Kugelmass (New Brunswick: Rutgers Univ. Press, 2003), 287–288.
30 Ibid., 289.

"Many more Haggadahs will yet be published before the 'ultimate' edition appears. And that will only be if, and when, history itself shall be fulfilled."

Yosef Hayim Yerushalmi[31]

---

31 Yosef Hayim Yerushalmi, *Haggadah and History: A Panorama in Facsimile of Five Centuries of the Printed Haggadah from the Collections of Harvard University and Jewish Theological Seminary of American* (Philadelphia: JPS of American, 1975), 85.

Bibliography

Articles

Ackerman, Walter I. "Jewish Education – For What?" *Jewish American Year Book*, vol. 70, 3–36. 1969. Accessed 13 August 2014, http://www.ajcarchives.org/AJC_DATA/Files/1969_3_SpecialArticles.pdf.

Adelman, Penina V. "A Drink from Miriam's Cup: Invention of Tradition among Jewish Women." *Journal of Feminist Studies in Religion* 10, no. 2 (1994): 151–166.

Alpert, Joan. "Maxwell House Hagaddah: Good to the Last Page." *Moment* (March/April 2009). Accessed 29 June 2010,
http://www.momentmag.com/maxwell-house-hagaddah-good-to-the-last-page/.

Bellows, Marcie and Marla J. Feldman. *Pesach: a season for justice*. Religious Action Center of Reform Judaism, 2004. Accessed 21 April 2014, http://rac.org/_kd_Items/actions.cfm?action=Show&item_id=331&destination=ShowItem.

Berman, Howard A. "Introducing the New Union Haggadah!" *Reform Judaism* (28 March 2014). Accessed 28 July 2014, http://www.reformjudaism.org/blog/2014/03/28/introducing-new-union-haggadah.

Bluver, Hannah. "The Ballad of the Four Sons." *The Jewish Magazine* (April 1998). Accessed: 5 April 1998, http://jewishmag.com.

Bokser, Baruch M. "Ritualizing the Seder." *Journal of the American Academy of Religion* 56, no. 3 (1988): 443–471.

Chenkin, Alvin. "Socio-Economic Data: Jewish Population of the United States, 1955." *Jewish American Year Book*, vol. 57, 119–130. 1956. Accessed 4 June 2014, http://www.ajcarchives.org/AJC_DATA/Files/1956_4_USSocioEcnomic.pdf.

Cohen, Carla. "Selecting Your Passover Haggadah," review of *A Passover Haggadah*, by Herbert Bronstein. *Politics and Prose: Bookstore/Coffeehouse*. Accessed 27 July 2014, http://www.politics-prose.com/passover-haggadah.

Cohen Ioannides, Mara W. "A Lost Liturgy." *CCAR Journal* (spring 1999): 79–83.

—— "H. Berkowitz and S.S. Cohon: Two Men Battle Over One Haggadah." *American Jewish Archives Journal* 58 (2008): 103–119.

Cygielman, David. "Home Shuling." *Reform Judaism* (winter 2012): 6–27.

Diner, Hasia. "Entering the Mainstream of Modern Jewish History: Peddlers and the American Jewish South." *Southern Jewish History* 8 (2005): 1–30.

Dushkin, Alexander M. "Editorial Statement." The Jewish Teacher: A Quarterly Magazine for Jewish Religious School 1, no. 1 (1916): 1–3.

—— "Editorial Statement." The Jewish Teacher: A Quarterly Magazine for Jewish Religious School 1, no. 3 (1917): 133–139.

—— "Fifty Years of American Jewish Education – Retrospect and Prospects." *Jewish Education* 37, no. 1–2 (1967): 44–57.

Edelman, Lily. "Leonard Baskin's New Haggadah: The Artist Celebrates the Movement 'from the green gloom of slavery to the hot orange of freedom." Review of *A Passover Haggadah* by Herbert Bronstein, *The National Jewish Monthly* (April 1974): 5–8.

Eisen, Arnold. "The American Jewish Experience." *The Jerusalem Quarterly* 38 (1986): 80–88.

—— "Imagining American Jews: Recent Visions and Revisions." *Conservative Judaism* 1988–1989: 3–20.

Ellenson, Ruth Andrew. Review of "The Open Door: A Passover Haggadah," by Sue Levi Elwell. *University of Southern California: Trojan Magazine* (winter 2003). Accessed 28 July 2014, http://www.usc.edu/dept/pubrel/trojan_family/winter03/whats-new.html.

Finkelstein, Louis. "The Oldest Midrash: Pre-Rabbinic Ideals and Teachings in the Passover Haggadah." *The Harvard Theological Review* 31, no. 4 (1938): 291–317.

Fishkoff, Sue. "New haggadot and a face lift for an old favorite." *Washington Jewish Week*, 7 April 2011, p. 30–31.

Friedenwald, Harry. "The Problem of Jewish Education from the layman's point of view." *The Jewish Teacher: A Quarterly Magazine for Jewish Religious School* 1, no. 1 (1916): 13–16.

Funny Passover Songs. N.d. Accessed 5 April 2014, http://holidays.jua.com/passover-songs.shtml.

Geiger, Abraham. "Israel's Native Energy." Reprint in *The Rise of Reform Judaism: A Sourcebook of its European Origins*, edited by W. Gunther Plaut, 125–127. New York: World Union for Progressive Judaism, 1963.

—— "Jewish Movements Today." *Wissenschaftliche Zeitschrift für jüdische Theologie* no. 1 (1835). Reprint in *The Rise of Reform Judaism: A Sourcebook of its European Origins*, edited by W. Gunther Plaut, 18–19. New York: World Union for Progressive Judaism, 1963.

Goldberg, J. J. "Pew Survey About Jewish America Got It All Wrong: With Flawed Comparisons, Study Reached Faulty Conclusions." *The Jewish Daily Forward*, 13 October 2013. Accessed 14 July 2014, http://forward.com/articles/185461/pew-survey-about-jewish-america-got-it-all-wrong/?p=all#ixzz37TssioRu.

Goldstein, Sidney. "American Jewry, 1970: A Demographic Profile." *Jewish American Year Book*, 3–88. 1971. Accessed 4 June 2014, http://www.jewishdatabank.org/Studies/downloadFile.cfm?FileID=2983.

—— "Jews in the United States: Perspectives from Demography." *Jewish American Year Book*, 3–59. 1981. Accessed 5 June 2014, http://www.acjarchives.org/AJC_DATA/Files/1981_3_SpecialArticles.pdf.

—— "Profile of American Jewry: Insights from the 1990 National Population Survey." *Jewish American Year Book*, 77–173. 1992. Accessed 5 June 2014, http://www.jewishdatabank.org/Studies/downloadFile.cfm?FileID=3004.

"Haggadahs." *Euclid Ave. Temple Bulletin*, 4 April 1930. Accessed 28 July 2014, http://americanjewisharchives.org/collections/ms0882/00257/m-s0882.00257.1930-04-04.pdf. Jacob Rader Marcus Center of the American Jewish Archives. Cincinnati Campus, Hebrew Union College – Jewish Institute of Religion, MS coll. 882.

"Haggadahs to Moscow." *News Letter: Central Conference of American Rabbis*, February 1992, p. 1. Jacob Rader Marcus Center of the American Jewish Archives. Cincinnati Campus, Hebrew Union College – Jewish Institute of Religion, MS coll. CCAR Nearprint, special topics/CCAR 1984.

Herder, Kate. "Memories of Yesterday." *OzarksWatch: Documenting Jews of theOzarks* 12, nos. 1 & 2 (1999): 60–64.

History. Union for Reform Judaism. n.d. Accessed 6 June 2014, http://urj.org/about/union/history/.

Ilan, Nachem. "For Whom Was the 'Farhi haggada' Intended? On the image of Egyptian Jews during the First Half of the 20th Century." *Jewish Studies an Internet Journal* 4 (2005). Accessed 20 June 2014, http://www.biu.ac.il/js/JSIJ/4-2005/Ilan.pdf.

Jacobs, Joseph. "Statistics of Jews: Jewish Population of the United States Memoir of the Bureau of Jewish Statistics of the American Jewish Committee." *Jewish American Yearbook*, vol. 16. 1914–1915, 339–378. Accessed 31 January 2014, http://ajcarchive.org/AJC_DATA/FILES/1914_1915_7_Statistics.pdf.

Jacobs, Rick. "Op-Ed: Synagogues must reach out to 'the unisnspired,'" *JTA: The Global News Services of the Jewish People*, 28 March 2012. Accessed 23 March 2012, http://www.jta.org/2012/03/28/news-opinion/opinion/op-ed-synagogues-must-reach-out-to-the-uninspired.

"Jewish Statistics." *American Jewish Yearbook*, vol. 1, 283–285. (1899–1900). Philadelphia: Jewish Publication Society. Accessed 4 November 2013, http://www.ajaarchives.org/AJC_DATA/Files/1899-_1900_7_Statistics.pdf.

"Jewish Statistics." *American Jewish Yearbook*, vol. 2, 623. 1900–1901. Accessed 2 June 2014, http://www.jewishdatabank.org/Studies/downloadFile.cfm?FileID=3024.

Johnson, Neil M. "The Missouri Synod Lutherans and the War Against the German Language, 1917–1923." *Nebraska History* 56 (1975): 136–144.

Kaplan, Allen S. "Small Congregations." *CCAR Journal* (summer 2000): 5–7.

Kaplan, Dana Evan. "Reform Jewish Theology and the Sociology of Liberal Religion in America: The Platforms as response to the perception of socioreligious crisis." *Modern Judaism* 20 (2000): 60–77.

Kaplan, Mordecai M. "A Program for the Reconstruction of Judaism." *The Menorah Journal* 6 (1920): 181–193. Reprint in *The Jew in the Modern World: A Documentary History*, 3rd edition. Edited by Paul Mendes-Flohr and Jehuda Reinharz, 558–561. New York: Oxford Univ. Press, 2010.

Kelman, Stuart. "Mishkan T'Filah: A reform Sidder." *Jewish Book Council*. n.d. Accessed 6 June 2014, http://www.jewishbookcouncil.org/book/mishkan-tfilah.

Levy, Richard. "The Challenge of the 'Principles." *CCAR Journal* (winter 2000): 7–11.

—— "Is It Time to Chart a New Course for Reform Judaism?" *Reform Judaism* (winter 1998). Accessed 4 June 2014, http://reformjudaismmag.net/rjmag-90s/1198rl.html.

Linfield, H. S. "Statistics of Jews." *Jewish American Year Book*, 227–281. 1927–1928. Accessed 3 June 2014, http://www.jewishdatabank.org/studies/downloadFile.cfm?FileID=3025.

Lipman, Steve. "The Telling, And the Retelling." *The New York Jewish Week*, 4 September 2012. Accessed 24 January 2013, www.thejewishweek.com/special_sections/special_holiday_issues/telling_and_retelling.

Markowitz, S. H. "The Educative Process in a Jewish Community." *The Jewish Teacher: A Quarterly Magazine for Jewish Religious School* 2, no. 2 (1934): 1–8.

Massarik, Fred. "Trends in U.S. Jewish Education: National Jewish Population Study Findings." *American Jewish Year Book*, vol. 77, 240–250. Philadelphia: Jewish Pub. Society, 1977. Accessed 13 June 2014, http://www.bjpa.org/Publications/details.cfm?PublicationID=20843.

Menitoff, Paul J. "Pittsburgh Principles: A Continuing Process." *CCAR Journal* (winter 2000): 12–15.

Meyer, Michael A. "Thank You, Moritz Loth: A 125-Year UAHC Retrospective." *Reform Judaism* (fall 1998): 30–39.

Michaelson, Jay. "All The 2014 Haggadah Info You'll Ever Need." *The Jewish Daily Forward*, 3 April 2014). Accessed 28 July 2014, http://forward.com/articles/ 195696/all-the-haggadah-info-youll-ever-need/#ixzz38nn40XN3.

Moran, Benjamin. "Two New Haggadot for your Passover Seder." *Interfaith family* (30 March 2012). Accessed 24 January 2013, www.interfaithfamily.com/holidays/passover_and_easter/Two_New_Haggadot_For_Your_Passover_Seder.

"A New Vision for Reform Judaism." *Reform Judaism* (fall 2012), 5.

Oseran, Joel. "Reform Judaism Worldwide." *Reform Judaism* (spring 2014), 32–33.

A Passover Haggadah Second Revised Edition Edited by Herbert Bronstein Illustrated by Leonard Baskin. CCAR Press. 2010. Accessed 20 July 2010, http://ccarnet.org/ccar-press/all-books/passover-haggadah/.

Person, Hara. "CCAR Haggadot: A Feast of Haggadah Choices." *Reform Rabbis Speak* 21 February 2014. Accessed 29 March 2014, http://ravblog.ccarnet.org/2014/02/ccar-haggadot-a-feast-of-haggadah-choices/.

Philipson, David. "The Beginnings of the Reform Movement in Judaism." *The Jewish Quarterly Review* 15, no. 3 (1903): 475–521.

"Post Your Perspectives about the Jewish Future." *Reform Judaism Online* (summer 2011). Accessed 6 June 2014, http://data.urj.org/rjmag/thinktank/.

Reform Judaism: A Centenary Perspective. Central Conference of American Rabbis 1976. Accessed 26 July 2000, http://www.ccarnet.org/platforms/centenary.html.

Reform Leadership Council Think Tank. "Proposed Vision Statement." *Reform Judaism* (fall 2012), 5.

Reimer, Jack. Review of *A Passover Haggadah*, by Herbert Bronstein, *Conservative Judaism* (spring 1974), 88–89.

Review of "The Open Door: A Passover Haggadah." by Sue Levi Elwell. *The Mothers Circle*, 2014. Accessed 28 July 2014, http://www.joi.org/motherscircle/index.php?page=education-Passoverhaggadot.

Review of "The Open Door: A Passover Haggadah." by Sue Levi Elwell. *Publisher's Weekly*, 18 February 2002. Accessed 24 January 2013, http://www.publishersweekly.com/978-0-88123-079-6.

Review of *A Passover Haggadah*, by Herbert Bronstein. *Hadassah Magazine* (March 1974), 27.

Sarna, Jonathan D. "American Jewish History." *Modern Judaism* 10, no. 3 (1990): 343–365.

Schnur, Susan. "Miriam's Goblet (Kos Miriam)." *Lillith* (spring 2000), n. pag.

Schwartz, Jim and Jeffrey Scheckner. "Jewish Population in the United States, 2000." *Jewish American Year Book*, 253–278. 2000. Accessed 6 June 2014, http://wwwjewishdatabank.org/Studies/downloadFil.dfm?FileID=3013.

Schwartz, Jim, Jeffrey Scheckner, and Laurence Kotler-Berkowitz. "Census of US Synagogues, 2001." *American Jewish Yearbook*, 112–150. 2002. Accessed 31 January 2014. http://www.jewishdatabank.org/Studies/downloadFile.cfm?FileID=3022.

Seligman, Ben "Socio-Economic Data: Recent Demographic changes in some Jewish Communities." *American Jewish Year Book*, vol. 54, 3–24. Philadelphia: Jewish Publication Society of America, 1953. Accessed 4 June 2014, http:///www.jewishdatabank.org/Studies/downloadFil.cfm?FileID=2965.

Seligman, Ben B. and Harvey Swados. "Jewish Population in the United States." *American Jewish Year Book*, 651–689. 1949. Accessed 3 June 2014, http://www.jewishdatabank.org/Studies/american_jewish_year_book_articles.cfm.

Seltzer, Robert. "This is Not the Way." *Reform Judaism* (winter 1998), 23–24, 26, 80.

Shapiro, Leon. "Soviet Jewry Since the Death of Stalin: A Twenty-five Year Perspective." *American Jewish Year Book*, vol. 79 (1979): 81–82. Accessed 5 August 2014, http://ajcarchives.org/AJC_DATA/Files/1979_3_SpecialArticles.pdf.

Shluker, Zelda. "Passover 2012: New Haggadot." *Hadassah Magazine* (January 2013). Accessed 24 January 2013, www.hadassahmagazine.org.

Sloan, Jacob. "Communal Affairs: Religion." *Jewish American Year Book*, vol. 57, 188–205. 1956. Accessed 5 June 2014, http://www.ajcarchives.org/AJC_DATA/Files/1956_6_USCommunal.pdf.

Stahl, Nanette. "The Venice Haggadah of 1609: A Treasure for the Ages." *Yale Univ. Library*. 2008. Accessed 29 March 2014,
http://www.library.yale.edu/judaica/site/exhibits/venicehaggadah/VeniceHaggadah.html.

"Statistics of Jews." *American Jewish Yearbook*, vol. 41, 588. 1939–1940. Accessed 31 January 2014, http://www.ajcarchives.org/main.php?GroupingId=10074.

Stevens, Elliot L. "The Prayer Books, They Are A'Changin'." *Reform Judaism* (summer 2006). Accessed 17 November 2008, http://urj.org//worship/mishkan/current//?syspage=article&item_id=3588.

Tabory, Joseph. "The Prayer Book (Siddur) As an Anthology of Judaism." *Prooftexts* 17 (1997): 115–132.

Temkin, Sefton D. "A Century of Reform Judaism in America." *American Jewish Year Book*, vol. 74, 3–75. 1973. Accessed 12 August 2014, http://www.ajcarchives.org/AJC_DATA/Files/1973_3_SpecialArticles.pdf.

Waxman, Maron L. Review of *The New Union Haggadah, Revised Edition* by Howard A. Berman and Benjamin Zeidman. Jewish Book Council ©2014. Accessed 28 July 20014, http://www.jewishbookcouncil.org/book/the-new-union-haggadah-revised-edition.

Weissbach, Lee Shai. "East European Immigrants and the Image of Jews in the Small-Town South." *American Jewish History* 85, no. 3 (1997): 231–262.

Wertheimer, Jack. "The American synagogue: recent issues and trends." *American Jewish Yearbook*, 7. 2005. Accessed 31 January 2014, http://%3A%2F%2Fresearch.policyarchive.org%2F10414.pdf&ei=MCzsUr2EHsupsATTx4CoBg&usg=AFQjCNGnpmyyci2vvx1f9R9ACorSQ17Hjw&sig2=RbcqaxyzPoJH7iWCYv1PMg&bvm=bv.60444564,d.cWc.

Wise, Isaac Mayer. "The Confirmation and the Bar Mitzvah." *Asmonean* 1854. Reprint in *The Jew in the Modern World: A Documentary History*, 3rd ed. Edited by Paul Mendes-Flohr and Jehuda Reinharz, 518–519. New York: Oxford Univ. Press, 2010.

Whitefield, Stephen. "Framing Florida Jewry." *Southern Jewish History* 10 (2007): 103–134.

Wildstein, Jeffery. "Hebrew in the Reform Movement." *CCAR Journal: A Reform Jewish Quarterly* (winter 2005): 82–91.

Wilensky, David A. M. "Looking for a new haggada?" Review of *Sharing the Journey: The Haggadah for the Contemporary Family* by Alan S. Yoffie. *The Times of Israel*, 22 March 2012). Accessed 24 January 2013, http://www.timesofisrael.com/looing-for-anew-haggada/.

Wollheim, William. "Reform Passover Haggadah Reaches Sales Milestone." Article for Temple Bulletins. attached to Elliot L. Stevens to Colleague, 20 January 1984. Jacob Rader

Marcus Center of the American Jewish Archives. Cincinnati Campus, Hebrew Union College – Jewish Institute of Religion, MS coll. CCAR Nearprint, special topics/CCAR 1984.

Zeitman, Kim "Leadership and Jewish Peoplehood North American and European Rabbinical Students Join Together at HUC-JIR/Jerusalem." *Chronicle* [HUC–JIR] 70 (2007), 8–9.

Zemel, Daniel G. "A Response to the Pittsburgh Principles." *CCAR Journal: The Reform Jewish Quarterly* (winter 2000): 48–51.

Zola, Gary Phillip. "Southern Rabbis and the Founding of the First National Association of Rabbis." *American Jewish History* 85, no. 4 (1997): 353–372.

Book Chapters

Abrams, Judith Z. "The Continuity of Change in Jewish Liturgy," in *Platforms and Prayer Books: Theological and Liturgical Perspectives on Reform Judaism*. Edited by Dana Evan Kaplan, 119–128. Lanham: Rowman & Littlefield, 2002.

Agus, Jacob B. "The Reform Movement," in *Understanding American Judaism: Toward the Description of a Modern Religion*, vol. 2. Edited by Jacob Neusner, 5–30. New York: KTAV Pub. House, 1975.

"American Conference." *Year Book of the Central Conference of American Rabbis 1890–91*. Cincinnati: Bloch, 1891. Reprint *Central Conference of American Rabbis Year Book Volumes I, II, III 1890–1983*, 123–125. New York: CCAR, n.d.

Ariel, Yaakov. "Miss Daisy's Planet: The Strange World of Reform Judaism in the United States, 1870–1930," in *Platforms and Prayer Books: Theological and Liturgical Perspectives on Reform Judaism*. Edited by Dana Evan Kaplan, 49–60. New York: Rowman & Littlefield Pub., 2002.

Arnow, David. "Passover for the Early Rabbis: Fixed and Free," in *My People's Passover Haggadah: Traditional Texts, Modern Commentaries*, vol. 1. Edited by Lawrence A. Hoffman and David Arnow, 15–20. Woodstock, Vermont: Jewish Lights Pub., 2008.

—— "Redemption: Blessing and Meal," in *My People's Passover Haggadah: Traditional Texts, Modern Commentaries*, vol. 2. Edited by Lawrence A. Hoffman and David Arnow, 109–136. Woodstock, Vermont: Jewish Lights Pub., 2008.

—— "The World of Midrash," in *My People's Passover Haggadah: Traditional Texts, Modern Commentaries*, vol. 1 & 2. Edited by Lawrence A. Hoffman and David Arnow, 47–70. Woodstock, Vermont: Jewish Lights Pub., 2008.

Association for the Reform of Judaism "Introduction." *Prayer Book*. Berlin: Association for the Reform of Judaism, 1848, "Introduction." Reprint *The Rise of Reform Judaism: A Sourcebook of its European Origins*. Edited by W. Gunther Plaut, 59–60. New York: World Union for Progressive Judaism, 1963.

Bamberger, Bernard J. "Introduction." *Reform Judaism: Essays by Hebrew Union College Alumni*. Edited by Abraham J. Feldman et al., 3–27. Cincinnati: HUC Press, 1949.

—— "Solomon B. Freehof in the Central Conference of American Rabbis," in *Essays in Honor of Solomon B. Freehof*. Edited by Walter Jacob, Frederick C. Schwartz, and Vigdor W. Kavalier, 97–104. Pittsburgh: Rodef Shalom Congregation, 1964.

Berkowitz, Herbert. "Why I am Not a Zionist," in *Reform Judaism: A Historical Perspective. Essays from the Yearbook of the Central Conference of American Rabbis*. Edited by Joseph L. Blau, 371–378. New York: KTAV Pub. House, 1973.

Borowitz, Eugene B. "How a Document Came to be Written." *Reform Judaism Today: Book Two What We Believe*, 157–201. New York: Behrman House, 1977.

Brody, Paula J. "Forward," in *Sharing the Journey: The Haggadah for the Contemporary Family*. Edited by Alan S. Yoffie. Illustrated by Mark Podwal, xi–xii. New York: CCAR, 2012.

Bronstein, Herbert. "Platforms and Prayer Books: From Exclusivity to Inclusivity in Reform Judaism," in *Platforms and Prayer Books: Theological and Liturgical Perspectives on Reform Judaism*. Edited by Dana Evan Kaplan, 25–40. Lanham, Maryland: Rowman & Littlefield, 2002.

Chorin, Aaron. *A Word in its Time*. Reprint *The Rise of Reform Judaism: A Sourcebook of its European Origins*. Edited W. Gunther Plaut, 33–34. New York: World Union for Progressive Judaism, 1963.

Christ, Carol P. and Judith Plaskow. "Preface," in *Womanspirit Rising: A Feminist Reader in Religion*. Edited by Carol P. Christ and Judith Plaskow, ix–xi. New York: Harper & Row, Pub., 1979.

Cohen Ioannides, Mara W. "Creating a Community: Who Can Belong to the Reform Syangogue," in *Who Is a Jew? Reflections on History, Religion, and Culture*. Edited by Leonard Greenspoon, 61–77. West Lafayette, Indiana: Purdue Univ. Press, 2014.

Cohon, Samuel S. "The Theology of the Union Prayer Book," in *Reform Judaism: A Historical Perspective: Essays from the Yearbook of the Central Conference of American Rabbis*. Edited by Joseph L. Blau, 257–284. New York: KTAV Pub., 1973.

Dreyfus, A. Stanley. "The *Gates* Liturgies: Reform Judaism Reforms Its Worship," in *The Changing Face of Jewish and Christian Worship in North America*. Edited by Paul F. Bradshaw and Lawrence A. Hoffman, 141–160. Notre Dame: Univ. Notre Dame Press, 1991.

Epstein, Marc Michael. "Illustrating History and Illuminating Identity in the Art of the Passover Haggadah," in *Judaism in Practice: From the Middle Ages through the Early Modern Period*. Edited by Lawrence Fine, 289–317. Princeton: Princeton Univ. Press, 2001.

Farber, Eli. "Preservation to innovation: Judaism in America, 1654–1880," in *The Cambridge Companion to American Judaism*. Edited by Dana Evan Kaplan, 23–42. New York: Cambridge Univ. Press, 2005.

Feur, Leon I. "Summary and Prospect," in *Retrospect and Prospect: Essays in Commemoration of the Seventy-fifth Anniversary of the Founding of The Central Conference of American Rabbis: 1889–1864*. Edited by Bertram Wallace Korn, 252–272. New York: CCAR, 1965.

Fischel, Walter J. "Introduction," in *"The Haggadah shel Pesach" in Marathi of the Bene-Israel*. New York: Orphan Hospital Ward of Israel, 1968.

Fram, Leon. "Reform Judaism and Zionism," in *Reform Judaism: Essays by Hebrew Union College Alumni*. Edited by Abraham J. Feldman et al., 174–195. Cincinnati: HUC Press, 1949.

Freehof, Solomon B. "Reform Judaism and Payer," in *Reform Judaism: Essays by Hebrew Union College Alumni*. Edited by Abraham J. Feldman, et al., 81–106. Cincinnati: HUC Press, 1949.
Friedman, Peter B., Sidney Goldstein, and Mark Alan Zober, "Factors Influencing Synagogue Affiliation: A Multi-Community Analysis," in *Building an Awareness of a Continental Jewish Community*, 11–24. North American Jewish Data Bank, Occasional Paper No. 3, May 1987.
Gartner, Lloyd P. "American Judaism, 1880–1945," in *The Cambridge Companion to American Judaism*. Edited by Dana Evan Kaplan, 43–60. New York: Cambridge Univ. Press, 2005.
— "Midpassage of American Jewry," in *The American Jewish Experience*. Edited by Jonathan D. Sarna, 224–233. New York: Homes & Meier Pub., 1986.
Gereboff, Joel. "One Nation, with Liberty and Haggadahs for All," in *Key Texts in American Jewish Culture*. Edited by Jack Kugelmass, 275–292. New Brunswick: Rutgers Univ. Press, 2003.
Gillman, Neil. "Theologically Speaking," in *My People's Passover Haggadah: Traditional Texts, Modern Commentaries*, vol. 1. Edited by Lawrence A. Hoffman and David Arnow, Woodstock, Vermont: Jewish Lights Pub., 2008.
Heschel, Susannah. "Orange on the Seder Plate," in *The Woman's Passover Companion: Women's Reflections on the Festival of Freedom*. Edited by Catherine Specter, Sharon Cohen Anisfeld, Tara Mohr, 208–213. Woodstock, Vermont: Jewish Lights, 2003. Accessed 11 April 2014, http://www.etzchaimflorida.org/wpress/wp-content/uploads/Orange-on-the-Seder-Plate.pdf
Hoffman, Lawrence A. "From Enslavement...," in *My People's Passover Haggadah: Traditional Texts, Modern Commentaries*, vol. 1. Edited by Lawrence A. Hoffman and David Arnow. Woodstock, Vermont: Jewish Lights Pub., 2008.
— "Peoplehood with Purpose: The American Seder and Changing Jewish Identity," in *My People's Passover Haggadah: Traditional Texts, Modern Commentaries*, vol. 1. Edited by Lawrence A. Hoffman and David Arnow. Woodstock, Vermont: Jewish Lights Pub., 2008.
Jacob, Walter. "The Influence of the Pittsburgh Platform on Reform *Halakhah* and Biblical Study," in *The Changing Face of Jewish and Christian Worship in North America*. Edited by Paul F. Bradshaw and Lawrence A. Hoffman, 25–39. Notre Dame: Univ. of Notre Dame Press, 1991.
Jacobs, Rick. "Afterword," in *The New Reform Judaism: Challenges and Reflections*. Edited by Dana Evan Kaplan, 319–321. Philadelphia: JPS, 2013.
Joel, Joseph A. "Passover in Camp: A Reminiscence of the War," in *An Anthology of Western Reserve Literature*. Edited by David R. Anderson and Gladys Haddad, 41–43. Kent: Kent State Univ. Press, 1992.
Kalmin, Richard."The formation and character of the Babylonian Talmud," in *The Cambridge History of Judaism Volume 4: The Late Roman-Rabbinic Period*. Edited by Steven T. Katz, 840–876. Cambridge: Cambridge Univ. Press, 2009.
Kaplan, Dana Evan. "Trends in American Judaism from 1945 to the present," in *The Cambridge Companion to American Judaism*. Edited by Dana Evan Kaplan, 61–80. New York: Cambridge Univ. Press, 2005.
Knobel, Peter S. "The Challenge of a Single Prayer Book," in *Platforms and Prayer Books: Theological and Liturgical Perspectives on Reform Judaism*. Edited by Dana Evan Kaplan, 155–170. Lanham, Maryland: Rowman & Littlefield, 2002.

Krause, Corinne Azen. "The Historical Setting of the Pittsburgh Platform," in *The Changing World of Reform Judaism: The Pittsburgh Platform in Retrospect*. Edited by Walter Jacob, 5–16. Pittsburgh: Rodef Shalom Congregation, 1985.

Kroloff, Charles A. "Unity within Diversity," in *Tanu Rabbanan: Our Rabbis Taught: Essays on the Occasion of the Centennial of the Central Conference of American* Rabbis. Edited by Joseph B. Glaser, 89–103. New York: CCAR, 1990.

Kugelmass, Jack. "Keys and Canons," in *Key Texts in American Jewish Culture*. Edited by Jack Kugelmass, 3–21. New Brunswick: Rutgers Univ. Press, 2003.

Lutsky, Vladimir Borisovich. "Chapter XII: Egypt in the Middle of the 19th Century (1841–76) Egypt After the Capitulation of 1840," in *Modern History of the Arab Countries*, translated by Lika Nasser. Moscow: Progress Publishers, for the USSR Academy of Sciences, Institute of the Peoples of Asia, 1969. Accessed 4 July 2014, https://www.marxists.org/subject/arab-world/lutsky/ch12.htm.

Mendes, H. Pereira. "The Beginnings of the [Jewish Theological] Seminary." *The Jewish Theological Seminary of American. Semi-Centennial Volume*, edited by Cyrus Adler, 36. New York: Jewish Theological Seminary of America, 1939. Reprint in *The Jew in the Modern World: A Documentary History*, 3rd edition, edited by Paul Mendes-Flohr and Jehuda Reinharz, 522–523. New York: Oxford Univ. Press, 2010.

Meyer, Michael A. "German-Jewish Identity in Nineteenth-Century America," in *The American Jewish Experience*. Edited by Jonathan D. Sarna, 45–61. New York: Holmes & Meier, 1986.

Milgrom, Jacob, commentator. "The Second Passover," in *The JPS Torah Commentary: Numbers*, 371–372. Philadelphia: Jewish Publication Society, 1990.

Neusner, Jacob. "Introduction," in *The Mishnah: A New Translation*, xiii–xlii. New Haven: Yale Univ. Press, 1988.

—— "Judaism in Freedom." *Understanding American Judaism: Toward the description of a modern religion. vol. II: Sectors of American Judaism: Reform, Orthodoxy, Conservatism, and Reconstructionism*. Edited by Jacob Neusner, 305–314. New York: KTAV Publishing House, 1975.

Plaut, W. Gunther. "The Pittsburgh Platform in the Light of European Antecedents," in *The Changing World of Reform Judaism: The Pittsburgh Platform in Retrospect*. Edited by Walter Jacob, 17–24. Pittsburgh: Rodef Shalom Congregation, 1985.

Regner, Sidney L. "The History of the Conference Part I: 1889–1964," in *Tanu Rabbanan: Our Rabbis Taught: Essays on the Occasion of the Centennial of the Central Conference of American Rabbis*, edited by Joseph B. Glaser, 3–14. New York: CCAR, 1990.

Rosen, Bernard C. "Minority Group in Transition: A Study of Adolescent Religious Conviction and Conduct," in *The Jews: Social Patterns of an American Group*. Edited by Marshall Sklare, 336–346. Glenco: The Free Press, 1958.

Rubinstein, Peter J. "The Next Century," in *Tanu Rabbanan: Our Rabbis Taught: Essays on the Occasion of the Centennial of the Central Conference of American Rabbis*. Edited by Joseph B. Glaser, 133–155. New York: CCAR, 1990.

Scult, Mel. "Americanism and Judaism in the Through ot Mordecai M. Kaplan," in *The Americanization of the Jews*. Edited by Robert M. Seltzer and Norman J. Cohen. 339–354. New York: New York Univ. Press, 1995.

Sherwin, Byron. "Thinking Judaism through: Jewish theology in America," in *The Cambridge Companion to American Judaism*. Edited by Dana Evan Kaplan, 117–131. New York: Cambridge Univ. Press, 2005.

Stern, Malcom H. "The 1820s: American Jewry Comes of Age," in *The American Jewish Experience*. Edited by Jonathan D. Sarna, 31–37. New York: Homes & Meier Pub., 1986.

Susser, Bernard and Charles S. Liebman. "American Jews: New Images," in *Choosing Survival: Strategies for a Jewish Future*, 61–89. New York: Oxford Univ. Press, 1999.

Umansky, Ellen M. "Spiritual Expressions; Jewish Women's Religious Lives in the Twentieth Century United States," in *Jewish Women in Historical Perspective*. Edited by Judith R. Baskin, 265–288. Detroit: Wayne State Univ. Press, 1991.

Weisman, Ze'ev. "Reflection of the Transition to Agriculture in Israelite Religion and Cult," in *Studies in Historical Geography and Biblical Historiography*. Edited by Gershon Galil and Moshe Weinfeld, 251–262. Boston: Brill, 2000.

Weissman Joselit, Jenna. "The Call of the Matzoh," in *The Wonders of America: Reinventing Jewish Culture, 1880–1950*, 219–264. New York: Henry Holt and Co., 1994.

Whitfield, Stephen J. "American Jews: Their Story Continues," in *The American Jewish Experience*. Edited by Jonathan D. Sarna, 284–293. New York: Holmes & Meier, 1986.

Wischnitzer, Mark. "Jewish Immigration into the United States: 1881–1948," in *To Dwell in Safety: The Story of Jewish Migration Since 1800*, 289. Philadelphia: Jewish Publication Society, 1948. Reprint in *The Jew in the Modern World: A Documentary History*, 3rd edition. Edited by Paul Mendes-Flohr and Jehuda Reinharz, 532. New York: Oxford Univ. Press, 2010.

Wise, Issac Mayer. "Reformed Judaism," in *Selected Writings of Isaac M. Wise: With a Biography*. Edited by David Philipson and Louis Grossman, 260–351. Cincinnati: Robert Clarke Co., 1900.

Yoffie, Eric. "Forward," in *The New Reform Judaism: Challenges and Reflections*. Edited by Dana Evan Kaplan, ix–xi. Philadelphia: JPS, 2013.

Zola, Gary Phillip. "The First Reform Prayer Book in America: The Liturgy of the Reformed Society of Israelites," in *Platforms and Prayer Books: Theological and Liturgical Perspectives on Reform Judaism*. Edited by Dana Evan Kaplan, 99–118. Lanham, Maryland: Rowman & Littlefield, 2002.

Books

Antin, Mary. *The Promised Land*. Boston: Houghton Mifflin Co., 1912.

Benjamin, [Israel Joseph]. *Three Years in America 1859–1862*, vol. 1, translated by Charles Reznikoff. Philadelphia: Jewish Publication Society of America, 1956.

Bial, Morrison David. *Liberal Judaism at Home: The Practices of Modern Reform Judaism*. New York: UAHC, 1971.

Bokser, Baruch. *The Origins of the Seder: The Passover Rite and Early Rabbinic Judaism*. New York: Jewish Theological Seminary, 2002.

Broner, E. M. *TheTelling*. San Francisco: HarperSanFrancisco, 1993.

Calof, Rachel. *Rachel Calof's Story: Jewish Homesteader on the Northern Plains*. Edited by J. Sanford Rikoon. Bloomington: Indiana Univ. Press, 1995.

Dershowitz, Alan M. *The Vanishing American Jew*. New York: Touchstone, 1997.

Dushkin, Alexander M. *Jewish Education in New York City*. New York: Bureau of Jewish Education, 1918.
Farber, Eli. *A Time for Planting: The First Migration 1654–1820*. The Jewish People in America. Baltimore: Johns Hopkins Univ. Press, 1992.
Freedman, Marcia. *Exile in the Promised Land*. Ithaca: Firebrand Press, 1990.
Glazer, Nathan. *American Judaism*. Chicago: Univ. of Chicago Press, 1957.
Glückel of Hameln. *The Memoirs of Glückel of Hameln*. Translated by Marvin Lowenthal. New York: Schocken Books, 1977.
Hackenburg, William B. et al. *Statistics of the Jews of the United States*. Philadelphia: UAHC, 1880.
Hallo, William, David Ruderman, and Michael Stanislawski. *Source Reader Heritage: Civilization and the Jews*. Westport: Praeger, 1984.
Hertzberg, Arthur. *The Jews in America: Four Centuries of an Uneasy Encounter: A History*. New York: Simon and Schuster, 1989.
Hoffman, Lawrence A. and David Arnow, eds. *My People's Passover Haggadah*, 2 vols. Woodstock: Jewish Lights Pub., 2008.
Kestenberg-Gladstein, Ruth. *The Jews of Czechoslovakia: Historical Studies and Surveys*. vol. 2. Philadelphia: The Jewish Publication Society of America, 1968.
Kotler-Berkowitz, Laurence, et al. *The National Jewish Population Survey 2000–01: Strength, Challenge and Diversity in the American Jewish Population*. New Haven: Berman Institute – North American Jewish Databank, updated January 2004. Accessed 6 June 2014, http://jewishfederations.org/local_includes/downloads/4606.pdf.
Kreitman, Esther Singer. *Deborah*. Translated by Maurice Carr. New York: St. Martin's Press, 1946.
Levy, Esther. *Jewish Cookery Book, on Principles of Economy, Adapted for Jewish Housekeepers, with the addition of many useful medicinal recipes, and other valuable information, relative to housekeeping and domestic management*. Philadelphia: n.p., 1871. Reprint Cambridge, CT: Applewood Books, 1988.
Levy, Richard N. A Vision of Holiness: The Future of Reform Judaism. New York: URJ Press, 2005.
Lugo, Luis, et al. A Portrait of Jewish Americans: Findings from a Pew Research Center Survey of U.S. Jews. Washington, DC: Pew Research Center, 2013.
Marcus, Jacob Rader. *United States Jewry 1776-1985*, vol. 3. Detroit: Wayne State Univ. Press, 1993. Marsden, George M. *Religion and American Culture*. Fort Worth: Harcourt Brace College Pub., 1990.
Meyer, Michael A. A Response to Modernity: A History of the Reform Movement in Judaism. New York: Oxford Univ. Press, 1988.
Meyerhoff, Barbara. *Number Our Days*. New York: E.P. Dutton, 1978.
Oesterley, W. O. E. and Theodore H. Robinson. *Hebrew Religion: Its Origin and Development*. New York: Macmillan, 1937.
Oppenheim, Samuel. *The Early History of the Jews in New York, 1654–1664: Some New Matter on the Subject*. New York: American Jewish Historical Society, 1909.
Petuchowski, Jakob J. *Prayerbook Reform in Europe: The Liturgy of European Liberal and Reform Judaism*. New York: World Union for Progressive Judaism, 1968.
Philipson, David. *The Reform Movement in Judaism*. New York: Macmillan Co., 1907. Reprint Forgotten Books, 2012.

Plaut, W. Gunther. *The Rise of Reform Judaism: A Sourcebook of its European Origins*. New York: World Union for Progressive Judaism, 1963.

A Portrait of Jewish Americans: Findings from a Pew Research Center Survey of U.S. Jews. Washington, D.C.: Pew Research Center, 2013. Accessed 31 January 2014, http://www.jewishdatabank.org/Studies/downloadFile.cfm?FileID=3088.

Rudavsky, David. Modern Jewish Religious Movements: A History of Emancipation and Adjustment. New York: Behrman House, 1967.

Schwartz, Jim, Vivian Klaff, and Frank Mott. *National Jewish Population Survey (NJPS) 2000–01*. New York: Jewish Federations of North America, 2001. Accessed 31 January 2014, http://www.jewishdatabank.org/Studies/details.cfm?StudyID=307.

Sheskin, Ira. *Religious Practices and Synagogue Attendance*, Edited by Laurence Kotler-Berkowitz. Storrs, Connecticut: North American Jewish Data Bank, 2013. Accessed 6 June 2014, http://www.jewishdatabank.org/Studies/downloadFile.cfm?FileID=2888.\

Sheskin, Ira and Arnold Dashefsky. *Jewish Population in the United States, 2010*. Edited by Arnold Dashefsky, Sergio DellaPergola, and Ira Sheskin. Storrs, Connecticut: North American Jewish Databank, 2011.

— *Jewish Population in the United States, 2012*. Edited by Arnold Dashefsky, Sergio DellaPergola, and Ira Sheskin. Storrs, Connecticut: North American Jewish Databank, 2013. Accessed 6 June 2014, http://www.jewishdatabank.org/Studies/downloadFile.cfm?FileID=2917.

— *Jewish Population in the United States, 2013*, Edited by Arnold Dashefsky, Sergio DellaPergola, and Ira Sheskin. Storrs, Connecticut: North American Jewish Databank, 2012. Accessed 6 June 2014, http://www.jewishdatabank.org/Studies/downloadFile.cfm?FileID=3111.

Silverstein, Alan. *Alternatives to Assimilation: The Response of Reform Judaism to American Culture, 1840–1930*. Hanover: Brandeis Univ. Press, 1994.

Temkin, Sefton D. *Creating American Reform Judaism: The Life and Times of Isaac Mayer Wise*. Portland: Littman Library of Jewish Civilization, 1998.

Trupin, Sophie. *Dakota Diaspora: Memoirs of a Jewish Homesteader*. Lincoln: Univ. of Nebraska Press, 1984.

Waxman, Chaim I. *Jewish Education Does Matter*. Tel Aviv University, School of Education, 2003. Accessed 13 June 2014, http://www.bjpa.org/Publications/details.cfm?PublicationID=3038.

Wise, Issac Mayer. *Reminiscences*. Edited and Translated by David Philipson. Cincinnati: Leo Wise and Co., 1901.

— *The World of My Books*. Translated by Albert H. Friedlander. Cincinnati: American Jewish Archives, June 1954.

Yerushalmi, Yosef Hayim. *Haggadah and History: A Panorama in Facsimile of Five Centuries of the Printed Haggadah from the Collections of Harvard University and Jewish Theological Seminary of American*. Philadelphia: JPS of American, 1975.

Correspondences

Berg, Martha L. Letter to author. 5 August 2010.
Berkowitz, Henry. Letter to Committee of the Central Conference of American Rabbis on Revision of the *Union Haggadah*, ©1922. Jacob Rader Marcus Center of the American Jewish Archives, Cincinnati Campus, Hebrew Union College – Jewish Institute of Religion, MS coll. 276, 3/7.
—— Letter to Samuel S. Cohon, May 1922. Jacob Rader Marcus Center of the American Jewish Archives, Cincinnati Campus, Hebrew Union College – Jewish Institute of Religion, MS coll. 25, 1/5.
—— Letter to Samuel Cohon, 9 April 1923. Reprint in Samuel S. Cohon, Solomon B. Freehof, Gerson B. Levi, and William Rosenau. "Report of Committee on Revision of Union Haggadah." Central Conference of American Rabbis Annual Convention, Cape May, New Jersey, 27 June–2 July 2, 1923. *Year Book of the Central Conference of American Rabbis*, vol. 33, 41–43. Cincinnati: CJ Krehbiel & Co., 1923.
—— Letter to Tobia Schnfarber, 23 March 1906. Jacob Rader Marcus Center of the American Jewish Archives, Cincinnati Campus, Hebrew Union College – Jewish Institute of Religion, MS coll. 34, 3/8.
—— Letter to William Rosenau, 8 December 1904. Jacob Rader Marcus Center of the American Jewish Archives, Cincinnati Campus, Hebrew Union College – Jewish Institute of Religion, MS coll. 34, 2/2.
Bloch, Charles S. Letter to J. Morgenstern, 31 July 1907. Jacob Rader Marcus Center of the American Jewish Archives, Cincinnati Campus, Hebrew Union College – Jewish Institute of Religion, MS coll. 34, 3/18.
Bronstein, Herbert. Letter to Members of the Central Conference of American Rabbis, 1 March 1972. Jacob Rader Marcus Center of the American Jewish Archives, Cincinnati Campus, Hebrew Union College – Jewish Institute of Religion, MS coll. Bronstein, copy new Haggadah.
—— "Re: Ltr. To Mara W. Cohen Ioannides – CORRECTED VERSION 8/22 BRONSTEIN," 24 August 2000.
Calisch, Edward N. Letter to Samuel S. Cohon, 6 May 1923. Jacob Rader Marcus Center of the American Jewish Archives, Cincinnati Campus, Hebrew Union College – Jewish Institute of Religion, MS coll. 276, 3/7.
Cohen, Steven M. Email to Judy Aronson. 13 December 2013.
Cohon, Beryl D. Letter to the Central Conference of American Rabbis, 1964. Jacob Rader Marcus Center of the American Jewish Archives, Cincinnati Campus, Hebrew Union College – Jewish Institute of Religion, MS coll. 34, 20/8.
Cohon, Samuel S. Letter to Henry Berkowitz, 9 May 1922. Jacob Rader Marcus Center of the American Jewish Archives, Cincinnati Campus, Hebrew Union College – Jewish Institute of Religion, MS coll. 276, 3/6.
—— Letter to Rabbi – –, 2 January 1919. Jacob Rader Marcus Center of the American Jewish Archives, Cincinnati Campus, Hebrew Union College – Jewish Institute of Religion, MS coll. 276, 3/6.
—— Letter to Sol. B. Freehof, 9 June 1922. Jacob Rader Marcus Center of the American Jewish Archives, Cincinnati Campus, Hebrew Union College – Jewish Institute of Religion, MS coll. 276, 3/6.

—— Letter to William Rosenau, 14 June 1921. Jacob Rader Marcus Center of the American Jewish Archives, Cincinnati Campus, Hebrew Union College – Jewish Institute of Religion, MS coll. 276, 3/6.

Feuer, Leon I. Letter to Albert M. Schaler, 26 April 1965. Jacob Rader Marcus Center of the American Jewish Archives, Cincinnati Campus, Hebrew Union College – Jewish Institute of Religion, MS coll. 34, 22/10.

Fields, Harvey J. Letter to author, 14 October 1999.

Fram, Leon. Letter to Samuel S. Cohon, 12 May 1922. Jacob Rader Marcus Center of the American Jewish Archives, Cincinnati Campus, Hebrew Union College – Jewish Institute of Religion, MS coll. 276, 3/6.

Frankel, Zacharia. Letter to the Second Rabbinical Conference in Frankfort, 18 July 1845. Reprint W. Gunther Plaut. *The Rise of Reform Judaism: A Sourcebook of its European Origins*, edited by W. Gunther Plaut, 87–89. New York: World Union for Progressive Judaism, 1963.

Freehof, Solomon B. Letter to Samuel S. Cohon, 2 April 1923. Jacob Rader Marcus Center of the American Jewish Archives, Cincinnati Campus, Hebrew Union College – Jewish Institute of Religion, MS coll. 276, 3/7.

—— Letter to Abraham J. Feldman, 18 March 1949. Rodef Shalom Congregational Archives, BA 70, FF 34.

Freehof, Solomon B., Samuel N. Deinard, Samuel Schwartz, and Samuel S. Cohon. Letter to the CCAR, ©1922. Jacob Rader Marcus Center of the American Jewish Archives, Cincinnati Campus, Hebrew Union College – Jewish Institute of Religion, MS coll. 276, 3/7.

Frisch, Ephraim. Letter to Samuel S. Cohon, 4 March 1922. Jacob Rader Marcus Center of the American Jewish Archives, Cincinnati Campus, Hebrew Union College – Jewish Institute of Religion, MS coll. 276, 3/6.

—— Letter to Samuel S. Cohon, 4 April 1923. Jacob Rader Marcus Center of the American Jewish Archives, Cincinnati Campus, Hebrew Union College – Jewish Institute of Religion, MS coll. 276, 3/7.

G., J. B. Letter to Colleague, 31 May 1973. Jacob Rader Marcus Center of the American Jewish Archives, Cincinnati Campus, Hebrew Union College – Jewish Institute of Religion, MS coll. Passover nearprint, 1.

Grossman, Rudolph. Letter to I[saac] S. Moses, 29 March 1903. Jacob Rader Marcus Center of the American Jewish Archives, Cincinnati Campus, Hebrew Union College – Jewish Institute of Religion, MS coll. 34, 1/17.

—— Letter to William Rosenau, 30 March 1903. Jacob Rader Marcus Center of the American Jewish Archives, Cincinnati Campus, Hebrew Union College – Jewish Institute of Religion, MS coll. 34, 1/17.

Haas, Louis J. Letter to Samuel Cohon, 1 January 1922. Jacob Rader Marcus Center of the American Jewish Archives, Cincinnati Campus, Hebrew Union College – Jewish Institute of Religion, MS coll. 276, 3/6.

Horowitz, Bethami. "Push-back about Cohen's Pew policy 'take-aways'." Email to NRJE, 14 December 2013.

Israelites of the City of Charleston. Memorial to the President and Members of the Adjunta of Kaal Kadosh Beth Elohim of Charleston, South Carolina. 23 December 1824. Reprint *A*

Documentary History of the Jews in the United States 1654–1875, 3rd edition, edited by Morris U. Schappes, 171–177. New York: Schocken Books, 1971.

Kahn, Robert I. Memo to CCAR Liturgy Commmittee, ©1970. Jacob Rader Marcus Center of the American Jewish Archives, Cincinnati Campus, Hebrew Union College – Jewish Institute of Religion, MS coll. Miscellaneous Correspondence from April 17, 1970 through 1972.

Landman, Isaac. Letter to Kohon [sic], 2 February1922. Jacob Rader Marcus Center of the American Jewish Archives, Cincinnati Campus, Hebrew Union College – Jewish Institute of Religion, MS coll. 276, 3/6.

Lefkowtiz, David. Letter to Samuel S. Cohon, 3 April 1923. Jacob Rader Marcus Center of the American Jewish Archives, Cincinnati Campus, Hebrew Union College – Jewish Institute of Religion, MS coll. 276, 3/7.

Le'Or Education Fund, *Cannabis Passover Seder* (Portland, OR: Le'OR Education Fund, 2016), cover letter.

Levy, Isaac J. Letter to Leonara and Ezekial Levy, 24 April 1864. Reprint "Confederate Passover." Accessed 7 February 2013, http://www.jewish-history.com/civilwar/seder.html.

Lilienthal, Max. Letter to Isaac Leeser, 24 November 1856. Reprint "Letters and Addresses. Letters on Reform Addressed to the Rev. I. Lesser." In *Max Lilienthal: American Rabbi: Life and Writings*, edited by David Philipson, 367–397. New York: Bloch Pub., 1915.

Mann, Louis L. Letter to Samuel S. Cohon, 28 March 1923. Jacob Rader Marcus Center of the American Jewish Archives, Cincinnati Campus, Hebrew Union College – Jewish Institute of Religion, MS coll. 276, 3/7.

Marcuson, Isaac E. Letter to Samuel S. Cohon, 1 January 1922. Jacob Rader Marcus Center of the American Jewish Archives, Cincinnati Campus, Hebrew Union College – Jewish Institute of Religion, MS coll. 276, 3/6.

Mielziner, M. Letter to Central Conference of American Rabbis, 2 December 1892. Reprint *Year Book of the Central Conference of American Rabbis*, vol. 4, 8. Cincinnati: Bloch Pub., 1894.

Mielziner, M. Henry Berkowitz, et al. Letter to P.P., ©1892. Jacob Rader Marcus Center of the American Jewish Archives, Cincinnati Campus, Hebrew Union College – Jewish Institute of Religion, MS coll. L. Miezimer, nearprint.

Morgenstern, Julian. Letter to Samuel S. Cohon, 19 December 1922. Jacob Rader Marcus Center of the American Jewish Archives, Cincinnati Campus, Hebrew Union College – Jewish Institute of Religion, MS coll. 276, 3/6.

Person, Hara. "RE: CCAR Yearbook inquiry." Email to author, 7 August 2013.

Pfaslzer, Elisi. Letter to Henry Berkowitz, 6 February 1922. Jacob Rader Marcus Center of the American Jewish Archives, Cincinnati Campus, Hebrew Union College – Jewish Institute of Religion, MS coll. 25, 1/26.

Philipson, Ludwig. Letter to the Directors of the Jewish Community in Brunswick, 26 March 1844. Reprint *The Rise of Reform Judaism: A Sourcebook of its European Origins*, edited by W. Gunther Plaut, 74–75. New York: World Union for Progressive Judaism, 1963.

Rosenau, William. Letter to Henry Berkowitz, 24 October 1904. Jacob Rader Marcus Center of the American Jewish Archives, Cincinnati Campus, Hebrew Union College – Jewish Institute of Religion, MS coll. 34, 2/2.

—— Letter to Henry Berkowitz, 24 December 1904. Jacob Rader Marcus Center of the American Jewish Archives, Cincinnati Campus, Hebrew Union College – Jewish Institute of Religion, MS coll. 34, 2/2.
—— Letter to Joseph Krauskopf, 4 September 1903. Jacob Rader Marcus Center of the American Jewish Archives, Cincinnati Campus, Hebrew Union College – Jewish Institute of Religion, MS coll. 34, 1/17.
—— Letter to Max Heller, 6 April 1905. Jacob Rader Marcus Center of the American Jewish Archives, Cincinnati Campus, Hebrew Union College – Jewish Institute of Religion, MS coll. 33, 4/26.
Rosenbaum, David. Letter to Samuel Cohon, 15 January 1922. Jacob Rader Marcus Center of the American Jewish Archives, Cincinnati Campus, Hebrew Union College – Jewish Institute of Religion, MS coll. 276, 3/6.
Sales Agents for the Conference, Bloch Publishing Co. Letter to Sir, 21 March 1910. Jacob Rader Marcus Center of the American Jewish Archives, Cincinnati Campus, Hebrew Union College – Jewish Institute of Religion, MS coll. 34, 5/12.
Schanfarber, T. Letter to M. J. Gries, 19 October 1905. Jacob Rader Marcus Center of the American Jewish Archives, Cincinnati Campus, Hebrew Union College – Jewish Institute of Religion, MS coll. 34, 3/4.
Schocken, Salman. Letter to Samuel A. [sic] Cohon, 18 April 1944. Jacob Rader Marcus Center of the American Jewish Archives, Cincinnati Campus, Hebrew Union College – Jewish Institute of Religion, MS coll. 276, 3/7.
Schwarz, Jacob D. Letter to Friend, 11 March 1949. Rodef Shalom Congregational Archives, BA 70, FF 34.
Stevens, Elliot L. Letter to Colleague, 20 January 1984. Jacob Rader Marcus Center of the American Jewish Archives, Cincinnati Campus, Hebrew Union College – Jewish Institute of Religion, MS coll. CCAR Nearprint, special topics/CCAR 1984.
—— Letter to Colleagues and Friends, February 1992. Jacob Rader Marcus Center of the American Jewish Archives, Cincinnati Campus, Hebrew Union College – Jewish Institute of Religion, MS coll. CCAR 4/CCAR 1992.
Washington, George. Letter to the Hebrew Congregation in New Port, Rhode Island, 17 August 1790. Reprint "Correspondence Between the Jews and Washington." In *A Documentary History of the Jews in the United States 1654–1875*, 3rd ed. Edited by Morris U. Schappes, 80. New York: Schocken Books, 1971.
—— Letter to the Hebrew Congregations in the Cities of Philadelphia, New York, Charleston and Richmond, 1790. Reprint "Correspondence Between the Jews and Washington." In *A Documentary History of the Jews in the United States 1654–1875*, 3rd ed. Edited by Morris U. Schappes, 83–84. New York: Schocken Books, 1971.
—— Letter to the Hebrew Congregation of the City of Savanah, 1789. Reprint "Correspondence Between the Jews and Washington." In *A Documentary History of the Jews in the United States 1654–1875*, 3rd ed. Edited by Morris U. Schappes, 78. New York: Schocken Books, 1971.
Wessel, Harvey E. Letter to Samuel S. Cohon, 24 March 1923. Jacob Rader Marcus Center of the American Jewish Archives, Cincinnati Campus, Hebrew Union College – Jewish Institute of Religion, MS coll. 276, 3/7.

Wolf, Horace J. Letter to Samuel S. Cohon. 29 March 1923. Jacob Rader Marcus Center of the American Jewish Archives, Cincinnati Campus, Hebrew Union College – Jewish Institute of Religion, MS coll. 276, 3/7.

Wolsey, Louis. Letter to Edward N. Calisch, 27 March 1923. Jacob Rader Marcus Center of the American Jewish Archives, Cincinnati Campus, Hebrew Union College – Jewish Institute of Religion, MS coll. 34, 13.7.

— Letter to Samuel S. Cohon, 24 December 1918. Jacob Rader Marcus Center of the American Jewish Archives, Cincinnati Campus, Hebrew Union College – Jewish Institute of Religion, MS coll. 276, 3/6.

Documents

About InterfaithFamily. n.d. Accessed 7 August 2014, http://www.interfaithfamily.com/about_us_advocacy/about_us_advocacy.shtml.

Article 16. Contitution of the German Confederation. Congress of Vienna, Vienna, 8 June 1815. Reprint *The Jew in the Modern World: A Documentary History*, 3rd edition. Edited by Paul Mendes-Flohr and Jehuda Reinharz, translated by Raphael Mahler, 165. New York: Oxford Univ. Press, 2010.

Association for the Reform of Judaism, Proclamation of the Association, Berlin, 1844. Reprint *The Rise of Reform Judaism: A Sourcebook of its European Origins*. Edited by W. Gunther Plaut, 57. New York: World Union for Progressive Judaism, 1963.

Columbus Platform. CCAR. 1937.

Constitution. New Israelitish Temple Association, Hamburg, 11 December 1817. Reprint *The Rise of Reform Judaism: A Sourcebook of its European Origins*. Edited by W. Gunther Plaut, 31–32. New York: World Union for Progressive Judaism, 1963.

Declaration of Principles. Pittsburgh Conference, Pittsburgh, Pennsylvania, 16–18 November 1885. Reprint *Year Book of The Central Conference of American Rabbis* 1890–91. Cincinnati: Bloch, 1891. Reprint *Central Conference of American Rabbis Year Book Volumes I, II, III 1890–1983*, 120–123. New York: CCAR, n.d.

Declaration of the Rabbinical Conference. Frankfort, July 1845. Reprint *The Rise of Reform Judaism: A Sourcebook of its European Origins*. Edited by W. Gunther Plaut, 89–90. New York: World Union for Progressive Judaism, 1963.

Declaration of the Rights of Man and of the Citizen. French National Assembly, Paris, France, 26 August 1789. Reprint *The Jew in the Modern World: A Documentary History*, 3rd edition. Edited by Paul Mendes-Flohr and Jehuda Reinharz. Translated by Benjamin Flower, 123. New York: Oxford Univ. Press, 2010.

Frederick William III, "Edict Concerning the Civil Status of the Jews in the Prussian State." 11 March 1812. Accessed 28 March 2014, http://germanhistorydocs.ghi-dc.org/sub_document_s.cfm?document_id=3650.

The Guiding Principles of Reform Judaism. CCAR Annual Meeting, Columbus, Ohio, 1937. Accessed 26 July 2000, http://www.ccarnet.org/platforms/Columbus.html.

"History." *United Hebrew Congregation*, 2012. Accessed 24 March 2015, http://www.unitedhebrew.org/AboutUs/History.aspx

Jacob, Walter. "70. Reform Haggadah." Questions and Reform Jewish Answers: New American Reform Responsa, 110–112. New York: CCAR, 1992.

Knobel, Peter, et al. Criteria for a New Haggadah. Ad Hoc Committee for Haggadah Development, 2 April 1997.
Melzner, Ralf and Stefanie Flamm. "New Rabbinical School Praised." *Abraham Geiger Kolleg*, 14 November 2000. Accessed 17 September 2011, http://abraham-geiger-kolleg.de.
Miami Platform. CCAR, 1997.
"Mission." *Hebrew Union College—Jewish Institute of Religion* 2015. Accessed 4 January 2015, http://huc.edu.
"Mission Statement." *Central Conference of American Rabbis* 17 January 2008. Accessed 4 January 2015, http://ccarnet.org.
Moss, David. "My Haggadah: The Book of Freedom." *David Moss Projects* 2015. Accessed 5 January 2015, http://davidmoss.com/projects/moss-haggadah/.
"The New Union Haggadah." *Central Conference of American Rabbis Press* 2014. Accessed 28 July 2014, http://www.ccarpress.org/shopping_product_detail.asp?pid=50125.
"Plan of the Prayer Book." *Year Book of the Central Conference of the American Rabbis 1891–92*, 15–16. Cincinnati, Ohio: Bloch Pub., 1892. Reprint Central Conference of American Rabbis Year Book Volumes I, II, III 1890–1983. New York: CCAR, n.d.
The Principles of the Society for Classical Reform Judaism. 1 February 2008. Accessed 29 July 2014, renewreform.org/our-principles/.
Reform Judaism: A Centenary Perspective. CCAR 1976. Accessed 5 December 2010, http://www.ccarnet.org/platforms/rabbis-speak/platforms/reform-judaism-centary-perspective/.
"Sharing the Journey: The Seder Leader's Guide." *Central Conference of American Rabbis* 2014, accessed 5 January 2015, http://www.ccarpress.org/shopping_product_detail.asp?pid=50236.
Society of the Friends of Reform. Declaration of Principle. 1842. Reprint *The Rise of Reform Judaism: A Sourcebook of its European Origins.* Edited by W. Gunther Plaut, 51. New York: World Union for Progressive Judaism, 1963.
"A Statement of Principles for Reform Judaism." Central Conference of American Rabbis Annual Conference, Pittsburgh, Pennsylvania, May 1999.
These are the Words of the Covenant. Hamburg Rabbinical Court, 1819. Reprint *The Jew in the Modern World: A Documentary History*, 3rd edition. Edited by Paul Mendes-Flohr and Jehuda Reinharz. Translated by S. Fischer and S. Weinstein, 187–189. New York: Oxford Univ. Press, 2010.
2014–2015 Prospectus. London: Leo Beck Institute, 2014.
The Union Haggadah. New York: Bloch Publishing Co., 1908. Advertisement. Jacob RaderMarcus Center of the American Jewish Archives, Cincinnati Campus, Hebrew Union College – Jewish Institute of Religion, MS coll. 34, 4/8.

Haggadot and Siddurim

אַ נײַע הגדה של פסח. New York: Workmen's Circle, 1991.
Angel, Marc D. הגדה של פסח הספרדים *A Sephardic PASSOVER HAGGADAH*. Hoboken, New Jersey: KTAV Pub., 1988.
Berman, Howard A. *The New Union Haggadah: Revised Edition.* New York: CCAR, 2014.

Bien, H. M. Easter Eve or The "New Hagodoh Shel Pesach." A Metrical Family-Fest Service. Cincinnati: Bloch Pub., 1886.

Bronstein, Herbert. הגדה של פסח [Haggadah Shel Pesach]: A Passover Haggadah: A New Union Haggadah. New York: Grossman Pub., 1974.

— הגדה של פסח Пасхальная Агада (New York: CCAR, 1992).

Cantor, Aviva. *An Egalitarian Hagada.* New York: Lillith Pub., 1982.

— "Jewish Women's Haggadah." *Womanspirit Rising: A Feminist Reader in Religion.* Edited by Carol P. Christ and Judith Plaskow, 185–192. New York: Harper & Row, Pub., 1979.

Central Conference of American Rabbis. "(Seder Haggadah.) Domestic service for the Eve of Passover." *Union Prayer Book*, 227–257. Chicago: Bloch Pub., 1892.

— *The Union Haggadah.* New York: Bloch Publishing, July 1905.

— *The Union Haggadah.* New York: Bloch Publishing, 1907.

— *The Union Haggadah.* New York: Bloch Publishing, 1908.

— *The Union Haggadah: Home Service for the Passover.* New York: Central Conference of American Rabbis, 1923.

— *The Union Haggadah: Home Service for the Passover.* New York: Central Conference of American Rabbis, 1923. Reprint 2011.

— *Union Prayer Book.* Chicago: Bloch Pub., 1892.

Cohen Ioannides, Mara W. and Stephen M. Cohen. *Haggadah: A Modern Edition.* 1st ed. n.p.: n.p., 1993.

Dayenu: A Special Contemporary Dayenu Created in Honor of the 40th Anniversary of the Birth of the State of Israel. New York: CLAL, 1988.

Elwell, Sue Levi. כל-דכפין The Open Door: A Passover Haggadah. New York: CCAR, 2002.

Einhorn, David. [Olat Tamid]: Book of Prayers for Jewish Congregations. Chicago: S. Ettlinger, 1896.

Fields, Harvey J. *Festival of Freedom* הגדה של פסח. Los Angeles: Wilshire Boulevard Temple, 1988.

Freedman, Ruth Gruber. *The Passover Seder.* New York: New American Library, 1983.

Frishman, Elyse D. *Mishkan T'filah: A Reform Siddur.* New York: CCAR, 2007.

Goldberg, Nathan. *Passover Haggadah* הגדה של פסח, New Revised Ed. New York: KTAV Pub., 1966.

Green, A. A. *The Revised Hagada: Home Service for the First Two Nights of Passover.* London: Greenberg & Co., 1897.

Gutstein, Z. Harry. *Passover Hagadah* הגדה של פסח. New York: KTAV Pub., 1949.

Haggadah for the Liberated Lamb, edited by Roberta Kalochofsky. Marblehead, Massachusetts: Micah Pub., 1985.

הגדה של פסח. Bombay: n.p., 1846. Reprint *"The Haggadah shel Pesach" in Marathi of the Bene-Israel.* New York: Orphan Hospital Ward of Israel, 1968.

הגדה של פסח. New York: Behrman's Book Shop, 1910. Reprint הגדה של פסח. New York: KTAV, 1951.

הגדה של פסח *Пасхальная Агада.* Jerusalem: Hotzot Bkal, ©1971.

הגדה של פסח *The Haggadah of Passover.* New York: Shulsinger Brothers Pub., 1954.

הגדה של פסח *Passover Haggadah.* Bloomfield Hills, MI: SKM Marketing, 2013.

הגדה של פסח *The Passover Haggadah.* Edited and translated by Philip Birnbaum. USA: Hebrew Pub. Co., 1976.

הגדה של פסח *[Haggadah Shel Pesach] Service for the Two First Night of Passover with an English Translation*, 7th (Stereotype) Edition. New York: L.H. Frank, 1863.

הגדה של פסח *Service for the First Two Night of Passover*, New Ed. New York: Star Hebrew Book Co., 1929.

Jackson, S[olomon] H. Service for the two first nights of the Passover, in Hebrew and English: According to the Custom of the German & Spanish Jews, translated by David Levi. New York: S.H. Jackson, 1837.

Joint Committee on Ceremonies, UAHC and CCAR, *Ceremonial for Opening the Door for Elijah*. New York: CCAR, 1942. Rodef Shalom Congregational Archives, BA 70, FF 34.

—— *Passover and the Contemporary Scene*. New York: CCAR, 1942. Rodef Shalom Congregational Archives, BA 70, FF 34.

"Judaic Treasures of the Library of Congress: The First English Translation of the Haggadah." *Jewish Virtual Library*, 2014. Accessed 29 March 2014, http://www.jewishvirtuallibrary.org/jsource/loc/Haggadah2.html.

Kalechofsky, Roberta. *Haggadah for the Liberated Lamb*. Marblehead: Micah, 1985.

Kaplan, Mordecia M., Eugene Kohn, and Ira Eisenstein. *The New Haggadah for the Pesah Seder*. New York: Behrman's Jewish Book House, 1941.

Kolatch, Alfred J. *The Family Seder: A Traditional Passover Haggadah for the Modern Home*. New York: Jonathan David Pub., 1967.

Lehmann, Marcus. *Hagadah Schel Pesach*. Frankfurt am Main: J. Kauffmann Berlag, 1935.

Le'Or Education Fund. *Cannabis Passover Seder*. Portlan, OR: Le'Or Education Fund, 2016.

Levi, David. *Service for the first two nights of the Passover, in Hebrew and English: according to the custom of the German & Spanish Jews*. New York: S.H. Jackson, 1837.

The Matteh Aharon Haggadah 1710. New York: The Disken Orphen Home, 1982.

Morris, Tamra L. ed. *Freedom Haggadahfor Soviet Jewry*. New York: CLAL and The National Conference on Soviet Jewry, 1987.

Moses, I[saac] S. *Seder Hagadah: Domestic Service for the Eve of Passover*. 2nd revised and enlarged ed. Chicago: I.S. Moses, 1898.

—— *Seder Hagadah: Domestic Service for the Eve of Passover*. 5th revised and enlarged ed. New York: Bloch Pub., 1907.

A Night of Questions – A Passover Haggadah. Edited by Joy D. Levitt and Michael J. Strassfeldl. Elkins Park: Reconstructionist Press, 2000.

Passover Haggadah. Naples, New York: Manischewitz Wine Company, 1988.

Passover Haggadah. DeLuxe Edition. N.p.: General Foods, 2004.

Philips, A. Th. פסח הוסדר של הגדה *Form of Service for the Two First Nights of the Feast of Passover with English Translation*, New Illustrated Edition. New York: Hebrew Publishing Co., 1859.

Roberts, Cokie and Stephen V. Roberts. *Our Haggadah: Uniting Traditions for Interfaith Families*. New York: HarperCollins, 2011.

Rosenau, William. סדר הגדה *Home-Service for Passover Eve*. New York: Bloch Pub., 1905.

Roth, Cecil. The Haggadah: A New Edition with English Translation. London: Soncino Press, 1959.

הגדה של פסח סדר. Amsterdam: Asher Anshel ben Eliezer and Issachar Ber ben Abraham Eliezer, 1695. Reprint *The Amsterdam Haggadah of 1695*. New York: Orphan Hospital Ward of Israel, 1974.

סדר של פסח הגדה. Altona: Joseph ben David, 1738. Reprint *The Leipnik-Rosenthaliana Haggadah*. New York: Orphan Hospital Ward of Israel, 1977.

סדר של פסח הגדה. Altona-Hamburg-Wandesbeck: Netanel ben Aaron Levi, 1772. Reprint *The Moshe Bamberger Haggadah*. New York: Orphan Hospital Ward of Israel, 1972.

סדר הגדה של פסח Service for the First Two Night of Passover, New Ed. New York: Star Hebrew Book Co., 1929.

The Shaare Rahamin Haggadah. Brooklyn: Congregation Shaare Rahamim, 1999.

Silver, Arthur M. *Passover Haggadah: The Complete Seder*. New York: Menorah Publishing Co., 1980.

Silverman, Morris. הגדה של פסח Passover Haggadah with Explanatory Notes and Original Readings. Hartford, Connecticut: Prayer Book Press, 1959.

Simkin, Ruth. *Like An Orange on a Seder Plate: Our Lesbian Haggadah* (n.p.: Ruth Simkin, 1999).

Stern, Chiam. *Gates of Prayer for Shabbat and Weekdays* שערי תפלה לשבת ויום חול: A Gender Sensitive Prayerbook. New York: CCAR, 1994.

A Soviet Jewry Freedom Seder. Chevy Chase: Congregation Ohr Kodesh, 1974.

Tabory, Joseph. *JPS Commentary on the Haggadah: Historical Introduction, Translation, and Commentary*. Philadelphia: JPS, 2008.

Tucson Jewish Feminist Haggadah. Tucson: Women's Division of the Jewish Federation of Southern Arizona and B'nai B'rith Hillel Foundation of the Univ. of Arizona, ©1994.

Wise, Isaac Mayer. *Minhag America; Tefilot B'nai Yeshurun* (Cincinnati: Bloch, 1857).

Yoffie, Alan S. *The Seder Leader's Guide to Sharing the Journey: The Haggadah for the Contemporary Family*. New York: CCAR, 2012.

—— *Sharing the Journey: The Haggadah for the Contemporary Family*. Illustrated by Mark Podwal. New York: CCAR, 2012.

Interviews

Bronstein, Herbert. Interview by author, 13 December 1996.

Ellenson, David. "Seminary of Unimaginable Ironies." *Reform Judaism* (summer 2011), 52–53, 61–62.

Elwell, Sue Levi. Interview by author, 14 February 2014.

Fox, Steve and Lance Sussman. "Rabbinic Road Out of a Wilderness." *Reform Judaism* (summer 2011), 54–57.

Freelander, Daniel. "Birth of a Synagogue Movement." *Reform Judaism* (summer 2011), 58–61, 64.

Kaplan, Dana Evan. Interview. *TCJ: Up Close*. The Jewish Channel, 17 March 2014. Accessed 22 July 2014, http://newsdesk.tjctv.com/2014/03/up-close-march-17–2014/.

Knobel, Peter. Interview by author, 7 August 2013.

Levy, Richard. Interview by author, 28 March 2014.

—— "Is It Time To Chart A New Course For Reform Judaism?" *Reform Judaism* (winter 1998), 10–12, 18–22, 54.

Podwel, Mark. "New Passover Seder Haggadah." *Religion & Ethics Newsweekly*, 15 January 2013. Accessed 30 March 2012, www.pbs.org/wnet/religionandethics/episodes/march-30–2012/new-passover-seder-haggadah/10622/.

Rosenfeld, Elie. "Elie Rosenfeld- Maxwell House Haggadah." *Jinsider*, 13 November 2008. Accessed 29 June 2010, https://www.youtube.com/watch?v=l_PL7PjL6NE.
Sarna, Jonathan D. "The Discontinuity of Continuity." *Reform Judaism* (winter 2012), 24–26.
Yoffie, Alan. Interview by author, 24 January 2014.
Zamore, Mary L. Interview by author, 10 January 2014.

Minutes and Reports

"Actions of the Executive Board 1989–1990." Central Conference of American Rabbis Annual Convention, Seattle, Washington, 22–28 June 1990. *Year Book of the Central Conference of American Rabbis*, vol. 100, 251–254. New York: CCAR, 1991.
Bamberger, Bernard J. "Report of the Committee on Liturgy." Central Conference of American Rabbis Annual Convention, Buffalo, New York, 10–15 June 1952. *Year Book of the Central Conference of American Rabbis*, vol. 62, 258–259. Philadelphia: Maurice Jacobs, 1957.
—— "Report of the Committee on Liturgy." Central Conference of American Rabbis Annual Convention, Atlantic City, New Jersey, 25–28 June 1956. *Year Book of the Central Conference of American Rabbis*, vol. 64, 83–84. Philadelphia: Maurice Jacobs, 1957.
—— "Report of the Committee on Liturgy." Central Conference of American Rabbis Annual Convention, Chicago, Illinois, 24–29 June 1958. *Year Book of the Central Conference of American Rabbis*, vol. 68, 102. Philadelphia: Maurice Jacobs, 1958.
Berkowitz, Henry. "Report of the Committee on Union Haggadah." *Year Book of the Central Conference of American Rabbis*, vol. 18, 132. Cincinnati: Bloch Pub., 1908.
—— "Report of the Committee on 'The Union Seder Haggadah." Central Conference of American Rabbis Annual Convention, Frankfort, Michigan, 2–8 July 1907. *Year Book of the Central Conference of American Rabbis*, vol. 15, 94–95. Cincinnati: Bloch Pub., 1908.
Berkowitz, Henry, J. Stolz, and H. G. Enelow. "Report of the Committee on Haggadah." Convention of the Central Conference of American Rabbis, 1903. *Year Book of the Central Conference of American Rabbis*, vol. 14, 83–85. Cincinnati: Bloch Pub., 1904.
Berkowitz, Henry, K[aufmann] Kohler, et al. "Report of the Committee on Seder Haggadah." Central Conference of American Rabbis Conference, Indianapolis, Indiana, 3 July 1906. *Year Book of the Central Conference of American Rabbis*, vol. 16, 83–84. Cincinnati: Bloch Pub., 1906.
Berman, Morton M. "Report of the Committee on Marriage, Family and the Home." Central Conference of American Rabbis Annual Convention, Asbury Park, New Jersey, 20–23 June 1955. *Year Book of the Central Conference of American Rabbis*, vol. 65, 69. Philadelphia: Maurice Jacobs, 1957.
Bronstein, Herbert. Minutes of Liturgy Committee Meeting, 29 November 1967.
CCAR Executive Board. "Actions of the Executive Board 1989–1990." Proceedings of the Central Conference of American Rabbis, Seattle, Washington, 22–29 June 1990. *Central Conference of American Rabbis Yearbook*, vol. 100, 251–254. New York: CCAR, 1991.
Chorin, Aaron. "The Rational of Reform," July 1844. Reprint *The Jew in the Modern World: A Documentary History*, 3rd edition, edited by Paul Mendes-Flohr and Jehuda Reinharz, 211. New York: Oxford Univ. Press, 2010.

Cohen, Simon, et al. "Report of Committee on Publications." Central Conference of American Rabbis Annual Convention, Montreal, Canada, 24–28 June 1948. *Year Book of the Central Conference of American Rabbis*, vol. 57, 43–46. Philadelphia: JPS, 1948.

Cohon, S[amuel] S. Response to "Report of Committee on Revision of the Haggadah." Central Conference of American Rabbis Annual Convention, Cincinnati, Ohio, 2–7 April 1919. *Year Book of the Central Conference of American Rabbis*, vol. 29, 57. Cincinnati: CJ Krehbiel & Co., 1919.

Cohon, Samuel S., Samuel N. Deinard, Solomon B. Freehof, and Samuel Schwartz. "Report of Committee on Revision of the Haggadah." Central Conference of American Rabbis Annual Convention, Washington, D.C., 13–17 April 1921. *Year Book of the Central Conference of American Rabbis*, vol. 31, 38. Cincinnati: CJ Krehbiel & Co., 1921.

Cohon, Samuel S., Samuel N. Deinard, Maurice Lefkovitz, et al. "Report of Committee on Revision of the Haggadah." Central Conference of American Rabbis Annual Convention, Cincinnati, Ohio, 2–7 April 1919. *Year Book of the Central Conference of American Rabbis*, vol. 29, 55–56. Cincinnati: CJ Krehbiel & Co., 1919.

Cohon, Samuel S, Solomon B. Freehof, Gerson B. Levi, and William Rosenau. "Report of Committee on Revision of Union Haggadah." Central Conference of American Rabbis Annual Convention, Cape May, New Jersey, 27 June – 2 July 1923. *Year Book of the Central Conference of American Rabbis*, vol. 33, 41–43. Cincinnati: CJ Krehbiel & Co., 1923.

Committee on Liturgy and Music Minutes, 2 March 1966.

Dreyfus, A. Stanley. "Report of the Liturgy Committee." Central Conference of American Rabbis Annual Convention, Cincinnati, Ohio, 15–19 June 1975. *Year Book of the Central Conference of American Rabbis*, vol. 85, 41–44. New York: CCAR, 1975.

—— "Report of the Liturgy Committee." Central Conference of American Rabbis Annual Convention, Toronto, Canada, 26–29 June 1978. *Year Book of the Central Conference of American Rabbis*, vol. 88, 39. New York: CCAR, 1979.

Fink, Joseph L. "Report of the Committee on President's Message." Central Conference of American Rabbis Annual Convention, Asbury Park, New Jersey, 20–23 June 1955. *Year Book of the Central Conference of American Rabbis*, vol. 65, 110–113. Philadelphia: Maurice Jacobs, 1957.

Franklin, Leo M., et al. "Report of the Committee on Publications." Proceedings of the Central Conference of American Rabbis, Cincinnati, Ohio, 2–7 April 1919. *CCAR Yearbook*, vol. 29, 44–49. Cincinnati: C. J. Krehbiel, 1919.

Franklin, Leo M., Ephraim Frisch, Samuel Hirshberg et al. "Report of the Committee on Publications." Central Conference of American Rabbis Annual Convention, Chicago, Illinois, 28 June – 4 July 1918. *Year Book of the Central Conference of American Rabbis*, vol. 28, 46–54. Cincinnati: CJ Krehbiel & Co., 1918.

Franklin, Leo M., Ephraim Frisch, I. E. Marcuson, et al. "Report of the Publications Committee." Central Conference of American Rabbis Annual Convention, Wildwood, New Jersey, 13 June – 7 July 7, 1916. *Year Book of the Central Conference of American Rabbis*, vol. 26, 50–61. New York: Bloch Pub., 1916.

Guttmacher, A., et al. "Report of the Publication Committee." 5 June 1910. Central Conference of American Rabbis Annual Convention, Charlevoix, Michigan, 28 June – 4 July 1910. *Year Book of the Central Conference of American Rabbis*, vol. 20, 40–41. n.p.: n.p., 1911.

Hahn, Aaron. Motion. Convention of the Central Conference of American Rabbis, Cleveland, Ohio, 14 July 1891, *Year Book of the Central Conference of American Rabbis 1890–91*, 26. Cincinnati: Bloch Pub., 1891. Reprint *Central Conference of American Rabbis Year Book Volumes I, II, III 1890–1983*. New York: CCAR, n.d.

Kahn, Robert I. "Report of Committee on Liturgy." Central Conference of American Rabbis Annual Convention, Boston, Massachusetts, 17–20 June 1968. *Year Book of the Central Conference of American Rabbis*, vol. 78, 90–92. New York: CCAR, 1969.

—— "Report of Committee on Liturgy." Central Conference of American Rabbis Annual Convention, Jerusalem, Israel, 6–10 March 1970. *Year Book of the Central Conference of American Rabbis*, vol. 80, 45. New York: CCAR, 1971.

—— "Report of Committee on Liturgy and Music." Central Conference of American Rabbis Annual Convention, Grossinger, New York, 12–15 June 1972. *Year Book of the Central Conference of American Rabbis*, vol. 82, 47–48. New York: CCAR, 1973.

Kliger, Sam. "Russian–Jewish Immigrants in the U.S.: Social Portrait Challenges, and AJS Involvement." *American Jewish Committee Commission on Contemporary Jewish Life*. Accessed 5 August 2014, http://www.ajcrussian.org/site/nlet/content2.aspx?c=chLMK3PKLxF&b=7718799&ct=11713359.

Krauskopf, Joseph. response to Henry Berkowitz, J. Stolz, and H. G. Enelow. "Report of the Committee on Haggadah." *Year Book of the Central Conference of American Rabbis*,vol. 14, 86. Cincinnati: Bloch Pub., 1904.

Krauskopf, Joseph and Henry Berkowitz. "Report of the Committee on a Pesach Haggadah." *Year Book of the Central Conference of American Rabbis*, vol. 13, 64. Cincinnati: Bloch Pub., 1903.

Mannheimer, S. and I. Schwab. "On Prayer-Book." Presented at the Convention of the Central Conference of American Rabbis, Cleveland, Ohio, 14 July 1891, *Year Book of the Central Conference of American Rabbis 1890–91*, 26–27. Cincinnati: Bloch Pub., 1891. Reprint *Central Conference of American Rabbis Year Book Volumes I, II, III 1890–1983*. New York: CCAR, n.d.

Marcuson, Isaac E. "Report of Committee on Publications." Central Conference of American Rabbis Annual Convention, New York, New York, 22–27 June 1943. *Year Book of the Central Conference of American Rabbis*, vol. 53, 47–49. Philadelphia: JPS, 1943.

—— "Report of Committee on Publications." Central Conference of American Rabbis Annual Convention, Cincinnati, Ohio, 23–26 June 1944. *Year Book of the Central Conference of American Rabbis*, vol. 54, 50–53. Philadelphia: JPS, 1944.

Marcuson, Isaac E., Ernst Appel et al. "Report of Committee on Publications." Central Conference of American Rabbis Annual Convention, Atlantic City, New Jersey, 25–27 June, 1945. *Year Book of the Central Conference of American Rabbis*, vol. 55, 47–49. Philadelphia: JPS, 1946.

Marcuson, Isaac E., Solomon N. Bazell, et al. "Report of Committee on Publications." Central Conference of American Rabbis Annual Convention, Charlevoix, Michigan, 18–23 June 1940. *Year Book of the Central Conference of American Rabbis*, vol. 50, 50–53. Philadelphia: JPS, 1938.

Marcuson, Isaac E., Solomon N. Bazell, et al. "Report of Committee on Publications." Central Conference of American Rabbis Annual Convention, Cincinatti, Ohio, 24 February – 1 March 1942. *YearBook of the Central Conference of American Rabbis*, vol.52, 52–53. Philadelphia: JPS, 1942.

Marcuson, Isaac E., Max C. Currick, Barnett A. Elzas, et al. "Report of Committee on Publications." Central Conference of American Rabbis Annual Convention, Detroit, Michigan, 27–30 June 1929. *Year Book of the Central Conference of American Rabbis*, vol. 39, 53–55. n.p.: n.p., 1929.

Marcuson, Isaac E., Solomon N. Bazell, Clifton H. Levy, and Nathan Stern. "Report of Committee on Publications." Central Conference of American Rabbis Annual Convention, Chicago, Illinois, 27 June – 1 July 1928. *Year Book of the Central Conference of American Rabbis*, vol. 38, 46–47. n.p.: n.p., 1928.

Marcuson, Isaac E., L. Elliot Grafman, and Solomon Landman. "Report of Committee on Publications." Central Conference of American Rabbis Annual, Milwaukee, Wisconsin, 22–24 June 1933. *Year Book of the Central Conference of American Rabbis*, vol. 43, 35–37. n.p.: n.p., 1933.

Marcuson, Isaac E., L. Elliot Grafman, Solomon Landman, Clifton Harby Levy, and Harry A. Merfeld. "Report of Committee on Publications." Central Conference of American Rabbis Annual, Wernersville, Pennsylvania, 14–18 June 1934. *Year Book of the Central Conference of American Rabbis*, vol. 44, 35–37. n.p.: n.p., 1934.

Marcuson, Isaac E., Elliot Grafman, Solomon Landman, Clifton Harby Levy, and Harry A. Merfeld. "Report of Committee on Publications." Central Conference of American Rabbis Annual Convention, Chicago, Illinios, 25–30 June 1935. *Year Book of the Central Conference of American Rabbis*, vol. 45, 35–37. n.p.: n.p., 1935.

Marcuson, Isaac E., Elliot Grafman, Solomon Landman, Clifton Harby Levy, Harry A. Merfeld, and Nathan Stern. "Report of Committee on Publications." Central Conference of American Rabbis Annual Convention, Cincinnati, Ohio, 2–6 November 1932. *Year Book of the Central Conference of American Rabbis*, vol. 42, 43–45. n.p.: n.p., 1932.

Marcuson, Isaac E., Benjamin Kelson, Solomon Landman, Clifton Harby Levy, and Harry A. Merfeld. "Report of Committee on Publications." Central Conference of American Rabbis Annual Convention, Cape May, New Jersey, 23–27 June 1936. *Year Book of the Central Conference of American Rabbis*, vol. 46, 53–55. n.p.: n.p., 1936.

Marcuson, Isaac E., Benjamin Kelson, Solomon Landman, Clifton Harby Levy, and Harry A. Merfeld. "Report of Committee on Publications." Central Conference of American Rabbis Annual Convention, Columbus, Ohio, 25–30 May 1937. *Year Book of the Central Conference of American Rabbis*, vol. 47, 39–42. Philadelphia: JPS, 1937.

Marcuson, Isaac E., Benjamin Kelson, Solomon Landman, Clifton Harby Levy, and Harry A. Merfeld. "Report of Committee on Publications." Central Conference of American Rabbis Annual Convention, Atlantic City, New Jersey, 21–26 June 1938. *Year Book of the Central Conference of American Rabbis*, vol. 48, 36–38. Philadelphia: JPS, 1938.

Marcuson, Isaac E., Benjamin Kelson, Solomon Landman, Clifton Harby Levy, and Harry A. Merfeld. "Report of Committee on Publications." Central Conference of American Rabbis Annual Convention, Washington, D.C., 13–18 June 1939. *Year Book of the Central Conference of American Rabbis*, vol. 49, 49–51. Philadelphia: JPS, 1938.

Marcuson, Isaac E., Sol. L. Kory, Clifton Harby Levy, Harry A. Merfeld, et al. "Report of Committee on Publications." Central Conference of American Rabbis Annual Convention, Providence, Rhode Island, 25–29 June 1930. *Year Book of the Central Conference of American Rabbis*, vol. 40, 40–42. n.p.: n.p., 1930.

Marcuson, Isaac E., Sol. L. Kory, Clifton Harby Levy, Norris Newfield, and Nathan Stern. "Report of Committee on Publications." Central Conference of American Rabbis Annual

Convention, Wawasee, Indiana, 17–21 June 1931. *Year Book of the Central Conference of American Rabbis*, vol. 41, 36–39. n.p.: n.p., 1931.

Marcuson, Isaac E., Aryeh Lev et al., "Report of Committee on Publications." Central Conference of American Rabbis Annual Convention, Montreal, Canada, 22–26 June 1948. *Year Book of the Central Conference of American Rabbis*, vol. 57, 58–61. Philadelphia: JPS, 1948.

Marcuson, Isaac E., Clifton Harby Levy, Morris Newfield, and Julian Morgenstern. "Report of Committee on Publications." Central Conference of American Rabbis Annual Convention, Cedar Point, Ohio, 16–30 June 1924. *Year Book of the Central Conference of American Rabbis*, vol. 34, 77–79. Richmond, Virginia: Old Dominion Press, 1925.

Marcuson, Isaac E., Julian Morgenstern, Morris Newfield, and Nathan Stern. "Report of Committee on Publications." Central Conference of American Rabbis Annual Convention, Cincinnati, Ohio, 20–23 October 1925. *Year Book of the Central Conference of American Rabbis*, vol. 35, 34–35. Richmond, Virginia: Old Dominion Press, 1925.

Mielziner, M., S. Mannheimer, S. Hecht, H[enry] Berkowitz, Isaac S. Moses. "Report of the Ritual Committee." *Year Book of the Central Conference of the American Rabbis 1892–93*, 96–100. Cincinnati, Ohio: Bloch Pub., 1893. Reprint *Central Conference of American Rabbis Year Book Volumes I, II, III 1890–1983*. New York: CCAR, n.d.

Minutes. New Amsterdam Council, 5 November 1655. Reprint "Asserting the Right to Fight." In *A Documentary History of the Jews in the United States 1654–1875*, 3rd ed. Edited by Morris U. Schappes, 6. New York: Schocken Books, 1971.

Morgenstern, Julian, Ephraim Frisch, Isaac Landman, and Isaac E. Marcuson, "Report of the Publications Committee." Central Conference of American Rabbis Annual Convention, Charlevoix, Michigan, 29 June – 6 July 1915. *Year Book of the Central Conference of American Rabbis*, vol. 25, 48–57. New York: Bloch Pub., 1915.

Moses, I[saac] S. Response to Henry Berkowitz, J. Stolz, and H. G. Enelow. "Report of the Committee on Haggadah." *Year Book of the Central Conference of American Rabbis*, vol. 14, 87–88. Cincinnati: Bloch Pub., 1904.

Motion on the Letter to Central Conference of American Rabbis, 2 December 1892. *Year Book of the Central Conference of American Rabbis*, vol. 4, 9. Cincinnati: Bloch Pub., 1894.

Narot, Joseph R. Minutes of the Liturgy Committee Meeting, New York City, 13–14 April 1965. Jacob Rader Marcus Center of the American Jewish Archives, Cincinnati Campus, Hebrew Union College – Jewish Institute of Religion, MS coll. 34.

——— "Report on the Committee on Liturgy and Music." Proceedings of the Central Conference of American Rabbis, Toronto, Canada, 21–25 June 1966. *Central Conference of American Rabbis Yearbook*, vol. 76, 62–65. New York: CCAR, 1966.

——— "Report of the Committee on Liturgy and Music." Proceedings of the Central Conference of American Rabbis, Los Angeles, California, 19–22 June, 1967. *Central Conference of American Rabbis Yearbook*, vol. 77, 53–55. New York: CCAR, 1967.

Philchik, Ely E. "Report of Committee on Publications." Central Conference of American Rabbis Annual Convention, Asbury Park, New Jersey, 20–23 June 1955. *Year Book of the Central Conference of American Rabbis*, vol. 65, 78–79. Philadelphia: Maurice Jacobs, 1957.

——— "Report of Committee on Publications." Central Conference of American Rabbis Annual Convention, Miami Beach, Florida, 24–27 June 1957. *Year Book of the Central Conference of American Rabbis*, vol. 67, 73–74. Philadelphia: Maurice Jacobs, 1958.

— "Report of Committee on Publications." Central Conference of American Rabbis Annual Convention, Chicago, Illinois, 24–29 June 1958. *Year Book of the Central Conference of American Rabbis*, vol. 68, 111–112. Philadelphia: Maurice Jacobs, 1959.

"Plan of the Prayer Book." *Year Book of the Central Conference of the American Rabbis 1891–92*, 15–16. Cincinnati: Bloch Pub., 1892. Reprint *Central Conference of American Rabbis Year Book Volumes I, II, III 1890–1983*. New York: CCAR, n.d.

Polish, David, Albert Goldstein, and Hyman J. Schachtel. Subcommittee on Haggadah, ©1960. Jacob Rader Marcus Center of the American Jewish Archives, Cincinnati Campus, Hebrew Union College – Jewish Institute of Religion, MS coll. 24, 20/11.

Poller, H. Leonard. "Report of the Committee on Liturgy." Proceedings of the Central Conference of American Rabbis, Jerusalem, Israel, 7–13 March 1988. *Central Conference of American Rabbis Yearbook,* vol. 98, 135–138. New York: CCAR, 1989.

— "Report of the Committee on Liturgy." Central Conference of American Rabbis Annual Convention, Cincinnati, Ohio, 21–26 June 1989. *Year Book of the Central Conference of American Rabbis*, vol. 99, 200–202. New York: CCAR, 1990.

"A Portrait of Jewish Americans." *Pew Research: Religion and Public Life Project*, 1 October 2013. Accessed July 14, 2013, http://www.pewforum.org/2013/10/01/jewish-american-beliefs-attitudes-culture-survey/.

Regner, Sidney L. Minutes of the Liturgy Committee Meeting, New York, New York, 29 May 1956. Jacob Rader Marcus Center of the American Jewish Archives, Cincinnati Campus, Hebrew Union College – Jewish Institute of Religion, MS coll. 34.

— Minutes of Liturgy Committee Meeting, 23–29 December 1959. Jacob Rader Marcus Center of the American Jewish Archives, Cincinnati Campus, Hebrew Union College – Jewish Institute of Religion, MS coll. 34.

— "Report of Committee on Publications." Central Conference of American Rabbis Annual Convention, Estes Park, Colorado, 23–28 June 1953. *Year Book of the Central Conference of American Rabbis*, vol. 63,143–145. Philadelphia: Maurice Jacobs, 1957.

— "Report of Committee on Publications." Central Conference of American Rabbis Annual Convention, Pike, New Hampshire, 22–27 June 1954. *Year Book of the Central Conference of American Rabbis*, vol. 64, 66–67. Philadelphia: Maurice Jacobs, 1957.

Regner, Sidney L., Bernard J. Bamberger, et al. Minutes of the Liturgy Committee Meeting, Hotel Sheraton—Gibson, Cincinnati, Ohio, 24 January 1956.

"Report of Committee on President's Message." Central Conference of American Rabbis Annual Convention, Frankfort, Michigan, 2–8 July 1907. *Year Book of the Central Conference of American Rabbis*, vol. 15, 118–119. Cincinnati: Bloch Pub., 1908.

Resolution. Year Book of the Central Conference of the American Rabbis 1891–92, 18 Cincinnati: Bloch Pub., 1892. Reprint Central Conference of American Rabbis Year Book Volumes I, II, III 1890–1983. New York: CCAR, n.d.

Rosenau, [William]. Response to I[saac] S. Moses' response to Henry Berkowitz, J. Stolz, and H. G. Enelow. "Report of the Committee on Haggadah." *Year Book of the Central Conference of American Rabbis*, vol. 14, 88. Cincinnati: Bloch Pub., 1904.

Rubin, Alvan D. "Report of Committee on Publications." Central Conference of American Rabbis Annual Convention, Minneapolis-St. Paul, Minnesota, 19–23 June 1962. *Year Book of the Central Conference of American Rabbis*, vol. 72, 108–109. Philadelphia: Maurice Jacobs, 1963.

—— "Report of Committee on Publications." Central Conference of American Rabbis Annual Convention, Philadelphia, Pennsylvania, 17–20 June 1963. *Year Book of the Central Conference of American Rabbis*, vol. 73, 79–80. Philadelphia: Maurice Jacobs, 1963.

Sack, Eugene J. "Report of Committee on Publications." Central Conference of American Rabbis Annual Convention, Bretton Woods, New Hampshire, 23–28 June 1958. *Year Book of the Central Conference of American Rabbis*, vol. 69, 108–110. Philadelphia: Maurice Jacobs, 1960.

—— "Report of Committee on Publications." Central Conference of American Rabbis Annual Convention, Detroit, Michigan, 21–26 June 1960. *Year Book of the Central Conference of American Rabbis*, vol. 70, 87–88. Philadelphia: Maurice Jacobs, 1961.

—— "Report of Committee on Publications." Central Conference of American Rabbis Annual Convention, New York, New York, 20–24 June 1961. *Year Book of the Central Conference of American Rabbis*, vol. 71, 108–109. Philadelphia: Maurice Jacobs, 1962.

Schulman, [??]. Response to "Report of Committee on Revision of the Haggadah." Central Conference of American Rabbis Annual Convention, Cincinnati, Ohio, 2–7 April 1919. *Year Book of the Central Conference of American Rabbis*, vol. 29, 57. Cincinnati: CJ Krehbiel & Co., 1919.

Silverman, Joseph, Isaac S. Moses, and Solomon Foster. "Report of the Committee on Publication." Central Conference of American Rabbis Annual Convention, Frankfort, Michigan, 26 June 1907. *Year Book of the Central Conference of American Rabbis*, vol. 15, 54–55. Cincinnati: Bloch Pub., 1905.

Sonneschein, S[olomon], H. Motion. Convention of the Central Conference of American Rabbis, Cleveland, Ohio, 14 July 1891. *Year Book of the Central Conference of American Rabbis 1890–91*, 27. Cincinnati, Ohio: Bloc Pub., 1891. Reprint *Central Conference of American Rabbis Year Book Volumes I, II, III 1890–1983*. New York: CCAR, n.d.

Sonneschein, S[olomon], Aaron Hahn, Low Schwab, Leo Mannheimer, and E. N. Calish, "Report by the Committee on Ritual." Convention of the Central Conference of American Rabbis, Cleveland, Ohio, 15 July 1891, *Year Book of the Central Conference of American Rabbis 1890–91*, 29–30. Cincinnati: Bloch Pub., 1891. Reprint *Central Conference of American Rabbis Year Book Volumes I, II, III 1890–1983*. New York: CCAR, n.d.

Stolz, Joseph, et al. "Report of Publication Committee." Proceedings of the Central Conference of American Rabbis, Frankfort, Michigan, 2 July 1908. *Central Conference of American Rabbis Yearbook*, vol. 18, 39–41. Cincinnati: S. Rosenthal & Co., 1909.

"Summary of Committee Activity 1990–91." Committees and Members. Central Conference of American Rabbis Annual Convention, Fort Lauderdale, Florida, 23–27 June 1991 and San Antonio, Texas, 6–9 April 1992. *Year Book of the Central Conference of American Rabbis*, vol. 101–102, 73–79. New York: CCAR, 1993.

"Summary of Committee Activity 1995–96." Committees and Members. Central Conference of American Rabbis Annual Convention, Jerusalem, Israel, 8–13 March 1995 and Philadelphia, Pennsylvania, 24–28 March 1996. *Year Book of the Central Conference of American Rabbis*, vol. 106–107, 341–352. New York: CCAR, 1997.

Wise, Jonah B. Response to "Report of Committee on Revision of the Haggadah." Central Conference of American Rabbis Annual Convention, Cincinnati, Ohio, 2–7 April 1919. *Year Book of the Central Conference of American Rabbis*, vol. 29, 58. Cincinnati: CJ Krehbiel & Co., 1919.

Speeches

Bokser, Baruch M. *From Sacrifice to Symbol – and Beyond*. Paper presented at The Solomon Goldman Lectures, edited by Byron L. Sherwin and Michael Carasik, vol. 5. Chicago: Spertus College of Judaica Press, 1990.

Brickner, Barnett. "President's Message." Presented at the Central Conference of American Rabbis Annual Convention. Proceedings of the Central Conference of American Rabbis, Asbury Park, New Jersey, 20–23 June 1955. *Central Conference of American Rabbis Yearbook*, vol. 65,10–11. Philadelphia: Maurice Jacobs, 1955.

Frankel, Zacharia. Statement on the language of prayer. Presented at The Reform Rabbinical Conference at Frankfurt, 17 July 1845. Reprint *The Jew in the Modern World: A Documentary History*, 3rd ed. Eited by Paul Mendes-Flohr and Jehuda Reinharz. Translated by J. Hessing, 203–204. New York: Oxford Univ. Press, 2010.

Glazer, Nathan. "Jews and the Urban Experience: A Historical Assessment." Keynote. Presented at the Jews and the Urban Experience, Cohn-Haddow Center for Judaic Studies, Temple Beth El, Bloomfield Hills, Michigan, 7 March 1999. Bloomfield Hills, Michigan: Wayne State Univ., 1999.

Gamoran, Emanuel. "Liberal Judaism and the Day School." Presented at The Jewish Day School: A Symposium. Central Conference of American Rabbis, Cincinnati, June 1950. Reprint in *The Jewish Teacher* 2, no. 2 (1951): 1–6.

— "Progress and Prospects in Jewish Education." Presented at the American Association for Jewish Education and the National Council for Jewish Education, Atlantic City, New Jersey, June 1949. Reprint in *The Jewish Teacher* 18, no. 3 (1950): 1–5.

Grossman, Louis. "A Message of the President to the Thirtieth Annual Convention of the Central Conference of American Rabbis," 2 April 1919. Central Conference of American Rabbis Annual Convention, Cincinnati, Ohio, 2–7 April 1919. *Year Book of the Central Conference of American Rabbis*, vol. 26, 108–130. Cincinnati: CJ Krehbiel & Co., 1919.

Kravitz, Leonard S. "A Response." Papers Presented at the UAHC 48th Biennial. Reprint *The Theological Foundations of Prayer: A Reform Jewish Perspective*. Edited by Jack Bemporad, 83–90. New York: UAHC, 1967.

Kaufmann Kohler. "American Judaism." *Hebrew Union College and Other Addresses*, 198–199. Cincinnati, Ohio: Ark Publishing Co., 1916. Reprint "The Concordance of Judaism and Americanism (1911)." *The Jew in the Modern World: A Documentary History*, 3rd edition. Edited by Paul Mendes-Flohr and Jehuda Reinharz, 525–526. New York: Oxford Univ. Press, 2010.

Krauskopf, Joseph. "Appendix B: Message of Rabbi Jos. Krauskopf, President of Central Conference of American Rabbis, to its Sixteenth Annual Convention, Cleveland, Ohio, July 3, 1905." Cleveland, Ohio, 2–6 July 1905 Convention. *CCAR Yearbook*, vol. 15, 175–203. Cincinnati: Bloch, 1906.

Jacobs, Rick. "At the End of Two Years." Presented at the Union for Reform Judaism Biennial, Washington, D.C., 18 December 2011. Accessed 30 July 2014, http://blogs.rj.org/blog/2011/12/18/at-the-end-of-two-years/.

— "Keynote Address." Presented at the Union for Reform Judaism Biennial, San Francisco, California. 12 December 2013. Accessed 4 January 2015, http://urj.org/biennial.

Jacobson, Israel. Dedication Address. Temple of Jacob, Seesen, 17 July 1810. Reprint *The Rise of Reform Judaism: A Sourcebook of its European Origins*. Edited by W. Gunther Plaut, 29–31. New York: World Union for Progressive Judaism, 1963.

Lilienthal, Max. "Modern Judaism." Thanksgiving 1865. Indianapolis, Indiana. Reprint *Max Lilienthal: American Rabbi: Life and* Writings. Edited by David Philipson, 444–453. New York: Bloch Pub., 1915.

Maier, Joseph. Concluding Address presented at the Brunswick Conference. June 1844. Reprint *The Rise of Reform Judaism: A Sourcebook of its European Origins*. Edited by W. Gunther Plaut, 79. New York: World Union for Progressive Judaism, 1963.

—— Statement for new prayer book. Paper presented at the Brunswick Conference, June 1844. Reprint *The Rise of Reform Judaism: A Sourcebook of its European Origins*. Edited by W. Gunther Plaut, 154. New York: World Union for Progressive Judaism, 1963.

Marcus, Jacob Rader. *The Future of American Jewry.* Presented at Dropsie College for Hebrew and Cognate Learning, Philadelphia, Pennsylvania, 2 June 1955. Cincinnati: American Jewish Archives, 1956.

—— *Impacts of Contemporary Life upon Judaism.* Presented at the Biennial Union of American Hebrew Congregations, Chicago, Illinois, 19 June 1933. Cincinnati: American Jewish Archives, 1969.

—— *The Periodization of American Jewish History.* Presented at the Fifty-Sixth Annual Meeting, American Jewish Historical Society, Coolidge Auditorium, Library of Congress, Washington, D.C., 15 February 1958. Cincinnati: American Jewish Archives, 1958.

—— *The Quintessential American Jew.* Presented at the Sixty-Sixth Annual Meeting of the American Jewish Historical Society, Boston, Massachusetts, 19 May 19, 1968. Cincinnati: American Jewish Archives, 1968.

Marcuson, Isaac E. "Conference Lecture—Judaism and Life." Presented at the Central Conference of American Rabbis Annual Convention, Buffalo, New York, 28 June – 4 July 1917. *Year Book of the Central Conference of American Rabbis*, vol. 27, 213–219. Cincinnati: CJ Krehbiel & Co., 1917.

Peleg, Kristene. "Prairie Harvests and Sukkoth: A comparison of Jewish holiday observances in three frontier memories." Paper presented at the 36th Annual Conference of the Association for Jewish Studies, Chicago, Illinois, 20 December 2004. Transcript.

Romain, Gemma. "The Jews of Nineteenth Century Charleston: Ethnicity in a Port City." Paper presented at the Seascapes, Littoral Cultures, and Trans-Oceanic Exchanges, Library of Congress, Washington, D.C., 12–15 February 2003. Transcript. Accessed 3 March 2008, http://www.historycooperative.org/proceedings/seascapes/romain.html.

Rosenau, William. "A Message of the President to the Twenty-Eighth Annual Convention of the Central Conference of American Rabbis." 28 June 1917. Central Conference of American Rabbis Annual Convention, Buffalo, New York, 28 June – 4 July 1917. *Year Book of the Central Conference of American Rabbis*, vol. 27, 182–212. Cincinnati: CJ Krehbiel & Co., 1917.

—— "A Message of the President to the Twenty-Seventh Annual Convention of the Central Conference of American Rabbis." 1 July 1916. Central Conference of American Rabbis Annual Convention, Wildwood, New Jersey, 13 June – 7 July 1916. *Year Book of the Central Conference of American Rabbis*, vol. 26, 172–193. New York: Bloch Pub., 1916.

Sarna, Jonathan D. Marshal Sklare Memorial Lecture. Paper presented at the annual meeting of the Association for Jewish Studies, 2002. Transcript.

Shevitz, Amy Hill. "Constructing Community, Constructing Section: Regional Culture and Jewish Community Across the United States." Paper presented at the 2006 Biennial Scholars' Conference on American Jewish History, Charleston, S.C., 5–7 June 2006.

Accessed 11 October 2007, http://www.cofc.edu/~jwst/pages/Shevitz,%20Amy%20-%20constructing%20section%20+.pdf

Silverman, Joseph. "Message of President Joseph Silverman." Presented at the Central Conference of American Rabbis Annual Convention, New Orleans, Louisiana, 5 – 10 May 1902. *Year Book of the Central Conference of American Rabbis*, vol. 12, 26 – 38. Cincinnati: Bloch Pub., 1902.

Tonnerre, Clermont. "Debate on the Eligibility of Jews for Citizenship." Presented at the French National Assembly, Paris, France, 23 December 1789. Reprint *The Jew in the Modern World: A Documentary History*, 3rd ed. Edited by Paul Mendes-Flohr and Jehuda Reinharz. Translated by J. Rubin, 123 – 125. New York: Oxford Univ. Press, 2010.

Wolf, Arnold Jacob. "A More Traditional and Radical Prayer Book." Paper presented at the UAHC 48th Biennial. In *The Theological Foundations of Prayer: A Reform Jewish Perspective*. Edited by Jack Bemporad, 92 – 100. New York: UAHC, 1967.

Yoffie, Eric. "Rabbi Yoffie's Remarks to the URJ Executive Committee March 2010." Presented at the URJ Executive Committee, New York, New York, 15 March 2010. Accessed 30 July 2014, http://urj.org/about/union/leadership/yoffie/?syspage=article&item_id=37320.

Index of Names

Aaron 3–5, 47, 50, 73
Abrams, Judith Z. 109
Ackerman, Paula 131
Ackerman, Walter 30f.
Agus, Jacob B. 97
Alexander, Alexander 11
Angel, Marc D. 41
Antin, Mary 25
Arnow, David 7–9, 13
Aronin, Ben 15
Auerbach, Isaac 49

Bacharach, Hava 25
Barsimon, Jacob 55
Beer, Jacob Herz 49
Benjamin, Israel Joseph 27–29, 31, 92, 95
Berkowitz, Henry 20, 63, 74–76, 80–84, 86f., 96–101, 103
Berman, Howard A. 151, 156–158, 164
Beruriah 23
Bettan, Israel 92
Bial, Morrison David 32, 124
Bien, H. M. 33
Birnbaum, Philip 38
Bokser, Baruch M. 3, 7f.
Borowitz, Eugene 133
Brody, Paula J. 152f.
Broner, E. M. 17
Bronstein, Herbert 1, 14, 20f., 72, 78, 92, 123–129, 132, 139, 155f., 161

Calish, Edward N. 73f.
Calof, Rachel 66
Cantor, Aviva 16f.
Chorin, Aaron 47, 50
Cohen, Gershon 10
Cohon, Samuel S. 20, 90, 92–95, 98–101, 103–105, 108, 117f., 125
Cowen, Lillith 14
Cowen, Philip 14

da Modena, Leone 11
Dershowitz, Alan M. 135, 146, 162

Dreyfus, A. Stanley 76, 109, 116, 124, 128f.
Dushkin, Alexander 29–31, 92, 95

Edelman, Lily 128
Einhorn, David 12–14, 53, 62, 70, 75, 86, 103
Eisen, Arnold M. 136
Eisenstein, Ira 38
Eleazar ben Samuel of Mayence 24
Elijah 10, 15, 19f., 25, 35, 41, 43, 83, 85f., 118, 139, 156
Elwell, Sue Levi 126, 142–146, 151, 162, 164f.
Epstein, Itzhak 16, 44

Farhi, Hillel 36
Felsenthal, Bernard 13
Fields, Harvey J. 41, 127
Fram, Leon 95, 101
Frank, L. H. 13f.
Frankel, Zacharias 52f.
Freedman, Marcia 17f.
Freehof, Solomon 20, 92, 94, 99f., 104, 109, 120
Freelander, Daniel 71, 108, 113, 159
Friedenwald, Harry 29
Friedländer, David 29, 48f.
Frisch, Ephraim 88, 92, 94f., 104

Gaon, Elijah 25
Garoran, Emanual 29
Geiger, Abraham 50f., 77, 141–143
Geller, Laura 146
Gereboff, Joel 11, 34, 44, 76, 112, 166
Gilbert, W. 11
Goldberg, Nathan 38
Goldstein, Albert 121f., 129
Goldstein, Elyse 132
Goldstein, Sidney 22, 117, 129, 135–137, 142, 158
Gratz, Rebecca 28
Green, A. A. 12, 35
Grossman, Louis 67, 93f.
Grossman, Rudolph 74, 81, 161

Index of Names

Gutheim, James 66
Gutstein, Z. Harry 38

Haas, Louis J. 95
Hahn, Aaron 73f.
Herder, Kate 33, 65
Herzog, Chaim 164
Hoffman, Lawrence 7–9, 13, 76, 126f., 138, 149

Jackson, Solomon H. 12
Jacob, Walter 71, 77, 80
Jacobs, Rick 59, 62, 64, 148, 152, 159, 162–164
Jacobson, Israel 49
Joel, Joseph A. 65
Joseph, R. 9

Kahn, Robert I. 124–126, 134
Kalechofsky, Roberta 16
Kaplan, Dana Evan 70, 106, 115, 117, 129, 134, 141, 148f., 159, 16–165
Kaplan, Mordecai M. 39
Kley, Eduard 49
Knobel, Peter 128f., 138, 142, 149, 164–166
Kohler, Kaufman 70f., 84, 103
Kohn, Eugene 38
Kolatch, Alfred J. 39f.
Krauskopf, Joseph 19, 80–82
Kreitman, Esther Singer 25
Krischen, Jerry 16
Kroloff, Charles A. 134f., 138
Kugelmass, Jack 44,

Landman, Isaac 88, 95f., 107
Leeser, Isaac 66–69
Lefkowitz, David 104
Lehmann, Marcus 38
Levi, Charles 74
Levi, David 12
Levitt, Joy D. 38, 43
Levy, Asser 56
Levy, Esther 28f.
Levy, Ezekiel 65
Levy, Isaac J. 65

Levy, Richard 58, 69, 131, 134, 138, 140f., 150, 164
Liben, Dan 15
Liebman, Haim 12, 14
Lilienthal, Max 61, 66–69
Lipman, Steve 155
Loth, Moritz 69

Mann, Louis 104, 108
Mannheimer, S. 33, 72–75
Marcus, Jacob Radar 45f., 57f., 62, 75, 81–84, 86–88, 116
Marcuson, Isaac E. 88, 92, 95, 100, 103, 105–107, 110
Markowitz, S. H. 22, 30
Maron, Benjamin 155
Mendelssohn, Moses 46
Menitoff, Paul J. 141, 163
Merzbacher, Leo 60, 66
Messiah 10, 19, 35, 83, 118
Michaelson, Jay 157
Mihaly, Eugene 123
Miriam 17f., 43, 139, 156
Morgenstern, Julian 84, 88, 95, 103, 105
Morris, Tamra L. 16
Moses 3–5,
Moses, Adolph 74
Moses, Isaac S. 14f., 33, 74f., 76, 81f.
Moss, David 164

Narot, Joseph R. 123f.
Neumark, Martha 131
Neusner, Jacob 97, 140

Obama, Barak 14
Opher, Ahron 121

Petuchowski, Jakob J. 48, 53
Pfaslzer, Elsi 98
Philippson, Ludwig 52
Philips, A. Th. 13, 32
Philipson, David 45–53, 67f., 70, 74
Pietersen, Solomon 55
Plaut, W. Gunther 47, 49–51, 127
Podwal, Mark 152
Polish, David 121f., 124

Index of Names

Poznanski, Gustav 60
Preisand, Sally 131

Rashi 23 f.
Reagan, Ronald 164
Reimer, Jack 128 f.
Rice, Abraham 66
Ritual Committee 74–76
Roberts, Cokie 16
Roberts, Steven 16
Rosen, Bernard C. 115
Rosenau, William 34, 74, 81 f., 90 f., 99 f.
Rosenbaum, David 94
Rosenfeld, Elie 13, 17
Roth, Cecil 39
Rubin, Alvan D. 122
Rubinstein, Peter J. 130, 135, 138, 152, 162

Saadia ben Joseph 47
Saadiah 10
Sarna, Jonathan 27, 56, 66, 112, 159
Schachtel, Hyman J. 121 f.
Schnur, Susan 18
Schocken, Salman 105, 117 f.
Schwab, Isaac 33, 72–74
Seltzer, Robert 109, 138 f.
Sexias, Moses 57
Shalom, Ima 23, 53, 62, 95, 109, 118–120
Shearith Israel 26, 58
Sheftal, Levi 57
Shluker, Zelda 155
Silver, Arthur M. 40
Silverman, Joseph 78, 80, 84
Silverman, Morris 39

Simkin, Ruth 18
Solomon, Hayyim 56
Sonneschein, Solomon H. 73 f.
Stein, Leopold 11 f., 76, 103
Stern, Jacob 59
Stern, M. A. 51, 59
Stern, Sigismund 51
Stevens, Elliot L. 76, 132 f., 138 f., 149, 155
Stiles, Ezra 57
Strassfeld, Michael J. 38, 43

Tabory, Joseph 1, 3, 8
Tiktiner, Rebecca 24
Turnoy, Gittel 65

Washington, George 17, 20, 57, 60, 62, 94, 107, 132, 147, 157, 163
Waxman, Chaim I. 31
Waxman, Maron L. 157
Wessel, Harvey E. 103 f.
Wilensky, David A. M. 155
Wise, Isaac 53, 61, 65–69, 72 f., 75, 78, 86, 88, 103, 133, 165
Wolf, Horace J. 104
Wolsey, Louis 92, 104

Yerushalmi, Yosef Hayim 1, 9 f., 122, 167
Yoffie, Alan 15 f., 151–155, 162, 165
Yoffie, Eric 163

Zamore, Mary L. 145, 151–155, 165
Zemel, Daniel G. 163
Zifroni, Daniel 11
Zunz, Leopold 49 f.

Index of Subjects

א נייע הגדה של פסח 42
affiliation 115, 130, 136, 142, 148, 157
Alliance Français Schools 36
Am Olam 65
American Revolution 58
Amsterdam Haggadah 11, 32, 37
anti-Semitism 10, 45, 78, 101, 109, 136
aphikoman 39
assimilation 28, 46f., 52, 65, 78, 89, 93, 109, 135f.

בדיק תחמץ 32, 34, 37f., 127
Bene Israel 36f.
Beth Elohim 59f.
bi-cultural 1, 58, 61, 79, 83, 115
Blessing and Washing 32
Bloch Publishers 82, 87f.
B'nai B'rith 70
Board of Jewish Ministers of Philadelphia 69
Breslau Conference 71
Brunswick Conference 52
bêt hadîn 67f.
Bureau of Jewish Education 29, 92

Cannabis Passover Seder 18
CCAR Press 152, 156f., 164f.
Centenary Platform 130
Central Conference of American Rabbis (CCAR) 2, 14, 19f., 33, 55, 72, 75, 78, 82, 84, 86f., 140, 161
Ceremonial for Opening the Door for Elijah 118
Charleston, South Carolina 56f., 59f., 62
Chase & Sanborn Coffees 14
Christian 11, 24, 26, 28, 45, 49, 58f., 61, 63f., 70f., 76, 93, 105, 116, 130
Church 11, 45, 76, 115
Civil Rights Movement 116f.
Civil Rights Seders 18
Classical Reform 34, 121, 134, 156, 162, 164f.
Columbus Platform 97, 108, 123

Committee 19f., 30, 42, 59, 73–78, 79–84, 86–94, 96, 98–100, 103, 105–107, 109f., 116, 118–126, 128, 132f., 137, 139, 142, 149, 163
– Ad Hoc 142
– Curriculum 30
– Executive Board 92, 121, 126, 132
– Liturgy 48, 60, 73, 76, 78, 82–84, 109, 120–125, 127–129, 149
– on Ceremonies 110, 118f.
– on Haggadah 74, 76, 80–82, 121
– on Liturgy 109, 120, 123–129, 132, 137
– on Liturgy and Music 123–126
– on Marriage, Family and the Home 120
– on Prayerbook 73f., 149
– on President's Message 86
– on Publications 88, 92, 103, 122
– on Revision of the Haggadah 90, 92–94, 96, 99f., 103
– on Ritual 74–76
– on Seder Haggadah 83f., 86
– on Social Action 116
– on Union Haggadah 87
Conference 2, 14, 16, 33, 52f., 55, 68–78, 80–84, 86–88, 90–94, 96, 99–101, 103, 105–110, 118–120, 122–126, 128, 130, 132–135, 137f., 140f., 150, 152, 154, 156f., 162–165
– Breslau 53, 71
– Brunswick 52
– Eastern 70f.
– Frankfurt 52f., 109
– Pittsburg 70f.
– of Rabbis 70
Conference of Rabbis 68, 70f.
Conference of Rabbis of Southern Congregations 70
confirmation 49, 61
Congregation Ohr Kodesh 16
Conservative 29, 68, 71, 89, 110, 113–115, 123, 128–130, 134, 147, 158
Conservative Judaism 68, 115, 128–130
Criteria for a New Haggadah 142

https://doi.org/10.1515/9783110524703-012

Dayēnû 9, 95
Dayenu
– A Special Contemporary Dayenu Created in Honor of the 40th Anniversary of the Birth of the State of Israel 15
Department of Synagogue and School Extension (DSSE) 29
Deuteronomy 6, 9, 23
Diskin Orphan Home of Israel 14
Dutch West India Company 55

Easter Eve or The "New Hagodoh Shel Pesach." A Metrical Family-Fest Service 33
Eastern Conference 70f.
Eastern European 24, 26, 78–80, 89–93, 99, 102, 106, 108, 112f., 118, 130, 139, 162f., 166
education 2, 14, 23–32, 36, 40–42, 45, 49, 61, 70, 81, 87, 94f., 97f., 116, 120, 126, 133, 152, 155, 159
Education Department of the Union 30
Egalitarian Hagada, An 17
Emancipation 26, 32, 45–48, 53, 56, 61, 66, 79
Enlightenment 26, 46, 48, 53, 57
Ethical Culture 72
Exodus 1, 3, 5, 9, 15–17, 35, 43, 85f., 98, 100, 102, 154f., 161

Family Seder: A Traditional Passover Haggadah for the Modern Home, The 40
feminist 16f., 41f., 125, 131, 142f., 145, 149, 151
Festival of Freedom 9, 161
Festival of Freedom הגדה של פסח 41
Four Questions 8, 43, 93, 98
Frankfurt Conference 52, 109
Frankfurt Society of Friends of Reform 51
Freedom Haggadah for Soviet Jewry 16

Gates of Prayer 129, 131f.
Gates of Repentance 132
Gemara 9
Genossenschaft für Reform in Judenthum 51

German 11–13, 38, 45f., 48–55, 58–67, 69, 73, 75–79, 81, 87, 89–91, 93, 105f., 108, 112, 118, 161
German Liberal Haggadah 11f.
Germany 1, 26, 49, 62, 64, 71
Glückel of Hameln 25
Gutenberg 10

Hadassah Magazine 128, 155
Hagadah Schel Pesach 38
Haggadah (pl. Haggadot)
– אַ נייע הגדה של פסח 42
– Amsterdam Haggadah 11, 32, 37
– *Cannabis Passover Seder* 18
– CCAR 2, 14f., 19f., 33f., 55, 75–78, 80–82, 84–88, 90–94, 96–102, 105, 110, 112, 116, 118f., 122–129, 137, 142–146, 148, 150–157, 159f., 162–166
– 1892 2, 33, 73–77
– 1905 2, 19f., 34, 55, 82–84
– 1907/1908 2, 84–88, 97–98
– 1923 2, 19f., 55, 90–94, 96, 99–103, 105–108, 110, 118–120, 122, 124–126, 129, 156f., 164, 166
– 1974 2, 14, 20, 78, 122f., 126–129, 155, 161
– 2002 1f., 56, 129, 143–145f., 164f.
– 2012 2, 15, 45, 60, 147–149, 151–155, 159, 165
– 2014 2, 15f., 48, 63, 76, 79, 89, 104, 107, 112–114, 117, 126, 132, 135f., 151–155, 157, 159, 164
– Ceremonial for Opening the Door for Elijah 118
– *Easter Eve or The "New Hagodoh Shel Pesach." A Metrical Family-Fest Service* 33
– *Egalitarian Hagada, An* 17
– *Family Seder: A Traditional Passover Haggadah for the Modern Home, The* 40
– *Festival of Freedom הגדה של פסח* 41
– *Freedom Haggadah for Soviet Jewry* 16
– *Hagadah Schel Pesach* 38
– *Haggadah: A New Edition with English Translation, The* 39
– *Haggadah for the Liberated Lamb* 16, 42
– Leipnik-Rosenthaliana Haggadah 32

Index of Subjects

- *Like An Orange on the Seder Plate: Our Lesbian Haggadah* 18
- *Mantua Haggadah* 11
- *Maxwell House Haggadah* 13f., 17
- *Moshe Bamberger Haggadah* 32
- *New Haggadah for the Pesah Seder, The* 38
- *New Union Haggadah, The* 2, 151, 156f., 164
- *Night of Questions – A Passover Haggadah, A* 38, 43
- *Olat Tamid* 12, 75
- *Passover and the Contemporary Scene* 119
- *Passover Hagadah* הגדה של פסח 38
- *Passover Haggadah, A* 2, 14, 78, 123, 128f., 156, 161
- *Passover Haggadah: The Complete Seder* 40
- *Prague Haggadah* 11
- *Revised Hagada: Home Service for the First Two Nights of Passover, The* 12, 35
- *Seder Leader's Guide to Sharing the Journey, The* 2, 154
- *Shaare Rahamin Haggadah, The* 42
- *Sharing the Journey: The Haggadah for the Contemporary Family* 2, 15, 151–155, 164f.
- *Siddur Saadiah* 9
- *Soviet Jewry Freedom Seder, A* 16
- *ShopRite* 38, 163f.
- *Shulsinger Brothers Publishing Company* 39
- *Star Hebrew Book Company* 34
- supplement 118, 138
- כל-דכפין *The Open Door: A Passover Haggadah* 2, 143, 145f., 164f.
- *Tucson Jewish Feminist Haggadah* 41f.
- *Venetian Haggadah* 11
- *Venice Haggadah* 11
- *Union Haggadah, The* 2, 19f., 34, 55, 82–84, 84–88, 90–94, 96–98, 99f., 103, 105–108, 110, 118–120, 124–126, 129, 156f., 164, 166

Haggadah: A New Edition with English Translation, The 39
Haggadah for the Liberated Lamb 16, 42

Hamburg Temple 49f.
hamôṣî 8
Har Sinai Verein 60, 62
Hebrew 10–13, 17, 24–26, 28f., 32–34, 36–38, 40, 46, 49, 52–54, 58–62, 69, 71f., 74f., 87, 91, 93, 108f., 123–125, 133, 144, 150–152, 154, 156, 160
Hebrew Congregation 20, 57, 113
Hebrew Sabbath School Union (HSSU) 29
Hebrew Union College (HUC) 16, 45, 53, 58, 72, 90, 131, 149
Hebrew Union College–Jewish Institute of Religion (HUC–JIR) 151, 159, 163, 165
Hillel 3, 42, 164

illustrations 10f.
immigration 45, 59, 61f., 78f., 105, 133, 166
- Second Wave 61f., 66
- Third Wave 78f., 105
interfaith family 16, 151f., 155, 165

Jacob ben Isaac Ashkenazi 24f.
Jewish Book Council 157
Jewish Daily Forward, The 157
Jewish Minister's Association 69
Jewish Teacher, The 29, 92
Jewish Theological Seminary 9, 29, 72
Joseph Ben Judah ibn Aqnin 23
Judah ibn Tibbon 24
Judeo-German 11
Judeo-Italian 11
Judeo-Marathi 37
Judeo-Spanish 11, 32

Ladino 49
Leipnik-Rosenthaliana Haggadah 32
Leviticus 4–6
Liberal 25, 32, 60, 68, 71f., 84, 106, 123, 163, 165
Liberal Judaism at Home: The Practices of Modern Reform Judaism 32
Like An Orange on the Seder Plate: Our Lesbian Haggadah 18
Liturgy Committee 76, 78, 109, 120–124, 127–129

maṣah 8f.
Mantua Haggadah 11
Maxwell House 13f., 17
Maxwell House Haggadah 13f., 17
merchant 13, 25, 37, 63f.
Minhag America 67f., 73, 75, 80, 88, 90, 100, 133, 165
Mishkan T'filah 149, 165
Moshe Bamberger Haggadah 32
Mothers Circle, The 145

National Jewish Monthly, The 128
National Jewish Population Survey 148, 157f.
New Amsterdam 55f.
New Haggadah for the Pesah Seder, The 38
New Union Haggadah, The 151, 156f., 164
New World 26, 53, 55, 58, 61, 65, 79f., 102
New York Jewish Week 155
Newport, Arkansas 33, 65
Newport, Rhode Island 56f.
Night of Questions – A Passover Haggadah, A 38f., 43
Numbers 5

Olat Tamid 12, 75
Old World 58, 65, 74, 77, 162
Open Door: A Passover Haggadah, The 143, 145f., 151, 164f.
orange 18, 145, 153, 156
Orthodox 14, 22, 29, 32, 34, 38f., 68, 72, 79, 90, 102, 108, 111–115, 127, 130, 132, 134, 147, 157, 158

Passover and the Contemporary Scene 119
Passover Hagadah הגדה של פסח 38
Peereboom 55
Pesaḥim 8
Pew Study 150, 157
Pittsburgh Conference 70f.
plagues 9, 18f., 20, 156
Platform 2, 20, 53, 62, 70–72, 77, 91, 94, 97, 106f., 123, 129–134, 138, 140f., 156, 163
– 1885 2, 69–72, 77, 80, 138, 163
– 1937 2, 4, 97, 107f.
– 1976 2, 20, 130

– 1997 2, 135, 138, 162
– 2000 2, 97, 125, 130, 134
– Centenary Platform 130
– Columbus Platform 97, 107f., 123
– Pittsburgh Platform 71, 77, 91, 106, 138, 163
– Statement of Principles for Reform Judaism, A 140f., 143
Prague Haggadah 11
prayerbook 1, 10, 13, 33, 49f., 52, 60, 67, 69, 73–76, 80, 88, 108f., 124, 139, 149f., 165f.
– *Gates of Prayer* 129, 131f.
– *Gates of Repentance* 132
– *Minhag America* 67f., 73, 75, 80, 88, 90, 100, 133, 165
– *Mishkan T'filah* 149, 165
– *Olat Tamid* 12, 75
– *Siddur Saadiah* 9
– *Union Prayer Book* 73, 75f., 81, 84, 88, 108f., 121, 124
public education 23, 26f., 32, 36

Rabbinical Literary Association of America 69
Reconstructionist 18, 38f., 43
redemption 3, 7, 10, 13, 15, 20, 85
Reform 1f., 11f., 13f., 16, 19–22, 29–33, 34f., 45–53, 55, 58, 60–62, 64–73, 75–78, 80f., 86–91, 93–109, 111–119, 121, 123–125, 127–135, 137–152, 154–166
Reform Judaism 1, 20, 47–53, 55, 58, 60, 62, 66, 68f., 71–74, 76, 80, 86, 89, 91, 93, 97, 99–106, 108f., 112f., 116f., 119, 123–125, 127, 129f., 133f., 137f., 140f., 143, 145f., 148f., 151f., 154, 156–165
Reform Leadership Council (RLC) Think Tank 151
Reformed Society of Israelites 60
Religious Action Center of Reform Judaism 16
Revised Hagada: Home Service for the First Two Nights of Passover, The 12, 35
Russia 14, 26, 41, 78
Russian 12, 40, 79, 112, 132f., 139, 161, 166

Sacrifice   4, 6–9, 41, 101
search for leavening   32, 41
Seder Leader's Guide to Sharing the Journey, The   154
Seder Plate   18, 32, 34, 38–41, 43, 145, 153
Shaare Rahamin Haggadah, The   42
Sharing the Journey: The Haggadah for the Contemporary Family   15, 151f., 154, 164
ShopRite   38, 163f.
Shulsinger Brothers Publishing Company   39
Siddur Saadiah   9
Social Action Committee   116
St. Catrina   54
Star Hebrew Book Company   34
State Bank of New York   14
Statement of Principles for Reform Judaism, A   140f., 143, 156
superstitious   19, 83, 86, 90, 118, 139
synagogue   11, 22, 24, 31, 35, 37, 40, 49f., 54, 58–61, 63f., 69f., 72f., 89–91, 94, 106, 108, 113–116, 123f., 130f., 135f., 147f., 158

Talmud   1, 6–8, 15, 19, 21, 23–25, 27, 40, 51, 96, 109, 153
Tanaḥ   47
Temple   3, 6–8, 23, 41, 50, 60, 64, 69, 95, 101, 104, 108, 114, 146, 155, 163

Temple Emanu-El   60, 104
Test for Leavening   34, 38
Times of Israel, The   155
Torah   3–6, 9, 23–25, 27, 46, 51, 58, 96f., 140, 162f.
Tucson Jewish Feminist Haggadah   41f.

Union for Reform Judaism (URJ)   148, 162
Union of American Hebrew Congregations (UAHC)   20, 29, 69, 89, 106, 147
Union Prayer Book   33, 73, 75f., 81, 84, 88, 108f., 121, 124
United Jewish Congregations of America   68

Venetian Haggadah   11
Venice Haggadah   11

Western Expansion   63
Wilshire Boulevard Temple   41
Wissenschaft des Judenthums   50, 55, 91
Wissenschaftliche Zeitschrift für judische Theologie   50
World Union for Progressive Judaism (WUPJ)   143

Yiddish   24f., 32, 42, 46, 54

Zionism   20, 101, 109

www.ingramcontent.com/pod-product-compliance
Lightning Source LLC
Chambersburg PA
CBHW030623230426
43661CB00053B/2117